Antipodal England

SUNY SERIES, STUDIES IN THE LONG NINETEENTH CENTURY

Pamela K. Gilbert, *editor*

Antipodal England

*Emigration and Portable Domesticity
in the Victorian Imagination*

Janet C. Myers

STATE UNIVERSITY OF NEW YORK PRESS

Cover illustration: Ford Madox Brown, *The Last of England* (1852–55).
Courtesy of Birmingham Museums & Art Gallery.

Published by
STATE UNIVERSITY OF NEW YORK PRESS
ALBANY

For information, contact State University of New York Press, Albany, NY
www.sunypress.edu

Production by Eileen Meehan
Marketing by Anne M. Valentine

Library of Congress Cataloging-in-Publication Data

Myers, Janet C., 1969–
   Antipodal England : emigration and portable domesticity in the Victorian imagination / Janet C. Myers.
      p. cm. — (SUNY series, studies in the long nineteenth century)
   Based on the author's doctoral thesis—Rice University, 2000.
   Includes bibliographical references and index.
   ISBN 978-1-4384-2714-0 (pbk. : alk. paper)
   ISBN 978-1-4384-2713-3 (hardcover : alk. paper)   1. English literature—19th century—History and criticism.   2. Emigration and immigration in literature.   3. Home in literature.   4. Women in literature.   5. Middle class women—England.   6. Women immigrants—Australia.   7. Australia—Emigration and immigration—Social aspects.   8. British—Australia—Social life and customs.   I. Title.
   PR468.E45M94 2009
   820.9'3526912—dc22

2008046866

10   9   8   7   6   5   4   3   2   1

Contents

List of Illustrations

Acknowledgments

The necessary insight and inspiration to bring this book into being came from my former teachers. I am grateful first and foremost for the superb guidance and intellectual stimulus I received at Rice University from Helena Michie and Robert Patten, who helped shape my thinking on all things Victorian—but especially emigration—when this book was in its earliest iterations. At the same time, Martin Wiener offered a historian's perspective that was invaluable, including an introduction to the wonderful story of the Tichborne Claimant. For initially drawing me to the Victorians and to some of the ideas around which this book would eventually cohere, I thank Susan Fraiman, Karen Chase, and Michael Levensen at the University of Virginia.

Colleagues at several institutions have provided intellectual support and friendship throughout the duration of this project. I have been privileged to be a part of two writing groups that have had a crucial impact on the book, including one at Rice University with Kay Heath, Louise Penner, Andrea Tinnemeyer, and Carolyn White. For their continued generous support and collaboration on matters related to both research and teaching, I thank Kay and Louise. Also while at Rice, Ginny Lane, Laurie Clements Lambeth, and Melinda Dougharty Bilecki provided necessary diversions from writing that ranged from haiku improvisation to forays into dog park culture. More recently, my colleagues in the English department at Elon University have supported and inspired both my research and the collective work we do every day. I am especially grateful to colleagues in my writing group—Barbara Gordon, Cassie Kircher, and Janet Warman—who invited me into their coterie and provided the intellectual support to sustain this project alongside the quotidian demands of academic life. Our collaboration over the years has been a source of great inspiration, and their perceptive readings have left an imprint throughout the book. And finally, I thank Deirdre McMahon, a dear friend and writing partner whose meticulous close readings and extensive expertise on the Victorians have also had a substantial impact on my writing and thinking about the period.

This book would not have been possible without various forms of institutional and material support. I wish to thank Rice University and Elon University for providing research funding to pursue archival work in England during the summers and Elon University for helping to defray the cost of permissions. I am also grateful for the dedication of librarians at my home institution, who helped me locate sources near and far, as well as librarians at the British Library, Bodleian Library, and The Women's Library, who provided assistance with archival research and helped with the reproduction of images. I thank the editors of the following journals for granting me permission to reproduce new versions of previously published material in chapters 2 and 4, respectively:

"Performing the Voyage Out: Victorian Female Emigration and the Class Dynamics of Displacement." *Victorian Literature and Culture* 29.1 (Spring 2001): 129–146. Copyright © 2001 Cambridge University Press. Reprinted with the permission of Cambridge University Press.

"'Verily the Antipodes of Home': The Domestic Novel in the Australian Bush." *Novel: A Forum on Fiction* 35.1 (2001): 46–68. Copyright NOVEL Corp. © 2001. Reprinted with permission.

I wish to acknowledge James Peltz, Allison Lee, and the production staff at SUNY Press, who have been wonderfully helpful and efficient, as well as the anonymous reviewers who read my manuscript for the press and offered incisive suggestions for revision. This book has been strengthened by all of their contributions.

Finally, I thank my family, especially Bob and Pat Myers, for supporting my work in innumerable ways, and Aidan and Clare Myers-Moran, for joyfully disrupting it whenever they had the chance. I dedicate this book to Alan Moran, who chose to entwine his fate with mine, and in so doing, to help me see firsthand the multiple and often ambivalent meanings of displacement.

Introduction

"Another English House in Another Country"

Imagining Home in the Empire

"Before concluding, we will just turn, in quiet thought, to dear Old England . . . We will not sigh, but go and make, as well as we can, another English house in another country." (Clarke 39)

*I*n a letter sent home to Britain in 1866, a recent emigrant to Australia complains about the size of a looking glass she had ordered to outfit her cabin aboard ship. At "only half the size of the one I paid for" (Clarke 41), Emilie Glen's looking glass serves as a potent reminder of the material importance of domestic objects in facilitating the recreation of English identity abroad.[1] Cabin fittings ranging from mirrors to bedding to cabinetry enabled middle-class emigrants like Glen to recreate familiar domestic spaces in the close cabins aboard ships, albeit on a smaller, more portable scale. Such replication in turn allowed emigrants to sustain essential domestic practices during a period of significant transition at sea. Passengers aboard ship, for instance, could adhere to the advice of one emigrant guide, which suggests that in preparation for dinner "even the most careless think it necessary to make some little change in their costume, and to spend at least five minutes at their cabin mirrors" (Silver, *S. W. Silver & Co.'s Colonial and Indian Pocket Book Series* 27). At sea, the act of looking in one's mirror ensures continuity with domestic rituals from home, allowing emigrants to "keep up appearances," not despite being aboard ship, but because of it. Imported onto the shore in Australia, such rituals would subsequently allow emigrants to recreate with partial success what one woman, writing for a newspaper published aboard a ship in 1862, envisions as "another English house in another country."

The imaginative leap described in this shipboard publication suggests that we must read Glen's looking glass not merely as a portable, material necessity, but also an apt metaphor for the self-reflexivity that was essential if Britons were to see themselves and their culture as capable of preservation and even re-invention despite the enormous geographical shift across continents that Australian emigration entailed. Taking this metaphor a step further, the inferior size of Glen's looking glass is evocative of the diminished sense of national identity that middle-class emigrants often experienced in the wake of leaving home, as they subsequently looked to their mirrors for evidence of their own Englishness. Throughout this study of Victorian emigration, I trace how the powerful confluence of these material and ideological meanings occurred and how they subsequently became attached to a new form of portable domesticity that enabled British emigrants throughout the second half of the nineteenth century to envision and to create the space that I am calling Antipodal England.[2]

VICTORIAN EMIGRATION, SETTLER COLONIALISM, AND POSTCOLONIAL STUDIES

My focus on middle-class emigration to Australia continues a conversation that was initiated more than a decade ago by Edward Said's landmark study, *Culture and Imperialism* (1993), which drew critical attention to the seemingly liminal role of the empire in nineteenth-century fiction. Arguing for a greater significance for empire than had previously been acknowledged, Said asserted that "[a]s a reference, as a point of definition, as an easily assumed place of travel, wealth, and service, the empire functions for much of the European nineteenth century as a codified, if only marginally visible, presence in fiction . . . scarcely ever more than named, rarely studied . . . or given density" (63). In the aftermath of Said's critique, a wealth of scholarship on British imperialism has since given this topic "density," including a host of influential studies by feminist critics who have skillfully examined the intersections between domesticity and imperialism in Victorian literature and culture.[3] At the same time, a growing body of scholarship, much of it in the social sciences, has focused on settler colonialism, a term whose precise definition is open to debate, but which typically refers to "societies in which Europeans have settled, where their descendants have remained politically dominant over indigenous peoples, and where a heterogeneous society has developed in class, ethnic, and racial terms" (Stasiulis and Yuval-Davis 3).[3] Two recent collections on the subject, one by Susan Pedersen and Sarah Elkins and the other by Annie E. Coombes, have called for renewed attention to settler colonialism with emphasis on what it can teach us about twentieth- and twenty-first-century nations and empires.

Antipodal England exists at the point of intersection between these two sub-fields within postcolonial studies, and by examining the complex appropriation of domestic ideologies and practices within the context of Australian colonial settlement, it seeks to show one way in which they overlap. Drawing on both areas of scholarship, I argue that just as ideals of home were of central importance to emigrants struggling to retain their national affiliation in the Australian colonies, this dynamic also applied in reverse—the Australian settler experience similarly helped to shape British conceptions of home and national identity. The liminality of emigration in the Victorian novel belies this centrality, seeming to reinforce a separation between the novel's primary subject, domestic life, and its secondary concern, the empire. In sub-plot after sub-plot, fictional emigrants disappear into or arrive from the colonies in ways that facilitate plot development but display a reticence on the part of novelists to represent the conditions of colonial life. This puzzling absence may account for the fact that Victorian emigration did not come under the scrutiny of literary critics until the last decade,[5] first in an edited collection by Rita S. Kranidis, and subsequently, in separate studies on female emigration by Kranidis and Diana C. Archibald.[6]

Despite its seeming marginality in the Victorian novel, Kranidis has begun persuasively to make a case for the importance of emigration, asserting that it was not merely "a series of isolated acts and events," but rather, that it constituted "a national trend suggestive of a predominant quest for an alternative mode of 'Englishness'" (*The Victorian Spinster* 23). As my opening quote suggests, the impetus to create such an alternative was powerful, and statistics about emigration as the empire grew bear out Kranidis's claim: estimates suggest that between 1821 and 1915, 10 million emigrants left Great Britain for non-European destinations (Woods 309). In Australia in particular, emigrants arrived so quickly and in such significant numbers that with an estimated immigrant population of three million by 1890, immigrants continued to outnumber native-born Australians descended from the British until the very end of the nineteenth century (Denoon 53). Textual evidence similarly supports the contention that emigration was "a national trend." Although fictional representations are oddly decentered, the proliferation of emigrant guides and the enthusiastic debates about emigration that punctuate contemporary periodicals indicate that emigration was a vital topic that impinged on the lives of many, if not most, Victorians.

While Australia loomed large within such discussions in the Victorian era, its role within such texts, and especially in literature, has received limited attention by critics.[7] Unlike India and Africa, which have been focal points for much of the recent work on empire, Australia was not subject to an administrative apparatus like the East India Company, nor did it play a significant role in relation to the empire's commercial ambitions. First occupied by the British as a penal colony in 1788, Australia was opened to free migration beginning in the 1830s, and it became home to millions of British and Irish emigrants throughout the century. In contrast to colonies in India and Africa, it was relatively autonomous, achieving self-government in 1855 and federation in 1901 (although citizenship rights at the time of federation did not extend to Aboriginal people). Through an analysis of the role of Australian emigration in the Victorian novel, I demonstrate why the revision of English identity that took place in Australia held more than a passing interest for the Victorians. Despite being pushed to the edges of the novel's range of vision, what is at stake in representations of colonial success or failure in Australia is nothing less than the integrity of British identity, and at times, of the British nation itself.

Such stakes are dramatized neatly in what is often perceived to be at the crux of settler colonialism: "The paradox of settler societies is that they simultaneously resisted and accommodated the authority of an imperialist Europe" (Stasiulis and Yuval-Davis 4). Marked both by the nature of their dependent relations with an imperial power and by an unusual degree of political and economic autonomy, settler societies embodied a tentative and ambivalent position with the empire. In the case of Canada, Australia, and New Zealand—sometimes termed the "white dominions"—strong imperial ties meant that "the dominant culture and institutions were fashioned directly on those of the 'mother' country (Britain)" (Stasiulis and Yuval-Davis 3–4). Yet despite such self-fashioning, these borrowings from imperial culture were complicated by the heterogeneous nature of colonial society. As James Hammerton notes, "the complex British rules which established social identity required revision in a pioneering colonial society like Australia," which was "a more primitive and egalitarian, albeit still socially stratified, society" (*Emigrant Gentlewomen* 63). Such stratification obviously complicates how we read the interactions between home and colony in the context of Australia. Donald Denoon, for instance, questions whether emigration alone can account for the maintenance of colonial ties to Britain given a large population of Irish emigrants who may have been less inclined toward loyalty to Britain (53).

Given these complexities, we can read the emigrant as a liminal figure who crosses geographical and textual boundaries, allowing us to track these tensions and to address the complex imbrications of domesticity and imperialism. Unlike British travelers abroad, who were the subjects of much scholarship throughout the 1990s,[8] Australian emigrants are inhabitants and not just visitors in the "contact zone" (Pratt, *Imperial Eyes* 4). As such, they permanently disrupt the binary oppositions that arise in the context of colonial encounter—including the boundaries between self and other, between colonizer and colonized. This is especially true in the case of Australia, where middle-class emigrants are precariously poised within a colonial space fractured by a shifting social hierarchy whose constituents—Aborigines, convicts, gold diggers, and free settlers of English, Scottish, and Irish descent—were classified according to race, ethnicity, economic status, and in some cases, reason for emigration. Within this fluid space, I identify a crucial paradox regarding the role of portable domesticity in colonial Australia: even as portable domesticity reinforces the values of British culture, it also subverts them, since the domestic practices that enable emigrants to transplant their national identity also initiate the process of settlement that gradually leads to the formation of a new national identity for Australia, and ultimately, to independence from Britain.

The "ambivalence of emplacement" that characterizes the conditions of emigration and settlement in a place like Australia is internalized by the emigrant/settler even at the level of language (Slemon 39), since Australia's status as an English-speaking colony results in textual productions by settler writers that are imbricated both in British and Australian literary traditions and are at times subversive in their relationship to imperialist power.[9] Textual representations of the emigrant/settler as a figure who is "not quite colonial" reveal a potentially wider spectrum of subject positions vis-à-vis nationality than simple binaries allow (Spence 2: 65). This broad spectrum in turn aids our understanding of the workings of empire both in the Australian colonies and in the imperial metropolis by illustrating that although the Antipodes signified for the Victorians a space that was socially and geographically far removed from Britain, events in Australia have reverberating effects that impact not only on settler and indigenous populations, but also on Britons back home.[10]

CO-OPTING DOMESTICITY FOR IMPERIAL AIMS

In his work on settler colonialism in Northern Ireland and Zimbabwe, Ronald Weitzer identifies two features of stable settler rule. The first involves maintaining control over indigenous populations by containing unrest or political agitation and minimizing involvement in indigenous affairs by the imperial power, while the second involves maintaining cohesion within the dominant settler population, a difficult task given the heterogeneous nature of settler societies (Weitzer 27–28). Weitzer's terms, when applied to Australia, suggest that simultaneous control over indigenous populations and a burgeoning group identity among settlers could work together to help minimize the pronounced cleavages within Australian society—between colony/metropole, settler/indigene, convict/free settler, and English/Scottish/Irish emigrants. *Antipodal England* reveals that one of the primary mechanisms for achieving these ends was domesticity.

As Annie E. Coombes reminds us, "ideas of 'self' and 'nation' were forged not only in response to the heterogeneous nature of the aspirations of the migrant and largely European communities . . . they *also* derived in response to the challenges presented by the reality of encountering indigenous peoples with highly differentiated political, cultural, and social structures" (3). Settlers in Australia responded to such challenges by exerting social control over indigenous domestic practices and familial arrangements. While the focus of this book is primarily on the specific ways in which English domesticity was transported to facilitate the creation of a home for British emigrants in Australia, it is also imperative to acknowledge the ways in which portable domesticity contributed to the exploitation of Australia's Aboriginal peoples—in many cases amounting to genocide—both through an ideology that presumed exclusion and through material practices that demarcated literal separations and enforced geographical displacement. In the case of Australia and other settler societies, cultural imperialism of this kind took many forms including "the outlawing of indigenous religions, customs and languages, forced removal of children from parents, and the imposition of European norms of gender roles, nuclear family institutions and forms of knowledge" (Stasiulis and Yuval-Davis 24–25).

While persistent and often violent interference in Aboriginal family systems was common from the colonial period onwards, popular and critical recognition of the systemic nature of such practices occurred only recently.[11] And while the literary, visual, and nonfictional texts I examine in the chapters that follow occasionally focus on colonial encounter, Aboriginal people and their culture typically remain either marginalized or remarkably absent from the accounts of emigration that I analyze. Such an elision points to the efficiency with which the policing of the domestic realm was carried out in Australia, and to the success of a policy of "strategic amnesia" that enabled Britons largely to disregard the catastrophic fate of Australia's indigenous peoples in the wake of British colonization and settlement (Anderson x). The conclusion of this study begins the exploration of how the domestic practices established by Victorian settlers continued to hold sway and influence twentieth-century social and racial policies, so that the tragic consequences of colonialism for indigenous peoples can be seen reiterated and reaffirmed in postcolonial Australia.

In addition to contributing to the project of controlling indigenous populations, domestic ideologies also play a crucial role in creating unity within the dominant settler group in Australia by helping to sustain a "myth of common ethnic origin" (Stasiulis and Yuval-Davis 19). Domesticity was able to help smooth over divisions within the settler population because it could reduce the distance between constituencies as diverse as convicts and free settlers or English and Irish migrants. This was possible in part because, as historians interested in the complex negotiations of class, gender, and nation in the Victorian era have ably illustrated, domestic ideology was inextricably bound up with conceptions of English national identity in the nineteenth century. Dror Wahrman, Leonore Davidoff, Catherine Hall, and John Tosh are among those scholars whose work has illuminated these connections to demonstrate how domesticity transcended class boundaries to become a marker—not of class per se—but of national character and "the conventional good life" (Tosh 4).[12] Davidoff and Hall's influential study, *Family Fortunes*, in particular, illustrates how the middling classes had cohered into a "powerful unified culture" by the middle of the nineteenth century, with the family serving as a focal point for class definition (23). The domestic culture that was the hallmark of this class gradually became essential to the national character of the English as "the middle-class view . . . [became] the triumphant common sense of the Victorian age" (Davidoff and Hall 28). By extension, the family—the heart of the domestic ideal—played a pivotal role in securing the health of the state and imposing a moral order that impacted "not only on relations between the sexes but also in definitions of who was properly part of the English nation. The 'teeming poor', the Irish, the gypsies, the unclean, all were consigned to the category of 'other'" (Davidoff and Hall 450). As this quotation implies, those groups within England who lacked access to a secure domestic and familial lifestyle were deemed to be outside of the nation.

By contrast, in Australia, such categorical distinctions were made first and foremost to demarcate the boundaries between settler and indigene, a project that diverted attention away from the less critical but still important borders between heterogeneous emigrant groups. As Jenny Sharpe has demonstrated in her study of Anglo-Indian women, women's domestic work in the British colonies is synonymous with the work of policing racial divides: "the domestic sphere is a space of racial purity that the colonial housewife guards against contamination from the outside. . . . The 'innocent space' of the home ceases to be innocent once racial segregation is considered part of domestic work" (92). In contrast to this stark segregation, the boundaries among settler constituencies based on ethnicity, class, or even reason for migration were blurred, and Antipodal domesticity became an attractive arena for refashioning emigrant identity because it was both portable and flexible enough to be co-opted by emigrants and settlers seeking affiliation within an emerging middle-class group. As a result, domesticity provided a source of cohesion within the heterogeneous emigrant populations. By examining its portability, I call attention to the constructedness of domesticity, identifying how it was shaped and disseminated in deliberate and highly specific ways in order to serve the needs of the empire. Although middle-class emigrants represent a very small subset of the emigrant population in Australia—by the 1890s, the middle and upper classes accounted for only about one quarter of all emigrants from Britain (Tosh 176)—their presence was vital to the creation of what one writer calls "our more roomy *Southern* England" (Hursthouse 3), a collective to which many other emigrant groups aspired to belong.

As I suggested in my opening analysis of the looking glass, my understanding of portable domesticity is grounded on the premise that "home" is significant both in its material and ideological forms, since "[d]omesticity denotes both a *space* (a geographical and architectural alignment) and a *social relation to power*" (McClintock 34). For middle-class Victorians, the ideological import of domesticity was equally as important as the material and spatial practices that helped define it. Davidoff and Hall have argued, for example, that because most middle-class families at the start of Victoria's reign lived in rented accommodation and mobility was common, "home" was defined less by actual structures than by ideological associations: "the form of the housing, the shell within which that space, 'a home', was to be made, was neither fully thought out nor secure. . . . In the early part of the period, 'home' was as much a social construct and state of mind as a reality of bricks and mortar" (357–8). To put it in the words of Charles Dickens, whose fiction is replete with portable families, "home" signifies more than just "[f]our walls and a ceiling" ("A Cricket on the Hearth" 44).

Because of the ideological significance attached to domesticity and the commonplace assumption that it was the "natural" purview of the English, it could be readily co-opted and pressed into the service of the empire. In the Antipodes, domesticity proved crucial to the success of colonial settlement given Australia's historical function as the receptacle of Britain's "superfluous" and unwanted populations. Britain's transported convicts in particular played a pivotal role in the history of Australian colonization,[13] because as Robert Hughes notes in *The Fatal Shore*, "[w]hat the convict system bequeathed to later Australian generations was . . . an intense concern with social and political respectability" (xiii). Working against what Hughes terms the "convict stain," subsequent generations of emigrants fetishized middle-class domesticity as a means of divorcing their experience from associations with convict transportation and exile while simultaneously reinforcing their connections to Britain. As my readings of a range of texts will illustrate, portable domesticity thus allowed for a rewriting of Australia's past and the expression of a wish-fulfillment "that 'real' Australian history had begun with Australian respectability—with the flood of money from gold and wool, the opening of the continent, the creation of an Australian middle class" (Hughes xiii).

In addition to helping to erase Australia's convict history, an emphasis on middle-class domesticity was also advantageous in serving as a corrective to the licentiousness and unbridled mobility associated with the "strike-it-rich-quick mentality" engendered by the 1851 gold rush (Brantlinger, *Rule of Darkness* 124). Figured by one novelist as "a valuable element in colonial society" (Spence 2: 255), the middle-class family and its ideals of industry, accountability, and moderation are set in direct opposition to the presumed rough, transient, and avaricious customs of gold diggers and short-term emigrants. Often figured as a stabilizing force in Britain,[14] the middle classes play an equally important role in colonial Australia, where models of middle-class family life are envisioned in emigrant guides, propaganda, and fiction as a primary means through which to steady the empire, both socially and economically, and to ensure colonial loyalty to Britain. This stabilizing function was so dramatic that in some cases, even marginalized subjects could reposition themselves as solid citizens of empire through the adoption of domestic practices and ideals, further contributing after mid-century to "a quite unprecedented theme of middle-class respectability" in Australia (Hammerton, *Emigrant Gentlewomen* 112). By standing in opposition to the seemingly dangerous

forms of economic and social mobility associated with emancipated convicts and gold diggers, portable domesticity thus enhanced the respectability of emigration and settlement in Australia and contributed to the
"myth of common ethnic origin" among settler populations (Stasiulis and
Yuval-Davis 19).

Through the consolidation of control over indigenous populations
and the maintenance of some degree of unity among settler groups, British
emigrants gradually generated the foundational myths around which Australian nationalism would eventually cohere. Yet while "[t]he dominant
history told a brave story of pioneers and settlers, soldiers and unionists,
almost always white, English-speaking and male" (Pettman 66), this gendered fiction elides not only an extensive indigenous history, but also the
significant role settler women played in Australia, particularly given the
prominence of domesticity within the settler project. While the cult of
domesticity in Britain markedly glorified women's moral responsibilities
in the home, it was a short leap from there to women's responsibilities
to the nation and by extension the empire. In his well-known essay "Of
Queen's Gardens," John Ruskin explicitly makes this connection, famously
asserting that woman's queenly function extends to the nation through her
duty "to assist in the ordering, in the comforting, and in the beautiful
adornment of the state" (106). This duty is fulfilled through the British
wife's seemingly inherent aptitude for making domesticity portable, since
"wherever a true wife comes, this home is always round her. The stars
only may be over her head; the glow-worm in the night-cold grass may be
the only fire at her foot: but home is yet wherever she is; and for a noble
woman it stretches far round her" (102–3). Although he emphatically rele-
gates woman to her "proper" sphere by glorifying her moral virtue, Ruskin
simultaneously alludes to a uniquely feminine capacity for mobility that
has far more radical implications. While women are figured in the passage above as agents of portable domesticity, they are also emphatically
embodiments of portable domesticity, since they both carry out the work
of making the home and are themselves the carriers of it; in the context
of the empire then, women not only perform the work of domesticity, in
Ruskin's language, through "ordering" and "comforting," but also through
"adorning" or representing it. The middle-class woman was particularly
well placed to perform such work because, as Carolyn Vellenga Berman
has argued, "[b]y embracing the seemingly humble duties of domestic life
as a mission of national stature, women of all classes (but especially the
middle classes) could prove their superiority to women of rank as caretak-
ers of the nation" (53). I propose to show that far from being mere passive
participants in the practices of imperialism, Victorian women in Australia

played a critical role as powerful cultural mediators who possessed a perceived aptitude for making domesticity portable.[15]

If Victorian women ensure that national identity is preserved through the transplantation of British domestic life in the colony, Victorian men, by contrast, are often figured as a weak link in the chain connecting England to the empire. One renowned emigration advocate, Caroline Chisholm, calls it "an act of national blindness" to support a system of colonization without women.[16] She insists, "[g]ive [male emigrants] help-mates, and you make murmuring, discontented servants, loyal and happy subjects of the State" (30). What is left potently unstated in Chisholm's imperative is the threat that male emigrants might turn to, even marry, non-British women, thus potentially destabilizing a presumptive British identity not only for the men themselves, but for their children. However, while the Australian colonies created an opening for a redefinition of women's place in the empire, Antipodal emigration also allowed for a more capacious set of gender norms for Victorian men. While this may seem counterintuitive given the ethic of mateship and the romance of the bush celebrated in so much of early Australian fiction, the conditions of colonial settlement necessitated that middle-class male emigrants, like their female counterparts, appropriate domestic values and practices as a means of negotiating displacement and retaining ties to Britain. Drawing on Tosh's work on masculinity, which cogently argues that domesticity was a critical component of masculine identity for most of the nineteenth century, this study explores the extent to which domesticity was crucial not only to women's efforts at self-definition in the Antipodes, but also to that of their male counterparts.

READING THE ARTIFACTS OF EMPIRE

Antipodal England relies on a conception of national identity as a construct that, like domesticity, is defined as much by a state of mind as it is by physical space (in this case, by geographical boundaries). My understanding owes much to Homi K. Bhabha's arguments about the performative nature of national identity and to Benedict Anderson's landmark study of nationalism, *Imagined Communities*. By emphasizing the cultural roots of nationalism—in religion, print culture, language, and kinship—Anderson makes it possible to theorize national identity not in terms of political or state ideologies, but in terms of cultural practices. One such practice that Anderson famously identifies as crucial to the emergence of European nationalisms was the development in the eighteenth century of print-capitalism. "[T]he novel and the newspaper," Anderson argues, "provided the technical means for 're-presenting' the *kind* of imagined community that is the nation" (25).

Building from Anderson, I examine the print-capitalism of Antipodal England in both its fictional and nonfictional guises. By exploring the narratological uses of emigration plots in Victorian novels by Charles Dickens, Anthony Trollope, Mary Elizabeth Braddon, and Catherine Helen Spence, I chart how the novel in particular helps to shape conceptions of national identity by dramatizing who does and who does not belong within a specified imagined community. One of the noteworthy features of Victorian literature that inspired this study was the consistent marginalization of emigration plots across a wide spectrum of novels as emigrants disappear into or arrive from the colonies with very little narrative detail. By attending closely to examples of such marginalization and to how novelists used the empire for strategic purposes, I demonstrate how the novel actually dramatizes the centrality of the colonies to Victorian conceptions of home and national identity. Issues of genre are central to this study, which focuses in part on how novelists manipulate the generic conventions associated with sensation fiction and domestic fiction in order to examine the effects of cross-cultural translation associated with emigration and colonial return.

While the novel presents a vision of what imaginings are possible, visual art and nonfictional sources such as memoirs, letters, and emigrant guides provide alternative "sites of cultural self-fashioning" that also impact upon constructions of national identity (Brantlinger, "Cultural Studies" 54). By juxtaposing novels with other genres I endeavor to broaden current scholarship on British imperialism by investigating what Deirdre David calls "the textual labor of empire building" (4), or in other words, the ways in which the imperial project depended not only upon territorial expansion and military activity, but also on various kinds of texts and writing. In the chapters that follow, I pair novels with archival sources such as letters written by governesses who emigrated to Australia, personal accounts of the Australian gold rush, and emigrant guides published by individuals or corporations such as S. W. Silver and Company, outfitters of emigrant ships. My analysis centers on how fictional plots and propaganda mirrored and helped to generate sometimes conflicting Victorian attitudes toward imperialism. By reflecting and changing the terms in which emigration was imagined and discussed, these textual representations worked at times to sustain or to critique the projects of imperialism and colonization; the fervor with which emigration and settlement is discussed, however, speaks to the centrality of these issues within the empire as a whole.

Rather than charting a historical trajectory of Antipodal emigration, I have chosen to order the chapters in a way that mirrors the process of emigration itself; chapters move from an emphasis on the transition from home to colony, including the liminal spaces of the emigrant ship and the Australian gold fields, to the reverse movement of emigrants returning to Britain, and finally, to the more permanent and lasting forms of colonial settlement in Australia. Through this trajectory, my argument clarifies the increasingly complex processes by which portable domesticity transformed the emigrant into the settler; these processes were recognized, disavowed, and deployed at key moments as both the link *and* the point of rupture between home and colony.

My argument in the first chapter, "Housekeeping at Sea and on Shore: Portable Domesticity and Emigrant Transformation," revolves around the centrality of domestic practices aboard emigrant ships, where idealized family life is modeled in order to "train" individual emigrants for the roles they will subsequently adopt in the colony. Beginning with one of the most famous icons of Victorian emigration, Ford Madox Brown's painting, *The Last of England* (1852–55), I analyze representations of shipboard life in emigrant guides and in the writings of Caroline Chisholm, a proponent of group emigration who founded the Family Colonization Loan Society to permit artificial "family" units to travel and settle together. I read the emigration plot in Charles Dickens's *David Copperfield* within this historical context, arguing that each of these texts encourages impoverished middle-class and working-class British emigrants to adhere to middle-class standards of behavior and propriety in an attempt to preserve order amid the cramped spaces of emigrant ships and later to harness the supposedly liberating potential of empire in the colonies. Within the logic of these texts, and particularly the novel, the emigrant ship becomes a primary locus for the affirmation and adoption of middle-class domestic values and practices; once mastered, the texts seem to argue, middle-class domesticity will transform those unable to achieve financial security within England into industrious and successful settlers in Australia.

Chapter 2, "Performing the Voyage Out: Victorian Female Emigration and the Gendering of Displacement," retains a focus on liminal spaces by examining accounts both of shipboard life and of the Australian gold diggings. I begin by analyzing a collection of letters written by unmarried middle-class women who emigrated to Australia under the auspices of the Female Middle Class Emigration Society (FMCES). Alongside their letters I read Anthony Trollope's *John Caldigate*, a novel about the Australian gold rush that thematizes many of the issues raised by the FMCES emigrants. Although Trollope's titular hero can successfully return to Britain after temporarily inhabiting the morally ambiguous space of the Australian gold diggings, his female companion cannot. Thus, I explore the extent to which in the novel and the letters performances of domesticity, leisure, and strategic amnesia enable female emigrants to maintain their affiliations with a British middle class aboard ship and in the colony. I argue that while the letters and the novel differ in their assessments of the success of such performances, both suggest that the rift caused by class and gender inequality within the British nation is widened in the context of emigration, creating a space for potentially empowering and often threatening forms of female self-assertion and independence. While such threats are ultimately contained within the logic of the novel, they continually resonate in the autobiographical accounts I examine.

The succeeding chapters of *Antipodal England* shift focus more explicitly to the personal and national implications of emigration for the returned emigrant and for the settler. Chapter 3, "The Fraudulent Family: Emigration, Colonial Return, and the Sensational Crimes of Empire," revisits the family, exploring how the resilience and portability I discuss in the first chapter is challenged when Victorian emigrants to Australia return to Britain and subsequently become embroiled in plots involving bigamy and fraud that signify their divided allegiances between home and colony. By pairing two wildly popular accounts of colonial return from Australia to Britain, one the fictional case of George Talboys in Mary Elizabeth Braddon's *Lady Audley's Secret* and the other the actual legal case involving the Tichborne Claimant, I endeavor to show how both accounts, though seemingly very different, draw on the genre of sensation fiction to dramatize and heighten pervasive Victorian anxieties about emigration and colonial return. In so doing, these accounts illustrate how emigration threatens the family, and by extension, the nation, by importing into its arenas the fluidity associated with bigamy and fraud.

The fourth chapter, "'Verily the Antipodes of Home': Narrating Domesticity in the Bush," explores the transplantation of literature itself—and the genre of the domestic novel in particular—as another form of portable domesticity, one that helped to ensure the success of settlement and to forestall the threats associated with colonial return that are explored in the previous chapter. In analyzing the transplantation of genre, I look at one of the first domestic novels written in Australia by a woman, Catherine Helen Spence's *Clara Morison*, which details the story of a Scottish governess who emigrates to Australia. To explore how the iconography of the domestic novel is transformed within this colonial setting, I discuss *Clara Morison* as a rewriting of another domestic novel to which it incessantly doubles back—Charlotte Brontë's *Jane Eyre*. I argue that Spence's novel exemplifies the portability of domesticity in two ways: by thematizing the role of British literature in enabling emigrants to maintain their ties to their home country despite displacement, and more literally, by rewriting the domestic novel and setting it in Australia, thereby demonstrating its adaptability.

Antipodal England concludes with "Portable Domesticity and Strategic Amnesia," which considers the reverberating legacies of nineteenth-century colonial settlement, particularly as they have recently come to light through investigations in the 1990s into the fate of what have become known as Australia's Stolen Generations. This label represents the tens of thousands of Aboriginal children who, over the course of roughly seventy years, were forcibly removed from their families and placed in the custody of institutions or foster homes in an attempt to enforce assimilation to Anglo culture. The investigative commission that examined their fates concluded that Australia's state and local governments had, from the late nineteenth century to the late 1960s, engaged in a systematic policy of genocide with respect to Australia's indigenous people. Under the auspices of bettering the education and future opportunities available to indigenous children, the Stolen Generations were lost not only to their families, but also to the Aboriginal culture from which they were forcibly divorced. The genesis of this policy during the period under study suggests that portable domesticity, in addition to being an important resource for British emigrants struggling to maintain their ties to home while negotiating geographical and cultural displacements, simultaneously functioned in ultimately devastating ways to fulfill one of the most insidious objectives of empire building: the British civilizing mission.

In her recent collection, *Rethinking Settler Colonialism: History and Memory in Australia, Canada, Aotearoa New Zealand, and South Africa*, Coombes argues that "an understanding of the political and cultural institutions and practices which shaped these colonial societies in the past can provide important insights into the available means for contesting its legacy of unequal rights by historically marginalized peoples in the present" (2). By examining settler colonialism and the origins of nationalism in Australia, this study aims in part to contextualize recent developments in the twentieth century and to help us better understand "the radical ambivalence of colonialism's middle ground" (Slemon 34). Settler nation-states are born out of such ambivalence, and in particular, out of two significant ruptures: the splitting off from indigenous populations and the splitting off from the imperial metropolis (Elkins and Pedersen 3). Such ruptures are made possible by transforming a "myth of common ethnic origins" into a myth of "common destiny," which orients settler societies around a

collective future rather than the past (Stasiulis and Yuval-Davis 19). Faced
with the enormous divide between metropole and colony—physical and
material, but also emotional and psychological—British emigrants looked
to the future to construct a national narrative that could incorporate and
ultimately transcend their former ideals associated with family, nation,
and home. In so doing, they were able to imagine and create "another English house in another country," a project whose partial successes have had
reverberating consequences for both Britain and Australia.

By examining the multifaceted ways in which portable domesticity
functioned in colonial Australia, *Antipodal England* illustrates how the
rhetoric and realities of "home" enabled British emigrants throughout the
second half of the nineteenth century to create a national identity that
was dependent upon but distinct from their English counterparts. These
imaginings and the material practices that sustained them suggest that
the forces of cultural production extend beyond geographical boundaries. Furthermore, the prevalence of such forces, as demonstrated in the
diverse cultural texts I discuss, suggests the central role that emigration and settlement played within the context of the empire as a whole.
This study exemplifies how, as a pivotal site for the expansion of British
colonial settlement, the space I have called Antipodal England offers a
nuanced and complex field for reconceiving the processes of colonial and
postcolonial identity formation.

Chapter One

Housekeeping at Sea and on Shore

Portable Domesticity and Emigrant Transformation

*f*ord Madox Brown's *The Last of England* (1852–55), one of the most famous icons of Victorian emigration, depicts a young family seated in the stern of the emigrant ship, *Eldorado* (Figure 1.1). Wearing traveling clothes, the couple appear to be middle class, and the distance they place between themselves and the other emigrants suggests a desire to maintain class status. This desire for maintenance is also apparent in the couple's posture: insulated against any intrusion by their fellow passengers, the bodies of the husband and wife are pressed closely together, their hands interlocking on the man's knee. A small child lies hidden within the folds of the woman's shawl, noticeable only because a tiny hand is held within the woman's own. The man holds an umbrella that shields his wife from the wind and also obstructs the view behind her of the white cliffs of Dover, which stand in as a metonymy for England. The husband and wife stare straight ahead, presumably engaging in an act of memory that will enable them to idealize England from abroad, despite the events that have evidently driven them from home.[1]

The couple's physical positioning up against the ship's rails and their fixed expressions suggest a desire to hold themselves apart from the other passengers aboard the ship. In their distressed gentility, they represent the fate of many middle-class Britons who could not maintain their class status at home and had to forestall degradation by emigrating to the colonies, where they could subsequently refashion themselves as respectable colonial settlers. The stoicism reflected in the husband and wife's fixed expressions and in their gripping hands exemplifies a desire for maintenance in

FIGURE 1.1. Ford Madox Brown, *The Last of England* (1852–55). Courtesy of Birmingham Museums & Art Gallery.

the face of their dramatically changing circumstances, and in the midst of members of all classes.

By contrast to the couple in the foreground, the figures in the background, seemingly working-class emigrants, are represented as less orderly and contained. These figures—clustered around the ship's rails—are all partially hidden or cut off by the painting's frame, leaving only fragments of bodies: a child's face, a woman's hands, grinning faces, a shock of red hair. Yet although we are not given visual access to this scene in its entirety, Brown provided viewers with several meta-texts through which to read *The Last of England* when he exhibited the painting for the first time in London in 1865. The first is a written description from the exhibition catalogue which provides a narrative framework for reading the painting, particularly the truncated figures in the background, while the second is a sonnet Brown included in the catalogue to accompany *The Last of England*.[2]

The following description of the painting from *The Exhibition of WORK, and other Paintings by Ford Madox Brown* highlights several competing narratives about emigration that circulated within Victorian Britain around mid-century:

> The husband is shielding his wife from the sea spray with an umbrella. Next them in the back ground, an honest family of the green-grocer kind, father (mother *lost*), eldest daughter, and younger children, makes the best of things with tobacco-pipe and apples, &, &. Still further back a reprobate shakes his fist with curses at the land of his birth, as though that were answerable for *his* want of success; his old mother reproves him for his foul-mouthed profanity, while a boon companion, with flushed countenance, and got up in nautical togs for the voyage, signifies drunken approbation. (136–7)

Whereas the greengrocer's family is "mak[ing] the best of things" aboard ship, the group behind them disrupts such a narrative of stability by playing out a small, but important, drama of contestation. While his drunken friend abets him, a young reprobate curses his native land, signifying his willingness to dismiss his home country and to adopt a new life and potentially, a new national identity. A small woman, his mother, according to Brown, taps at her son's shoulder and tugs at the sleeve of his coat to still his shaking fist. The mother's attempt to silence her son might represent both a rebellion against the disparagement of their homeland and a desire to arrest the transformation that comes with changing national allegiances. The juxtaposition of all these scenes in the painting—the middle class couple's desire for maintenance, the working-class family's attempt to make the best of things, and the reprobate's encounter with his mother—represents emigration as a family drama. Furthermore, such scenes underscore the competing narratives of maintenance and transformation that are central to Victorian representations of emigration.

The circular shape of the painting mirrors these thematics by isolating and enclosing the family circle, while simultaneously cutting off the figures in the background who represent various threats to this domestic unit.[3] Interestingly, Brown's painting suggests that women are the ones who are primarily responsible for preserving the family and engaging in acts of maintenance that will ensure loyalty to Britain, sometimes despite transformation. Like the mother in the background, the wife in the fore-ground of the painting is represented as the individual responsible for defusing her husband's resentment toward his native land. In the 1865 catalogue, Brown says of the wife that "[t]he circle of her love moves with her" (136). Indeed, as a figuration of the angel in the house, the female emi-grant in Brown's painting wears a bonnet that Lucy Rabin rightly suggests imitates the circling of a halo.[4] Although the husband's face is darkened by his raised collar and by the hat pulled down toward his brooding eyes, the wife's face is bright, her expression calm.

The sonnet that Brown wrote to accompany his painting further rein-forces the angelic quality of the emigrant wife and the sanctity of her fam-ily circle. The first eleven lines of the sonnet are written in the voice of the husband lamenting the fact that his family has been forced to leave England, while the turn comes in the final three lines, where an unnamed speaker describes the wife's hope for the future:

"The last of England! o'er the sea, my dear,
Our home's to seek amid Australian fields.
Us, not the million-acred island yields
The space to dwell in. Thrust out! Forced to hear
Low ribaldry from sots, and share rough cheer
With rudely nurtured men. The hope youth builds
Of fair renown, bartered for that which shields
Only the back, and half-formed lands that rear
The dust-storm blistering up the grasses wild.
There learning skills not, nor the poet's dream,
Nor aught so loved as children shall we see."
She grips his listless hand and clasps her child,
Through rainbow-tears she sees a sunnier gleam,
She cannot see a *void*, where *he* will be. (Brown, *The Exhibition* 136)

The differences between the husband and the wife's views of emigra-tion are pronounced, and they involve the issue of whether or not it is possible to remain unchanged by the experience of displacement. The hus-band conceives of his emigration as punishment and even exile: "Thrust out! Forced to hear/Low ribaldry from sots, and share rough cheer/With rudely-nurtur'd men." Imagining numerous assaults against his class sta-tus and moral character through association with lower-class men, the husband envisions the voyage out as a point of rupture between his past and his future: "The hope youth builds/Of fair renown, barter'd for that which shields/Only the back." Exchanging hopes of success and respectability for the rude comforts of a colonial home, "that which shields/Only the back," the husband goes bitterly forward toward a future that he envisions as devoid of the privileges of his class—among them, literature and learning. Despite his outwardly stoic appearance, the husband presumably cannot discipline his brooding mind from continually revisiting, and lamenting over, the past.

The wife, on the other hand, envisions a continuity between past and future that is absent in the husband's dark imaginings of "half-form'd lands that rear/The dust-storm blistering up the grasses wild." While the husband ties his family's happiness absolutely to the place he and his wife have loved as children, the wife conceives of home, not in terms of place, but in terms of the people who comprise her domestic happiness—her family. As "She grips his listless hand and clasps her child," the wife performs the work of maintenance that enables her to protect and enclose her family circle. The final line of the sonnet, "She cannot see a *void*, where *he* will be," implies that as long as she and her husband are together, she can imagine a future filled with hope and happiness. Unlike her husband, she "sees a sunnier gleam" when she looks to the future because she believes in the impenetrability—and the portability—of her family.[5]

Inspired by the departure of Thomas Woolner, a Pre-Raphaelite poet and sculptor who emigrated to Australia in July, 1852, Brown's painting and its meta-texts capture many of the competing narratives that circulated in Victorian Britain at the height of "the great emigration movement" (Brown, *The Exhibition* 136). Among these narratives were possibilities for continuity or rupture, success or failure, memory or forgetting. Contemporary representations of emigration, like Brown's painting, frequently dramatize these tensions playing out within the context of the family. In many cases, these representations deploy a discourse of discipline to mediate between the competing pressures imposed upon the emigrant during the voyage out.

The success of social discipline, as Michel Foucault has famously demonstrated in *Discipline and Punish*, resides in its potential for mobility; through its capacity to occupy various social institutions, discipline quietly pervades all aspects of our lives. In the continuously mobile space of the voyage, the power of discipline is linked specifically to domesticity and its portable unit: the family. In this chapter, I explore how disciplinary discourses on housekeeping and domestic life are used to negotiate the tensions between maintenance and transformation that invariably accompany the act of emigration. In a variety of texts, including emigrant guides, emigrant propaganda, and Charles Dickens's novel, *David*

Copperfield, I analyze representations of emigrant success in maintaining ties to Britain through the practices of portable domesticity, then go on to show how such success is complicated by the possibilities for transformation associated with emigration, particularly with respect to class. As Rita Kranidis astutely notes, "[t]he possibility of transformation and change of individual attributes believed to be intrinsic to those who fit neatly into a socioeconomic class (or who are firmly placed national subjects) then may be said to constitute the main threat of unclaimed spaces such as the ship and those only slightly more delineated spaces, the colonies" (*The Victorian Spinster* 158). Yet the potential for transformation, while threatening, is also tied to the liberatory promise of colonial space, and it is the balance between these competing drives that is at stake in the process of emigration. Whereas Brown's painting and contemporaneous emigrant guides reveal a deep ambivalence about the extent to which maintenance and transformation can coexist, Dickens's novel, in keeping with the emigration propaganda for Caroline Chisholm's Family Colonization Loan Society, holds out a fantasy that colonists can maintain their national identity and allegiance despite the inevitable changes brought on by emigration.

DISCIPLINARY DOMESTICITY
AND THE PROJECT OF MAINTENANCE

The genre of the emigrant guide or handbook was created in response to the dramatic increase in emigration that began in the late 1830s and continued into the second half of the nineteenth century.[6] The format of these guides or handbooks is fairly standardized; most contain information about a designated colonial locale as well as practical hints for intending emigrants regarding both life on board an emigrant ship and in the colony of their choosing. The guides are typically tailored to the needs of a male reader, but they address readers both from the working class and from the middling classes. Although there are occasionally guides that specifically cater to a particular type of emigrant—for instance, men with capital or men traveling to the gold rush—most address a broader audience that cuts across class boundaries. Some of these guides are written by corporations, such as S. W. Silver & Company, outfitters of emigrant ships, while others are written by individuals who rely on their personal experience in the colonies to advise other emigrants. Thus, although the authors' purposes for writing may be commercial or simply personal, most guides and handbooks focus to some extent on imperial interests and the greater good of Britain and the empire.

While these guides represent a diversity of opinions on the subjects of emigration and colonization, one of the interesting features that they share in common is a similar rhetorical stance designed to guide readers and their expectations. More specifically, such guides attempt to direct readers interested in emigration in two ways: first, they endeavor to adopt an unbiased and honest approach to their subject in order to moderate or discipline the expectations of readers; and second, they provide readers with practical instructions about how to implement a disciplined approach to emigrant life, especially aboard ship. This focus on discipline is a key feature in many of the guides, seemingly regardless of authorship or audience.

Because they needed to negotiate between competing popular narratives about Australian emigration as a source of utopian success or dismal failure, writers of emigration guides to the Australian colonies typically adopt a rhetorical stance that moderates between these two extremes. By exercising restraint in discussing the merits and logistics of emigration, such writers try to regulate the expectations of eager readers and potential emigrants; they do so by employing what one such writer calls "a language of *moderation*" that focuses on representing the realities associated with emigration and dispelling the popular myths (Hursthouse 28). In a handbook published by S. W. Silver and Company, a corporation that published a series of emigrant guides addressing readers interested in a range of colonial locations, the authors describe the propensity for some guides and handbooks on the colonies to assume a "literary" rather than a "scientific" treatment of their subject, faulting such guides for their tendency to be colored by an individual author's personal impressions and limited experience. Purporting instead to approach the subject from a scientific or objective point of view, the authors of the series of *S. W. Silver & Co.'s Handbook for Australia and New Zealand* define the value of their series exclusively in terms of practicality: "Each Pocket Book will be replete with details, the purpose being rather to provide the voyager with a useful store of facts than to give him an amusing book for an hour's pleasure" (iii–iv). In similar fashion, the authors promise "to exercise in the most scrupulous manner a double impartiality" in balancing the advantages and disadvantages of emigration and distinguishing between Australia and New Zealand as possible destinations. By promising objectivity and impartiality, these guides encourage readers to value factual information and to be suspicious of the many popular myths that either glorified or vilified the Australian colonies.

Charles Hursthouse, author of an emigration guide comparing New Zealand and Australia with Canada and the United States, identifies one source of such myths by offering a hypothetical description of two families who respond to their emigrant experiences in differing yet stereotypical ways. One family emigrates during the harvest month and immediately writes home with news of a paradise, and another family, accustomed to "silver forks, slippers, and soft-beds," is beset by troubles and immediately writes home with news of their disappointments. Neither family, according to Hursthouse, is correct in their hasty assessments; instead, "[a]fter the short experience of twelve months they would probably agree in representing the country neither as a paradise nor the utter reverse; but as a very fair country, in which, with common industry and activity, moderate success, at least, was *certain*" (83–4). Writing with the benefit of his own personal experience and reflection on life in various colonies, Hursthouse thus promotes the use of restraint in treating the subject of emigration and colonial life, even going so far as to regard such treatment as a moral obligation on the part of writers of guides and handbooks.[7] Hursthouse explains,

> if we rather understate than overstate—if we tell the emigrant that although the colony *does* yield him a clear stage, he will not win the battle unless he fights—that industry, energy, perseverance, qualities essential to success in the old country, are (if in a less degree) still essential to success in a new country; we shall, at least, have the satisfaction of knowing that we don't *deceive* him. . . . And thus it is, that in seeking to direct a stream of emigration to any particular locality, not only common honesty, but common good policy, true self-interest, should lead us to paint our picture in such sober colours that the emigrant shall recognise and acknowledge the *truthfulness* of the sketch, when brought face to face with the actual original. (28–29)

What is noteworthy about the above quote is Hursthouse's emphasis on truth and verisimilitude, a focus that echoes the emphasis in S. W. Silver's guides on objectivity and practicality. This focus is designed to temper the expectations of eager emigrants who might otherwise be too readily influenced by the more dramatic stories of success and failure. Hursthouse's emphasis on "industry, energy, and perseverance" is also an important feature of emigrant guides as a genre. Most guides place a premium on these or similar qualities and encourage potential emigrants to be aware that success in the colony requires, above all things, discipline and hard work. Despite the fact that these guides address a diverse audience, especially in terms of class, this emphasis is a common feature that works to moderate the expectations of readers, and perhaps even dissuade those unaccustomed to hard work.[8]

Rather than linking colonial success to factors such as class status, occupation, age, or gender, emigrant guides consistently represent hard work as *the* key to prosperity in the colonies. H. Smith Evans, in *A Guide to the Emigration Colonies*, writes that "[t]he timid, the discontented, the idler, and the drunkard, are the only parties who are not eligible for emigration. Labour is the passport to wealth and independence" (4). Likewise, Captain Maconochie writes that "[i]n conducting a great scheme of emigration, the mother country much more readily sends out her worst than her best; and the helplessness that loses ground at home, is not likely to gain it at the antipodes" (7). Equating a willingness to work with eligibility for successful emigration, emigrant guides recommend disciplined approaches to emigrant life that complicate traditionally rigid British class distinctions, as this example from the *Australian and New-Zealand Passengers' Guide* will demonstrate:

> It is useless for any one to emigrate who cannot carry with him health, strength, industry, and a strong determined will to overcome all difficulties, to endure disappointment, and patience to wait results. In those lands of the Antipodes a man cannot indulge in the genteel profession of living on his wits. He must put his shoulder to the wheel. He must be prepared to dig and delve and build, to plough and sow and reap. He has, however, this satisfaction for his energy and patient industry, that he labours for a tangible something, for a truly remunerative living, not a bare subsistence—a living that means, with continued determined labour and economy, an honourable independence, a home and lands and property, a comfortable old age, and the satisfaction that he leaves his family well provided. (4)

In its delineation of the kind of industry required in the Antipodes, this guide invokes what might be traditionally regarded in Britain as a working-class ethic that values physical labor as an honorable and worthy pursuit. Yet interestingly, the rewards for such labor are framed in terms that invoke a middle-class ethic, which typically values property as well as intangibles like independence and comfort. What this passage suggests is that the kinds of social distinctions that were rigidly upheld in Britain become less important and less distinct in the colony, where working with one's hands is regarded as equally important as "living on [one's] wits."[9] Such class transformations were equally complex aboard emigrant ships, where class distinctions were artificially maintained through the segregation of passengers according to rank into first-class, second-class, and steerage accommodations. Such distinctions were particularly important given the history of convict transportation and the consequent associations of Australian emigration with moral degeneration. One diarist, Reverend John Davies Mereweather, recognizes the threats associated with cross-class encounters aboard ship and asks "[w]hy not introduce, if not wholly, at least partially, the discipline of the convict ship on board the cheap emigrant ship?" (31). While such discipline might serve as an antidote to the legacies of convict transportation, it was also perceived as important because, as Patricia Clarke notes, the 14,000 mile voyage to the Antipodes also involved very real dangers and discomforts:

> Travel by sea in the nineteenth century was often a hazardous undertaking, and for emigrants traveling as far as Australia and New Zealand, it was especially so. The voyage, usually by sailing-ship, rarely took less than three months and often much longer; it traversed extremes of climate from the intense and humid heat at the Equator to the icy gales and storms of the southern ocean; it was usually uncomfortable, cramped, regimented and tedious; the food was dreary and monotonous, if not actually lacking in essentials; and severe seasickness and serious epidemic diseases were common. (24)

In responding to such physical dangers associated with shipboard life, physician James Fraser published *The Emigrant's Medical Guide* in 1853. In it, he concedes to the increasing amenities afforded by sea travel in the mid-nineteenth century, but argues that the close proximity of individuals from different classes aboard ship constitutes a legitimate public health threat that requires diligent attention on the part of all emigrants. He writes that "a crowded emigrant ship is 'a prison,' in which, without an intelligent acquaintance with, and application of, the laws of Hygiene, or the art of preserving health, the more malignant forms of disease may lead to results as disastrous as the destructive agency of the elements" (13).[10]

Fraser's emphasis, not on natural disaster, but on personal neglect, highlights the need for passengers to be vigilant with respect to hygiene and health aboard emigrant ships. Although many of his warnings are directed most pointedly to the steerage passengers who inhabit exceptionally close quarters, Fraser is nonetheless quick to point out that the middle-class body is not immune to contagion. In fact, middle-class emigrants are equally susceptible and open to attack, "for, although their better physical condition on embarking may enable them to resist disease a *little longer*, the ultimate effect will be the same" (14). Fraser's comment underscores the extent to which the class system aboard ship—even as it rigidly segregates passengers by rank into first class, second class, and steerage compartments—has the potential to break down, thus undermining the distinctions that emigrants like Brown's couple so avidly hope to keep in place. Aboard ship, disease is the great leveler that can quickly destroy the social distinctions so carefully nurtured within British society. The performance of hygienic and domestic rituals thus becomes imperative for class preservation, not only as a means of "keeping up appearances," but more importantly, of fending off the imagined "contamination" of the lower classes.

One way to protect against such threats was for emigrants to create an insular "home" aboard ship. It is therefore ironic that unlike the manual labor that is required of new settlers in the colony, often regardless of their class status, the work aboard ship, like that described above, is primarily the work of middle-class domesticity. P. B. Chadfield, author of *Out at Sea; or, The Emigrant Afloat,* describes an emigrant ship as "a floating home for the many families on board; partaking in a great measure of the character of a house, a ship presents the somewhat novel spectacle of several grades and conditions of men, and their families, for a time domesticated in one habitation" (30). Providing emigrants with minutely-detailed instructions regarding "the requirements and wants in housekeeping at sea" (11), Chadfield describes the fitting out of a cabin, or in other words, the creation of a portable household within the small shipboard spaces allotted to emigrants, as one of the most important domestic duties aboard ship. While first-class passengers occupied private quarters, their second-class counterparts lived in small cabins which housed several emigrants together, and the steerage passengers occupied communal (sometimes partitioned) spaces below decks.[11] For second-class and steerage passengers, housekeeping duties included setting up their living spaces for occupancy, keeping them clean, preparing meals, and washing dishes and utensils. In addition to providing emigrants with explicit directions about what to take on the journey and what to wear aboard ship, Chadfield's guide also includes recipes and instructions for cooking meals with the available provisions. He writes: "From the recipes already given, very tolerable dinners may be provided, if the emigrants themselves will take the trouble to prepare them; if not, they have themselves only to blame" (23). Like the members of the greengrocer family in Brown's painting who take comfort in the small luxuries still available to them, Chadfield emphasizes the emigrant's agency in making the best of conditions aboard ship. He requires of his readers the discipline and diligence that are characteristic features of the emigrant guide as a genre.

In addition to attending to the practical aspects of portable domesticity like fitting out a cabin and preparing meals, emigrants are encouraged to engage in very structured forms of leisure that become the "work" of shipboard life. Among the intellectual occupations and leisure pursuits recommended are the following: establishing schools and newspapers, pursuing a course of reading or study, keeping a journal, playing games, dancing, sporting, and sewing. *S. W. Silver & Co.'s Colonial and Indian Pocket Book Series and Voyager's Companion* is typical in advocating an engagement in useful occupations aboard ship:

> And yet it is just as well for the most light-hearted bird of passage to give himself some **Occupations**. A daily task gives zest to amusement and respectability to idleness. Indeed, a sea day is a long day without work of some kind. Two or three important books, above the easy reading class, may advantageously be attacked for a couple of hours, and the Pocket Book Log and Chart may very well ask for thirty minutes' attention. Ladies are fortunate in the ever ready resources of the needle and the crochet-hook. (27)

Silver's guide highlights the way in which emigrants, regardless of gender or class, are assimilated to a middle-class ideal of domesticity aboard ship. The pursuits recommended above—reading books "above the easy reading class," writing, and sewing—all assume middle-class occupations. And yet, as I have suggested, while a few guides are targeted specifically to the middle classes, the majority are directed at a wide audience, only occasionally addressing directly a subset of emigrants by class or occupation. While the notion of "respectable idleness" alluded to above resonates with the position of the British middle-class woman, who had to occupy her time with work while simultaneously creating the illusion of leisure, such guides prevent the potential feminization of male emigrants when placed in an analogous position by coding "play" aboard ship *as* work. In the passage above, Silver's guide also carefully delineates separate domestic occupations for women versus men. Through such strategies, emigrant guides defuse anxieties about the gendering of domestic work, while simultaneously assimilating the lower classes to a middle-class ethic that will help them succeed in the colony.[12] By couching the potential for social transgression within a rhetoric of proper restraint, anxieties about class mobility are less threatening than they might otherwise be.[13]

By encouraging discipline, introspection, and intellectual improvement, emigrant guides frame the emigrant ship as a space in which middle-class emigrants can engage in the practices of maintenance that will enable them to pass through the voyage unchanged, while lower-class emigrants can emulate middle-class models of success. Such a framework is also evident in the rhetoric associated with an organization founded in 1850 to promote emigration to the British colonies: Caroline Chisholm's Family Colonization Loan Society. The society's purpose, outlined by Chisholm in *The A. B. C. of Colonization*, was to provide financial assistance in the form of loans primarily to working-class and lower middle-class emigrants who might not otherwise be able to emigrate. Committed to the belief that the family was the key to successful colonization, Chisholm developed a system that enabled emigrants to band together in family groups comprised of individuals of all ages, who lived together aboard ship and ideally, continued to support one another in the colony, forming what she called "bush-partnerships" (16). By capitalizing on the disciplinary power inherent in these collective groups, wherein individual emigrants were responsible for all the members of their "family," Chisholm created a system of self-regulation to ensure the protection of female emigrants and children aboard ship, to guarantee the repayment of debts, and to promote colonial loyalty to Britain.

In writing about Chisholm's work in a piece for *Household Words*, W. H. Wills describes the promises elicited from embarking emigrants of the Family Colonization Loan Society. One such promise resonates clearly with the rhetoric of emigrant guides and their emphasis on structured leisure: Chisholm's emigrants resolved "to encourage and promote some well-advised system of self-improvement during the passage" (Wills 228). Likewise, participants pledged the following:

> We . . . endeavour, individually and collectively, to preserve the order of a well-regulated family during our passage to Australia, and to organise and establish a system of protection that will enable our female relatives to enter an emigrant ship with the same confidence of meeting with protection, as respectable females can now enter our steamers, trains, and mail-coaches. (qtd. in Wills 228)

Founded on the principles of self-help, Chisholm's society incorporates a pledge that echoes the disciplinary rhetoric of emigrant guides, particularly with its emphasis on "preserv[ing] the *order* of a *well-regulated* family" (italics mine). In addition, the oblique reference to female chastity in the passage above insists on the idea of maintenance, ensuring that there is no threat of a fall for female emigrants. Reacting against the notorious "moral threats to unaccompanied women" that received undue attention in the popular press (Kranidis, *Victorian Spinster* 158), Chisholm suggests that an organized system of emigration is safe and practical for female as well as male emigrants.

On March 30, 1850, Charles Dickens published a collection of letters written by British emigrants in Australia to serve as an endorse-
ment of Chisholm's newly-founded organization. This piece, entitled
"A Bundle of Emigrants' Letters," appeared in the inaugural edition of
Household Words contemporaneous with the serialization of *David Copperfield*.[14] Like the *Household Words* article, Dickens's novel endorses certain features of Chisholm's model of emigration, and there are numerous
aspects of the emigration plot in *David Copperfield* which suggest that
Dickens was influenced both by the rhetoric of emigrant guides and by
Chisholm's model of family emigration.[15] Dickens's description of the
steerage compartment of the emigrant ship in *David Copperfield* represents the diversity of age and occupation that was the hallmark of Chisholm's emigration system. Whereas governmental emigration schemes
placed restrictions on eligibility for emigration based on age and on the
number and ages of children within a family, Chisholm required only
the voucher of "good character," insisting that successful colonization
required a wide spectrum of individuals. In *David Copperfield*, Dickens
seems to agree:

> From babies who had but a week or two of life behind them, to crooked
> old men and women who seemed to have but a week or two of life before
> them; and from ploughmen bodily carrying out soil of England on their
> boots, to smiths taking away samples of its soot and smoke upon their
> skins; every age and occupation appeared to be crammed into the nar-
> row compass of the 'tween decks. (662)

The literal transplantation of English soil, soot, and smoke described
in this passage resonates with Chisholm's vision of emigration as the
wholesale transfer of English life to the colonies—a transfer made possible
through the portability of domesticity, and more particularly, the family.
Within the crowded space of the emigrant ship, represented by Dickens as
a society in microcosm, the work of domesticity is underway even before
the ship sails: "some, already settled down into the possession of their
few feet of space, with their little households arranged, and tiny children
established on stools, or in dwarf elbow-chairs; others, despairing of a
resting-place, and wandering disconsolately" (662). Like the writers of
emigrant guides, Dickens tethers the ability to create a home aboard ship
to success, while the inability to find "a resting-place" is linked early on to
the potential for failure, both aboard ship and in the colony.

This capacity for portable domesticity presumably comes naturally to
the Peggottys. Prior to their departure for Australia, the members of the

Peggotty household are already accustomed to living within unconventional family structures. David is amazed to discover, for instance, that Emily and Ham are Mr. Peggotty's niece and nephew, not his children, and that Mrs. Gummidge is biologically unrelated to the other inhabitants of the boathouse. David is equally surprised when he learns that the Peggottys live at Yarmouth in a ship that has been converted into a home. This unusual abode—a model of portable domesticity—is represented as a tidy, comfortable, and insular domestic space. As a young child, David is especially charmed by the fact that the ship had once been functional at sea: "That was the captivation of it to me. If it had ever been meant to be lived in, I might have thought it small, or inconvenient, or lonely; but never having been designed for any such use, it became a perfect abode" (24). David's comments highlight a central irony about domesticity: whereas "real" homes and families often fail to meet the excessive expectations of Britain's domestic ideal, those homes and families that are not so rigidly bound by conventional expectations often more closely approximate the ideal. Yet as John Tosh notes, "no reality could have matched the depth of emotional need invested in the idea of home. The Victorians were driven by their sense of social alienation to set up an exacting standard which hardly anyone could meet" (50). The unconventional homes and families that are a hallmark of Dickens's fiction, including Peggoty's boathouse and Wemmick's Castle in *Great Expectations*, depart from this "exacting standard" in interesting ways. The boathouse, for instance, is idealized as an unconventionally "delicious retreat" (25) that is perfectly self-contained and self-sustaining. Yet it is also mobile and flexible, able to accommodate readily an extension of the family when David and Peggotty arrive.

Given the adaptability of their family unit, the Peggottys would seem predisposed to successfully meeting the challenges posed by emigration, and indeed, together with the Micawbers, they comprise a family group that travels together and maintains an alliance in the colony which proves beneficial to all parties and which echoes Chisholm's notion of the ideal "bush partnership." Even before they leave England, the Micawbers appear to have learned something from the Peggottys about the domestic discipline that will be required of them aboard ship. In a parody of the necessities of sea travel, Dickens describes the Micawber children on the evening prior to their emigration to Australia, outfitted in their traveling clothes and wearing wooden spoons strapped to their bodies. As he serves his wife and children punch in the small tin pots they will utilize aboard ship, Mr. Micawber speaks about the restraint and self-discipline that their emigration will require of them: "The luxuries of the old country . . . we abandon. The denizens of the forest cannot, of course, expect to participate in the refinements of the land of the Free" (657). Partially immobilized by their snug-fitting garments, the members of the Micawber family humorously embody their willingness to relinquish some of the freedoms they have enjoyed at home. As they learn to equate domesticity with proper restraint, they begin to perform the roles that will be required of them as emigrants and settlers.

In addition to having secured their provisions for the voyage, Micawber proudly describes to Betsey Trotwood the "domestic preparations" his family is engaged in to groom themselves for the colonial occupations of farming and raising stock (630). The Micawber children are individually tasked with learning through observation to milk cows, to understand the habits of pigs and poultry, and to drive cattle. Micawber, on the other hand, has "directed some attention . . . to the art of baking" (631), while Mrs. Micawber is busy corresponding with her family in hopes of reuniting them with her husband prior to their departure. This role reversal, in which Micawber temporarily exchanges his writing for domestic work while Mrs. Micawber does the opposite, is suggestive of the way gender roles are transformed and adapted even before the family departs for colonial Australia. While domesticity is often integrated into conceptions of masculinity aboard ship and in the Antipodes, women are simultaneously charged with the work of cultural mediation that ensures that the family stays together and that its individual members maintain their loyalty to Britain.

Such loyalty is evident once the Micawber family reaches Australia and Mr. Micawber is able to repay all the debts he had incurred in Britain. In the colony, where he is no longer plagued by the threat of arrest and coercion, Micawber is presumably motivated to repay these debts either through an appropriate sense of duty or through a desire to further his burgeoning political career. Either way, he ironically becomes a model British citizen only by leaving his native land. His success resonates with one writer's speculations that by being kept "under the influence of home associations and public opinion" Caroline Chisholm's emigrants "would remain more English, more patriotic, than they now usually are, to their own infinite advantage, as well as that of the mother-country" (Maconochie 12). Micawber's ability to maintain his ties to his home country is certainly in keeping with the popular ethos of self-help to which Chisholm's colonization scheme is indebted. Her assumption was that working-class emigrants could be trusted to repay the money they had borrowed—money donated by generous members of the public—because they would be bound both by ties of nationalism and by ties of family. According to Chisholm, emigrants who had accepted loans "would feel a desire, a longing to do something worthy the confidence placed in them by the nation" (14). Where such patriotic feelings failed to instill a sense of duty in the debtor, Chisholm also relied on a "code of honour" among the members within a family group, since one emigrant's failure to repay a loan automatically became the responsibility of the collective. This model of a self-regulating system of discipline and surveillance is consistent with the rhetoric of emigrant guides, and it helps to account for Micawber's ability to engage in a form of maintenance that enables him to retain his ties to Britain while in Australia despite his prior financial indiscretions in his home country.

MAINTENANCE AND TRANSFORMATION IN TENSION

An 1858 illustration published in London and entitled "Welcome Given in Melbourne Australia to a Primrose from England" visually dramatizes the process of maintenance that I have argued is associated with portable domesticity in the context of emigration (Figure 1.2). The image depicts a group of men, women, and children gathered in a Melbourne shop around a flowerpot containing a primrose that has recently arrived from the home country. In the center of the picture, a shopkeeper stands watch over the scene, and three gentlewomen kneel on the floor huddled around the flower, heads bowed in thought with expressions that evoke the workings of memory. To the left and right of this grouping in the center, the faces of young men and in one case, of a young family, echo the thoughtful, nostalgic expressions of the figures in the center.

Like the emigrant ships discussed earlier, the Melbourne shop in this illustration represents a potentially chaotic space in which individuals from all classes intermingle. Such intermingling is especially evident in a gathering at the doorway of the shop, where a crowd of people including a gloved gentleman, a soldier, and a female servant wait to gain access to the shopkeeper and his latest import. The gentleman pays a figure seated at the entrance, presumably the price of admission. Inside the shop, some of the trappings typically associated with a rough, wild, and transient life in Australia are present in the picture—pistols dangle from one man's belt; pipes and rope hang from the ceiling of the shop; rifles and tools are gripped by several of the working men; and the rigging of a ship sits in the harbor. Yet counteracting these images are others associated with maintenance and community that suggest how all of these diverse figures are united by a sense of loyalty and by feelings of nostalgia for their home country. In particular, a family of four seated in the right-hand corner of the picture's frame echoes the family in *The Last of England*. Like the

FIGURE 1.2. "Welcome Given in Melbourne Australia to a Primrose from England," *Illustrated London News* (1858). Courtesy of Bodleian Library, University of Oxford, N. 2288g.6.

couple in the latter portrait, the father in "Welcome Given in Melbourne Australia" appears somewhat dejected, while the mother bows her head and closes her eyes with a more reverent expression. It is as if the mere presence of the flower, a vibrant emblem of portable domesticity, exerts a mesmerizing effect on all of the onlookers, taming and domesticating what might otherwise be a potentially unruly scene.

While the reverence inspired by the imported flower from England is likely the first thing the viewer notes in examining this illustration, another striking feature is the repetition throughout the scene of hands that either gesticulate toward the flowerpot at the center, or enclose other hands. Despite the obvious theme of maintenance underlying this nostalgic portrayal of emigrant life, the representation of these hands dramatizes a more subtle, opposing impulse—the possibility of transformation. As Bruce Robbins has argued in *The Servant's Hand*, hands were important markers within the Victorian class system, since they were the part of the body most vulnerable to physical contact between members of various classes.[16] Here, the numerous outreaching hands, which are uniformly genteel, with elongated, tapered fingers and delicate curvatures, represent the possibilities for class transformations in Australia. Despite the fact that members of all classes are differentiated throughout the illustration through their dress, the commonalities among the figures' hands suggests that class difference can be homogenized, and thus, that class mobility is possible in this new setting. The uniformity of these emigrant hands suggests that each figure in the picture, from the gentlewomen in the foreground to the working men with their rifles, is presumably ennobled and even transformed by being in the presence of the primrose and the nostalgic longing for Britain and "home" that it generates.[17]

In order to see how the tensions between maintenance and transformation that are made concrete in "Welcome Given in Melbourne Australia" are echoed in Dickens's novel, we must first return to the rhetoric of emigration guides. Although the emigrant's journey aboard ship allows for the domestic practices that serve to maintain national and class affiliations, George S. Baden-Powell in *New Homes for the Old Country* alludes to the contradictory possibilities of transformation that accompany the voyage out. In his guide, Baden-Powell advocates a longer voyage over a shorter one, arguing that the time spent aboard ship will enable the emigrant to discipline his mind in preparation for colonial life. Speaking about the emigrant to Australia and New Zealand, he writes:

> In the seventy days of rounding the Cape in a large vessel, he must be able to glean an immense amount of experience from the many on

board, who are able and willing to tell him all they know of the country whither he is bound. He will land with less thought of and regret for home, and with more knowledge of what is best to do. He will have had time to think over his position and make up his mind; he will have formed some sort of correct idea of his newly adopted land; whereas after a short voyage he would be suddenly set down, after a week's semi-sea-sickness, in a land of strangers, with all his home ties and ideas still strongly influencing him, and with but very vague notions of what to do or how to do it. (449)

Baden-Powell's comments highlight the emigrant's journey as a crucial period of transition and even transformation. As he describes it, the physical distance traversed during the emigrant's journey corresponds to a process of psychological distancing from the home country that enables the emigrant to gradually forge new national ties with his adopted country. During a long sea journey, the emigrant gains the experience, knowledge, and resolve that will enable him to succeed in the colony, whereas during a shorter journey the emigrant experiences a period of idleness that breeds indecision and homesickness.

The competing narratives of maintenance and transformation evident in Baden-Powell's description of shipboard life conjoin in the rhetoric of housekeeping and in the middle-class ideal of comfort, which is frequently evoked in emigrant guides as a measure of the emigrant's success both aboard ship and in the colony. Chadfield writes of his own experience as a passenger, noting that "[i]t was a common remark, during our voyage to the Australasian Colonies, that 'we had only just learned to make ourselves comfortable when the voyage was nearly over'" (4). Hursthouse likewise notes that "in a well-regulated ship, with good officers and pleasant society, such is the variety of amusement, such the absence of monotony, that I have known passengers get so comfortable on board, become so much at home, as almost to appear sorry when the voyage was ended" (67–8). This nostalgia for the voyage, a surprisingly common narrative thread in emigrant guides and letters,[18] is consistent with the gradual transfer of identification that Baden-Powell associates with the passage. The ability to make oneself comfortable aboard ship demonstrates qualities of perseverance and adaptability that emigrants will need as settlers in a new country. As a trope of maintenance, the ideal of comfort also implies a sense of continuity with life in Britain, confirming that portable domesticity, as a set of values and practices that create a notion of "home," is crucial to successful emigration.

Yet the nostalgia involved in memorializing the ship as "home" also underscores a desire to remain in a liminal stage that can forestall the transformation that occurs once an emigrant leaves the ship and becomes a colonial settler. Hursthouse refers to passengers leaving Britain for the first time as "embryo emigrants" (66). This appellation frames the ship as an insular space in which the emigrant grows and transforms, relying on available resources to achieve full potential. The implication of rebirth embedded in this designation also suggests the irreversibility of emigration: the emigrant can be transformed, but he or she often cannot transport that new identity back home. As Patrick Brantlinger notes, "[a]ll those who are superfluous or redundant at home can discover roles for themselves in the colonies. . . . Numerous characters in Victorian fiction experience secular rebirths in the Bush; even convicts can strike it rich and be redeemed, though they generally must stay in the land of their redemption" (*Rule of Darkness* 123). The title page of *Hetherington's Useful Handbook for Intending Emigrants: Life at Sea and the Immigrant's Prospects in Australia and New Zealand*, which addresses readers interchangeably as "emigrants" and "immigrants," represents as seamless the dramatic exchange that occurs in the transfer of identification from the home nation to the colony. Such a smooth transition is made possible in part because emigrants, in learning to "settle" aboard ship, are already training themselves to inhabit their new identities as colonial settlers.

This potential for the voyage out to represent a period of transition and transformation is ultimately apparent in Dickens's *David Copperfield*, despite the fact that, on the evening prior to his departure, Micawber casually undermines the gravity of emigration by minimizing the distance between Britain and Australia: "The ocean, in these times, is a perfect fleet of ships. . . . It is merely crossing . . . merely crossing. The distance is quite imaginary" (659). Although Micawber represents the voyage out as a period of stasis—a mere crossing—the distance he travels *is* consequential, for it leads to a profound transformation in his status and fortune. Leaving Britain a perennial debtor with numerous unfulfilled expectations, he achieves financial and professional success in the colony, rising to become a respected colonial Magistrate. Even prior to leaving England, Micawber has already begun, with characteristic relish, to transform himself to meet the requirements of the new role that he will adopt on board ship:

> In his adaptation of himself to a new state of society, he had acquired a bold, buccaneering air, not absolutely lawless, but defensive and prompt. . . . In his rough clothing, with a common mariner's telescope under his arm, and a shrewd trick of casting up his eye at the sky as looking out for dirty weather, he was far more nautical, after his manner, than Mr. Peggotty. (655)

Micawber's hyperbolic performance, while contradicting his own assertion that emigration is "merely crossing," simultaneously suggests that the voyage out is a crucial period during which competing narratives of maintenance and transformation collide.

This contradiction between Micawber's representation of emigration as stasis and the reality of his transformation is consistent with the rhetoric of the emigrant guides discussed above. Yet unlike these historical documents, *David Copperfield* holds out a fantasy that colonists can maintain their national identity and their loyalty to Britain despite the inevitable processes of transformation that emigration entails. Thus, while Dickens's representation of the Micawber family's emigration is invested with humor and irony, their colonial success should not automatically be discredited as merely a sensationalist ploy. J. S. Tait, author of an emigration guide for the middle classes, insists that agricultural knowledge was often a liability rather than an asset in the colonies because "the chances are that the British agriculturist would have to unlearn nearly all he knew. . . . The emigrant who can most quickly forget his former experience, and who has the greatest amount of unprejudiced intelligence and plenty of energy, will be the most likely to succeed" (19–20). Micawber possesses both of these latter qualities, and his subsequent success as a farmer is consistent with Tait's allusion to the possibility for colonial rebirth or transformation. Another guide directed at middle-class emigrants to Canada would also apply to Australia in its insistence that "male and female, if they expect to prosper, must be willing and accustomed to work;—the idle, the drunken, and the desponding, have no business there, where all is energy of mind and body" (Doyle 49). As Coral Lansbury contends, Micawber's "boundless enthusiasm" and "incorrigible optimism" are the qualities that enable his colonial success (95). While hard work is not Micawber's forte in Britain, his energy and adaptability, evidenced in the dramatic shifts of emotion in each letter documenting his arrest and subsequent release from debt, render him fit to cope with the requirements of colonial life.

When Mr. Peggotty returns to Britain and reports to David on the success of his party, the news of Micawber is surprising: "I've seen that theer bald head of his, a perspiring in the sun, Mas'r Davy, 'till I a'most thowt it would have melted away. And now he's a Magistrate" (712). Mr. Micawber's new public persona—as a Magistrate and a writer—is legitimated through the addition of "Esquire" after his name. Ironically, while this title is traditionally tied to land and ownership, Micawber earns the right to affix the title to his name only by severing his physical connection to Britain. Like many of the figures in "Welcome Given in Melbourne Australia" whose hands reflect a newfound gentility, Micawber's new authority does not

reflect an entitlement granted by birth, but rather a gradual class transformation brought on by his transplantation to Australia, which Dickens
clearly viewed in the 1850s as "a land of promise and social rehabilitation
for various basically honest characters who deserve better lives than they
can make for themselves in Britain" (Brantlinger, *Rule of Darkness* 121).

Micawber, of course, is not the only emigrant in *David Copperfield*
who benefits from this transformative power of emigration. Lansbury
asserts that "if a joyful future for the Micawbers would have been illogical
in England, it was acceptable in Australia. A country where a prostitute
could marry a decent working man was quite capable of restoring Wilkins
Micawber to permanent solvency" (103). Lansbury refers here not just to
Micawber, but also to Martha, whose reformation in Australia was also in
keeping with contemporary propaganda about female emigration and the
prospects of marriage for single women. Belonging to the capacious Victorian category of "superfluous women," Martha, Emily, and Mrs. Gummidge are all redeemed in the colony. Each of the three women receives
a marriage proposal, and although only Martha chooses to accept, the
invitations themselves are represented as signs of recuperation. Emily, living among people who can only speculate about her past, is relieved of the
stigma of her fallenness, but she nonetheless continues to seek redemption
through service to others. No longer superfluous, she becomes in Australia
indispensable to her friends and neighbors, who rely on her help whenever
there is trouble. Mrs. Gummidge, who is scarcely recognizable in Mr. Peggotty's description, is also disciplined and industrious in the colony: "She's
the willingest, the trewest, the honestest-helping woman, Mas'r Davy, as
ever draw'd the breath of life. I have never know'd her to be lone and lorn,
for a single minnit, not even when the colony was all afore us, and we was
new to it" (711).[19]

By leaving behind certain painful remembrances, the Micawbers and
the Peggottys eventually succeed in achieving a measure of class ascension and domestic comfort that is signaled by their ability to move out
of the bush and into Port Middlebury. Superficially, Dickens's representation of these transformations in *David Copperfield* functions as propaganda, corroborating the myths about Australia that would later be
reified by the gold rush—the promise of rebirth, the unlimited potential
for financial success, and the abundant prospects for single women with
respect to marriage. Yet Dickens's faith in the transformative power of
emigration may also reflect his own fantasies and anxieties with regard
to class ascension. Dickens's personal struggle to rise from the lower
ranks and achieve respectability as an author is mirrored in *David Copperfield* in semi-autobiographical fashion. Although he had achieved great

professional success by the time he wrote the novel, the emigration plot nonetheless holds out a fantasy that hard work, and not birth, might be the legitimate measure of one's status.

Yet this plot also assumes that emigrants can have the best of both worlds: they can remake themselves in the colony and still remain loyal to their home nation. Mrs. Micawber is the character who most firmly believes in this possibility. Like Baden-Powell, Mrs. Micawber identifies the voyage as a potentially pivotal moment of transformation: "From the first moment of this voyage, I wish Mr. Micawber to stand upon the vessel's prow and say, 'Enough of delay: enough of disappointment: enough of limited means. That was in the old country. This is the new. Produce your reparation. Bring it forward!'" (660). Echoing the rhetoric of the emigrant guide as well as Brown's representation of the emigrant wife, Mrs. Micawber frames the voyage as a crucial period of transition, and possibly rebirth. Furthermore, she attributes to Micawber the resolve and self-discipline that he eventually demonstrates, foreshadowing the eminent position to which he will rise in the colony. When Mr. Peggotty later describes Micawber as a man who "turned to with a will" in the bush (712), it is evident that a genuine transformation has occurred.

Yet according to Mrs. Micawber, such a transformation is not inconsistent with the project of maintenance. Prior to their departure for Australia, Mr. Micawber expresses his willingness to sever his ties with Britain, arguing that he has no wish for his family to return because "[Britannia] has never done much for me" (659). Yet Mrs. Micawber reproaches her husband, claiming—with Chisholm—that emigration creates a bridge between Britain and the colony. Her argument, like Chisholm's, rests on the assumption that individual action is reflected on a national scale:[20]

> And in doing that . . . feeling his position—am I not right in saying that Mr. Micawber will strengthen, and not weaken, his connexion with Britain? An important public character arising in that hemisphere, shall I be told that its influence will not be felt at home? Can I be so weak as to imagine that Mr. Micawber, wielding the rod of talent and power in Australia, will be nothing in England? I am but a woman; but I should be unworthy of myself, and of my papa, if I were guilty of such absurd weakness. (660–1)

Mrs. Micawber's questions of David prior to her family's departure speak to contemporary anxieties about whether emigration deprived Britain of potentially valuable resources and wealth, thereby benefiting the new colony rather than the home nation. But despite her interrogatory tone, Mrs. Micawber remains insistent that her husband's personal success in the colony will have imperial implications. Underneath the self-effacing claim that she is "but a woman," her arguments highlight the important role of women as cultural mediators who bear a responsibility for the maintenance of national identity (a role that Brown also emphasizes in *The Last of England*).

Chisholm similarly associates nationalism, not explicitly with women, but with the domestic realm. As she describes it, nationalism is an inherited aspect of identity that is nurtured through stories told in domestic settings, "at the hearth's fire-side." In the following passage, Chisholm suggests that British nationalism is not merely linked to a domestic ideal; it is actively constructed through domesticity:

> The spirit which has made our soldiers and sailors triumphant all over the world is not an artificial one; the feeling that has made the flag of victory wave wherever England's banners have been carried, is not created by the thrilling thunder of the canon, the loud call of the trumpet, or the martial strains of the pibroch, but it is one that glows in man's bosom, that he carries into the battle-field, and one which Britons in a special manner inherit from the land of their birth, nurtured and cradled by the relation of the deeds of their sires, at the hearth's fire-side. (33)

In Chisholm's estimation, national identity does not inhere in the patriotic performances commonly associated with nationalism—rather, it is created and sustained through the circulation of narratives within the most intimate of circles: the family. Because of their inherent portability, or their propensity for circulation, such narratives become critical for maintaining national identity throughout the experience of displacement.[21]

In *David Copperfield*, narratives do succeed in bridging the gap between Australia and Britain. Prior to his departure, Micawber hints that he will perform the role of cultural transmitter when he promises to spin yarns aboard ship (659). And despite Micawber's attempts to protect Mr. Peggotty from hearing the story of Ham's death, this news eventually penetrates the bush when a visitor from Britain brings an old newspaper into their home in Australia. News travels in the opposite direction as well. When Mr. Peggotty returns home, he takes Australian newspapers with articles written by Mr. Micawber, including a published letter to David. In what may be a fantasy about his own authorial power, Dickens describes in this letter the role of David's latest novel in maintaining colonial loyalty to Britain: it is read even in the bush. Mr. Micawber assures his friend that his novel has indeed breached the gap between Britain and

Australia: "You are not unknown here, you are not unappreciated. Though 'remote,' we are neither 'unfriended,' 'melancholy,' nor (I may add) 'slow.' Go on, my dear sir, in your Eagle course! The inhabitants of Port Middlebury may at least aspire to watch it, with delight, with entertainment, with instruction!" (713). Micawber's letter defies the common assumption that the Antipodes are devoid of intellectual life—an assumption that emigrant guides also refute—while simultaneously insisting that loyalty to Britain is possible despite his displacement. Drawing on his British literary inheritance, Micawber attests to the power of narrative to create and sustain national identity.

Ultimately, the most important storyteller in *David Copperfield* is neither Micawber nor David, but Dickens himself. In "A Bundle of Emigrants' Letters," Dickens imagines Australia as an Antipodal England where new and old narratives can coexist:

> From little communities thus established, other and larger communities will rise in time, bound together in a love of the old country still fondly spoken of as Home, in the remembrance of many old struggles shared together, of many new ties formed since, and in the salutary influence and restraint of a kind of social opinion, even amid the wild solitudes of Australia. (88)

Here, portable domesticity and the stories told about "Home" create the conditions for the kind of disciplined restraint that is associated with the project of maintenance described in emigrant guides. Dickens's vision of "civilization in the bush" is made possible in part by what he imagines in *David Copperfield* as the role of narrative in sustaining British national identity in Australia.

Dickens's use of the emigration plot in *David Copperfield* endorses Chisholm's conviction that British emigrants "will uphold as a body the moral banner of England unsullied in the Bush" (Chisholm 33). However, later in his career, Dickens's faith in the potential for emigration to benefit both Britain and the colonies began to reflect more of the ambivalence that I have identified in Brown's *The Last of England* and in nineteenth-century emigrant guides. By the time he published *Great Expectations*, more than a decade after he redeemed the Micawbers and the Peggottys, Dickens's attitude toward colonial redemption seems to have shifted, particularly with respect to Australia's convict history. In *Great Expectations*, Abel Magwitch's return to Britain highlights anxieties about the potentially negative repercussions of colonial progress and the tenuous linkages between home and colony (anxieties that I will examine in more depth in chapter

3). Such repercussions, however, were far from Dickens's mind in *David Copperfield*, a novel in which he embraces a transformation that attests to the power of domesticity, and the family, to discipline even the most errant of characters. The effectiveness of such discipline is also central to the accounts of emigration that I examine in chapter 2, which similarly detail how the work of maintenance serves an essential role—in this case primarily for single, middle-class women—in facilitating successful emigration while initiating personal transformation within the liminal spaces aboard ship and on shore.

Chapter Two

Performing the Voyage Out

*Victorian Female Emigration
and the Gendering of Displacement*

A famous 1862 debate between William R. Greg and Frances Power
Cobbe highlighted the prospect of female emigration as a solution
to the perceived problems posed by Britain's "superfluous women," those
single, unmarried "ladies," typically from among the middle classes,
who were unlikely to pair off and thereby fulfill their "natural" roles as
wives and mothers.[1] Arguments in favor of such a scheme suggested that
the emigration of superfluous women, like the emigration of Caroline
Chisholm's family groups, could function to stabilize the empire. Single
female emigrants, the reasoning went, would satisfy national demands
both at home and abroad—simultaneously restoring a numerical balance
between the sexes in Britain while also providing wives for British colonists throughout the empire. However, the seeming logic of this solution
was questioned well before this debate came to a head, as evidenced by an
1853 color cartoon entitled "Alarming Prospect—The Single Ladies off to
the Diggings" (Figure 2.1) and also for decades afterwards, as evidenced
by a series of emigrant letters, a memoir, and a novel that are the focal
points of this chapter.

In a clever play on prospecting for gold, the cartoon vividly illustrates
the unsettling possibility that female middle-class emigration might function not to shore up domestic norms, but rather, to challenge them by
creating opportunities for novel forms of female self-assertion and independence. The image depicts a crowd of respectably-dressed young women
busily boarding a ship presumably bound for Australia. Their expressions
are alternately smug and self-assured and are universally suggestive of

FIGURE 2.1. "Alarming Prospect—The Single Ladies off to the Diggings." Courtesy of Bodleian Library, University of Oxford, John Johnson Collection, Emigration 1, Alarmingprospect.

pleasure. On the docks, a handful of men forlornly watch them depart, and the cartoon's captions suggest that these would-be suitors are fruitlessly pleading with offers of marriage and economic security in an effort to induce the women to stay on their native soil.

Yet what about this scene makes it worthy of its title—"Alarming Prospect?" Is it the prospect of genteel "ladies" embarking on a long sea journey and participating in life at the diggings? Is it the association of "ladies" with the unfeminine attributes of class ambition and avarice that were routinely linked with Australian "gold fever?" Is it their self-assurance and apparent disregard for male authority as they leave home without remorse, rejecting their suitors as they go? While a combination of these factors is likely in play, each individual cause for alarm calls into question the ways in which class and gender norms might be undermined by the very act of emigration.

The erosion of gender norms in particular is evident in the cartoon in various ways. In a humorous assault on British masculinity, the men pictured are symbolically emasculated, both because they are visually outnumbered and overpowered by the women, who seem literally to crowd them out of the picture's frame, and because their impotency is parodied in a series of interrelated phallic symbols.[2] Yet of greater interest to the concerns of this chapter are the ways in which the image erodes and redefines traditional notions of British femininity by rejecting marriage and motherhood and privileging women's independence, ambition, and adventure.

The cartoon's captions first and foremost illustrate this point. One woman tells her suitor, "A Cottage! Fiddle-de dee-Sir!," while another with an exceptionally self-assured expression quips, "Bother yer Hundred Pounds, and House in the Public line! A likely start indeed!" A third woman already on board ship curses the man she leaves behind, calling him "A Twopenny Ha'penny fellow!" In responding to the unnarrated pleas of their male suitors, who presumably offer safety and security at home in lieu of emigration, the women express disdain toward middle-class marriage and the protections that go along with it, implying by way of contrast that their prospects in the colonies are far more exciting and potentially lucrative.

Other elements of "Alarming Prospect" similarly suggest the erosion of class and gender norms through an eschewal of marriage and motherhood. The cartoon's title invokes prospecting for gold and the image itself calls to mind popular associations of female emigration with another form of prospecting known as "husband hunting." However, rather than endorsing the notion that these women look to better marriage prospects or class mobility in the colonies, the cartoon suggests that the women have a different aim in mind altogether: independence. A prominent symbol in the center of the cartoon—an abandoned baby bassinet—supports this reading. Sitting on the dock bearing a sign that reads "Glass/with care," the bassinet is noteworthy especially because of the utilitarian function it serves; its "precious cargo" in this case is not an infant, as one might expect, but a fragile possession that is being carefully transported to Australia. The bassinet seems to belong to no one in particular, and as if to further emphasize the lack of maternal concern associated with it or the conspicuously absent infant, an abandoned little dog looks on from the dock with what can only be described as a forsaken expression. Rejecting conventional middle-class domestic life—a "Cottage," "a House in the Public line," or a baby in a bassinet—these female emigrants stand ready to substitute marriage and motherhood at home for independence and colonial adventure, an "Alarming Prospect" indeed.

THE RENOVATION OF FEMALE EMIGRATION

Like the women depicted in "Alarming Prospect," Maria Rye and Jane Lewin envisioned an unconventional role for British female emigrants. Debates about female emigration to the British colonies throughout the Victorian era routinely capitalize on the crucial role women could play in consolidating the empire through the civilizing mission. Advocates of female emigration frequently publicized the benefits of "matrimonial colonization," a rendering of what is now called republican motherhood that defines women's place in the nation in terms of their domestic and reproductive roles.[3] But the founding in 1862 of the Female Middle Class Emigration Society (FMCES) by two educated middle-class women, Rye and Lewin, marked a departure from this conventional approach to female emigration. The work of the FMCES was carried out in the spirit of energy and determination that characterized the period of growing feminist activity in the 1860s, when the British rhetoric about "superfluous" women was reaching the tenor of a national crisis.[4] While campaigns for improving female education and employment opportunities were long-term solutions to the problem, emigration offered a more immediate palliative. Concerned primarily with the plight of single, middle-class women, Rye and Lewin saw in emigration an alternative plot to the tragic denouement in poverty and spinsterhood that awaited a large proportion of Britain's population of single, unemployed women. Ignoring the civilizing mission and the inducements for genteel women to marry or to become domestic servants in the colonies,[5] Rye and Lewin instead focused on creating a class-differentiated access into colonialism by enabling single middle-class women, most of whom were governesses, to emigrate safely and to obtain professional employment in the colonies, most often in Australia and New Zealand.[6]

A letter Rye published in the *Times* discussing the purpose of the FMCES clearly demonstrates her dramatic departure from the rhetoric of the civilizing mission. Here, Rye inserts her female emigrants into a heroic discourse of colonialism commonly reserved for men:

> I would remind all who are hesitating about the advisability of emigration to remember, that in olden times ten men brought evil tidings of Canaan itself; yet the land was a good land, in spite of the wretched report, and it fared mightily well with those who had courage to march on and possess it. The matter is now virtually in the hands of the women of this country. They must decide their own fate. (*Times*, April 29, 1862)

Whereas the rhetoric of the civilizing mission emphasizes women's philanthropic capabilities, Rye's discourse of self-determination displaces a typical concern for the welfare of others with an explicitly feminist (and middle-class) preoccupation about female individuation: the imperative to "decide their own fate" (an imperative the women in "Alarming Prospect" seem similarly ready to embrace). Likening emigration to the Biblical pilgrimage for the land of Canaan, Rye affords her own work monumental status. Likewise, she ascribes a novel mission to her female emigrants—to consider themselves and their own well-being. Creating a counter-narrative to the history of emigration as the passive act of shoveling paupers and convicts from Britain's shores,[7] Rye invests her emigrants, often labeled distressed and "superfluous" women, with a powerful sense of agency and purpose.

In addition to challenging the stereotypes associated with matrimonial colonization and the feminine civilizing mission, Rye and Lewin also challenged those linking female emigration to promiscuity, drunkenness, and sexual scandal.[8] Attuned to the dangers posed by the inevitable mixing of classes and sexes in the close quarters of emigrant ships, the founders of the FMCES sought to distance their governesses, described by Rye as "the right set of girls" (*Times*, June 21, 1862) and "women of sterling worth" (*Times*, April 29, 1862), from lower-class emigrants. The latter group represented the possibilities of social descent and moral degradation and were frequently featured in complaints that one FMCES emigrant frames against "[f]ilth, drunkenness, swearing and 'horrid' people" (Clarke 27). Such distancing is evident in a letter Rye wrote to the *Times* in which she insisted that her governesses would prove themselves "vastly superior to the hordes of wild Irish and fast young ladies who [had] hitherto started as emigrants" (April 29, 1862). To ensure such an outcome, Rye and Lewin urged their emigrants to differentiate themselves by maintaining their class distinction throughout the experience of displacement.

But doing so required vigilance on the part of the FMCES emigrants, who had to negotiate the liminality of being single women—not wives—aboard emigrant ships and in the colonies. As Anne McClintock has argued, this liminality placed single, working women in a precarious relation to the imperial divide: "Tasked with the purification and maintenance of boundaries, they were especially fetishized as dangerously ambiguous and contaminating" (48). As such, single middle-class women became a locus, not of stability as anticipated, but of instability and fracture within the nation.

To counteract this position of liminality, the FMCES emigrants engaged in performative strategies—what I will call strategies of self-maintenance—that enabled them to preserve their class distinction, and in many cases, to perform upward mobility.[9] Of central importance to these performances was a notion the governesses had of themselves as members of an "imagined community" they shared with the British middle classes.[10] In the sections that follow, I endeavor to historicize the roles of both class and gender within such a national community by examining a collection of letters from the colonies that the FMCES emigrants wrote to Rye and Lewin alongside an autobiographical and a fictional account of female middle-class emigration.[11] In the letters, I analyze the performative strategies that the FMCES emigrants used to maintain their class distinction—or their affiliation with an imagined community of the British middle classes—throughout the experience of displacement. These strategies included the adoption of a discourse of rights, the performance of portable domesticity, or the replication of British domestic life aboard emigrant ships and in the colonies, and the exercise of strategic amnesia that enabled the governesses to preserve an illusion of class distinction irrespective of the realities of their circumstances. These strategies of self-maintenance served different functions at various stages of displacement. Aboard emigrant ships, such strategies enabled the governesses to negotiate their liminal class status and to maintain their class distinction. In the colonies, where the rigid social distinctions upheld in Britain dissolved, these strategies led the governesses to adapt their notions of success to an ideal of female individualism that was not so rigidly bound by class constraints. While this new ideal was empowering for many of the governesses, it nonetheless destabilized their connections to Britain because their new identities often could not be transported back home.

The problematic issue of the emigrant's return home to Britain is often thematized in Victorian autobiographies and fictional accounts of emigration, including two texts that I juxtapose with the FMCES letters, Mrs. Charles Clacy's *A Lady's Visit to the Gold Diggings of Australia 1852–53* and Anthony Trollope's *John Caldigate*. These texts about Australian emigration explore the most pressing issue raised in the letters, namely the single middle-class woman's precarious liminality in relation to home and colony, while similarly exposing the rifts in the British nation created by class and gender hierarchy. In Trollope's novel in particular, the instabilities that challenge the nation in the FMCES letters are greatly magnified when Euphemia Smith, a widowed middle-class emigrant, fails to perform effectively the strategies of self-maintenance that would allow her to maintain her class distinction. Although she also strives for independence and for the right to decide her own fate, the empowerment she subsequently achieves is not figured in the novel as a form of liberation from class constraints (as it is in the letters), but rather, as a dangerous challenge to the status quo in Britain. Whereas the FMCES governesses often acknowledge that the relative freedom they experience in the colony compensates for what they have left behind, Mrs. Smith refuses to accept a marginalized position in relation to the nation, and she subsequently returns to Britain and places a legal claim on John Caldigate. Unlike the FMCES letters, which testify to the renovating power of the colonial to make new roles available to women, Trollope's novel suggests that such power has dangerous consequences for single women who violate conventional gender roles, as Mrs. Smith does when she becomes a gold prospector in the colony. While they differ in this respect, however, both the letters and the novel reveal the disruptions in the imagined community caused by class and gender hierarchy, and in so doing, they expose the unstable foundations on which the project of colonialism is grounded.

PERFORMING THE VOYAGE UP: "BETWEEN-DECKS" ON SHIP AND ON SHORE

Under the auspices of the Female Middle Class Emigration Society, Rye, and later Lewin, were active in helping 302 single, middle-class women to emigrate between the years 1861 and 1886.[12] Although the cumulative influence of their efforts over twenty years was relatively minor, Rye and Lewin's work is remarkable precisely because they persisted when public support waned and colonial authorities insisted that the services of the educated classes were not needed in the colonies. In her discussion of the society's eligibility requirements, which demanded that emigrants possess both education and practical domestic training, Rita S. Kranidis notes that the FMCES founders attempted to establish a niche for their emigrants by "construct[ing] a new class and gender category, one that would satisfy the expressed needs of the colonists while attempting to rescue distressed gentlewomen at home" (*The Victorian Spinster* 30). In negotiating these competing pressures, the founders of the FMCES created a rupture in the nationalist discourse that depicts single, middle-class women as "superfluous" to the nation by virtue of their gender and class. Rye and Lewin refused to accept this definition of themselves and their potential emigrants, and Rye publicized instead the enormous potential for single middle-class women to achieve success in Australia and New Zealand: "there is plenty of work here for women who know how to do it . . . for women who can take care of themselves, and intend to walk uprightly, it is a place where they must get on in the long run" (*Times*, May 29, 1863).

The ability of Rye and Lewin's emigrants to "walk uprightly" by performing strategies of self-maintenance was exceptionally important aboard emigrant ships, which were liminal spaces involving special dangers and anxieties for women with respect to class. Despite their middle-class status, most of the FMCES emigrants were obliged for financial reasons to travel "between-decks," or in second-class accommodations also occupied by working-class emigrants who could afford to pay their own way. As one emigrant guide explains, the social distinctions upheld in the context of emigration were quite simple: "Emigrants to a colony may be divided into two classes: those who pay their own passage out, and those who are assisted out" (Hursthouse 59–60).[13] Because most of the governesses required the assistance of loans granted by the FMCES,[14] they shared an uncomfortable alliance not just with working-class emigrants, but also with steerage passengers, most of whom were poor emigrants sent out through government-sponsored schemes. These associations caused an unbearable affront to the gentility of some governesses, like Miss Cary, an emigrant to New Zealand, who writes: "I can assure you, to me the passage was most trying. We had food enough, I had so many things of my own, I did not suffer as much as others, but oh Miss Lewin, no Lady should come out on those emigrant ships" (Clarke 36). Interestingly, Cary's vague complaint about the voyage out has little to do with the physical realities of life on board ship; by her own account, she fared well throughout a journey during which others presumably suffered. Instead, the voyage poses threats to her modesty and gentility that are specifically tied to her class and gender status (she warns Lewin only against "Ladies" traveling out on ships). To counter such affronts, Cary is careful in her letter to highlight the exceptional nature of her own circumstances during the voyage by enumerating the benefits she enjoyed aboard ship: she had enough to eat, she had her own possessions on board, and she suffered little. These privileges firmly align her, not with the "others" who suffered, but with the most enfranchised passengers, or those who traveled first class.

In addition to the problems posed by the mixing of classes aboard ship, female emigrants also had to cope with challenges to their respectability generated by the close proximity of living spaces for men and women. Louisa Dearmer, a prolific correspondent to Jane Lewin, warns of the tragic consequences that sometimes occurred before the ships reached their destinations: "There is one sad thing I feel bound to mention: so many of the girls sent out, particularly in English vessels, but in others as well, get ruined on board ship; when they arrive here they have no character and go on the town" (Clarke 102). In emigrants' letters like this one and in Rye and Lewin's discourse about female emigration, the story of the fallen woman performed a policing function that served as a potent warning to middle-class women whose behavior was expected to be beyond reproach. The direct correlation in Dearmer's account between impropriety aboard ship and ruin in the colony was a familiar narrative that the founders of the FMCES circulated in an effort to deter impropriety. They were also careful in selecting vessels for their emigrants, but beyond this source of protection they could only advocate self-determination. Their stress on individual agency and the imperative for their middle-class emigrants to "decide their own fate" translates in the emigrants' letters into characteristic preoccupations with propriety, with class stratification, and with strategies of self-maintenance.

One such strategy, which is evident in Cary's letter above, was to align oneself with the privileges of first-class travel and thereby to perform upward mobility. Many of the governesses do this by adopting a discourse of rights regarding their treatment and comfort aboard ship that is consistent with the project of female individualism alluded to in Rye's letter to the *Times*. For instance, Margaret Pyman complains bitterly because she had to pay for her wine whereas other passengers were given a bottle of sherry each week: "It was not that I cared for or required it, but I did not choose to be deprived of my rights" (Clarke 45). Although perhaps objecting solely on principle, Pyman's rhetoric of rights represents an attempt to assert her own will and to modify circumstances that were beyond her control. A lack of space, privacy, or equitable treatment are the governesses' most frequent grievances, all of which are evident in Maria Atherton's complaint: "Being short of room they placed four of us in a Cabin not so large as the others which contained only two persons. We had no light and no air and were therefore quite unable to retire to our berths . . . we were the only parties deprived of a seat at the Table in the second Cabin and obliged to stand or seat ourselves on boxes" (Clarke 35). Not comfortable in or out of her cabin, Atherton displays a characteristic sensitivity about her status "between decks" as a second-class passenger; to assuage such anxieties she and other FMCES emigrants stridently defended their rights to everything to which they were entitled, thereby performing the upward mobility that could forestall the alternative drive to class degradation.

Among the necessities that concerned them were the cabin fittings that second-class passengers required for the journey since "any small material comforts, so necessary on a long sea voyage, had to be provided by the passengers themselves" (Clarke 25). These included everything needed to replicate a domestic "household" in one's own cabin: pillows, mattresses, bedsteads, bedding, folding chairs, pots and dishes, mess utensils, lamps and candles, cabinets, and articles for personal hygiene. Whereas advertising geared toward male emigrants bound for the gold diggings tended to capitalize on the items they would require once in Australia, such as those included in an 1852 advertisement by the Gutta Percha company (Figure 2.2), the FMCES emigrants seem to have focused their preparations almost exclusively on the domestic items required for shipboard life, a fact that highlights the uncertainty of their future prospects in the colonies. The FMCES assisted its emigrants in obtaining their cabin fittings, and those governesses who were unprepared because they did not receive all the items they needed often complained in defense of their rights. Emilie Glen wrote: "Silver's did not send all the things I paid for. There was no toilet pail and the looking glass was about half the size of the one I paid for. I found the cupboard ordered was not needed as there was one in the ship, so the Carpenter, whom they sent, took it back with them" (Clarke 41). The shortcomings of Glen's looking glass attest to the significance of personal hygiene and self-presentation in maintaining status aboard ship. Having paid for the privileges associated with domestic life, many governesses were frustrated when they did not receive all the tools necessary to perform their daily rituals of bathing, dressing, and dining.

Such rituals are discussed at length in guides and catalogs like Eneas Mackenzie's *The Emigrant's Guide to Australia*, which often include comprehensive lists of the necessary fittings, clothing, and food a second-class passenger would require for the journey, instructions about how to dress appropriately for the varying climates and how to maintain good health, and recipes and instructions for cooking aboard ship or in the bush. McClintock has argued that the idleness typically associated with middle-class women was actually "a laborious and time-consuming

TO EMIGRANTS!

The following **GUTTA PERCHA ARTICLES** will be found of Great Value to Emigrants, especially such as are proceeding to the

GOLD DIGGINGS.

GUTTA PERCHA LINING FOR BOXES.

| BUCKETS. | LIFE BUOYS. | WASHING BOWLS. |
| DRINKING MUGS. | FLASKS. | SYPHONS. |

GUTTA PERCHA TUBING.

| SUCTIONS FOR PUMPS. | CARBOYS FOR GUNPOWDER. |
| JUGS. | MINERS' CAPS. |

SOLES FOR BOOTS AND SHOES.

TO KEEP THE FEET DRY is of the utmost importance to the Emigrant. This may be secured by the use of Gutta Percha Soles, which are perfectly Waterproof, Cheaper, and more Durable than Leather. They can be put on with ease by any one. This cannot be too extensively known amongst Australian Emigrants, as it is now difficult to find a Shoemaker in that country.

Gold Washing Vessels of every variety of shape may be had to order.

Directions to Emigrants for lining Boxes with Gutta Percha Sheet, (so as to preserve the contents from injury by Sea Water), also for putting on Soles of Boots and Shoes, &c., may be had **GRATIS** on application to any of the Gutta Percha Company's dealers.

N.B. The Company's Illustrated Circulars, containing Instructions to Plumbers for joining Tubes, lining Tanks, &c., will be forwarded (post-free) on receipt of three Postage Stamps.

The GUTTA PERCHA COMPANY, Patentees,

18, WHARF ROAD, CITY ROAD, LONDON.

FIGURE 2.2. "To Emigrants!," *British Journal* (1852). Courtesy of Bodleian Library, University of Oxford, John Johnson Collection, Emigration 1, To Emigrants.

character role performed by women who wanted membership in the 'respectable' class" (161). When performing such a role, a middle-class woman had the double burden of working to conceal every sign of her labor. Although emigrant guides and cabin fittings quite literally made domesticity portable, the work of domesticity, and by extension self-main-tenance, must have been exceptionally arduous, especially when it was performed in the confined spaces of second-class cabins, which generally housed two or even three women.

Despite such difficulties, however, the cabin fittings allowed the FMCES emigrants to perform important domestic rituals aboard ship that deliberately replicated the leisured pace of middle-class domestic life. One of the most crucial of such shipboard rituals was dining. *S. W. Silver & Co.'s Colonial and Indian Pocket Book Series and Voyager's Companion* explicitly compares morning coffee to the Magna Carta and asserts that "the supreme shipboard duty is dinner at 6 P.M. It is a business, a ceremony, an obligation, and a pleasure combined. All things lead up to it; time is reckoned by its hour; it is expected; it is desired; and it demands preparation" (27). Meals, because they occurred at regularly scheduled intervals, performed a crucial function by continuously reit-erating the social stratification of passengers by rank, or in other words, by redrawing boundaries that were too easily transgressed in the close confinement of the ships. What one wore to dinner, where one sat and with whom, and what one ate and drank all served as indexes of class. Figured in the Silver's guide as "among the chief ends of life" (20), eating and drinking aboard ship thus enabled the display and performance of an enfranchised status.[15]

Receiving the attention and favor of the ship's captain, who dined with the first-class passengers, was also depicted as a sign of esteem and respectability that brought one closer to coveted first-class status. Several emigrants describe activities sanctioned by ship captains that replicate the patterns of middle-class leisure. Rosarie Winn makes it clear that such activities implied respectability by association: "We brought out a Paper called the *Dudbrook Chronicle* weekly, which I used to help the Captain to write and which I contributed an article every now and then. . . . We used to have a Debating Society on board which met twice a week to discuss different topics and we kept it up during the whole voyage, but only the Gentlemen, of course carried on the debates" (Clarke 39). As a testament to the propriety of life on the ship and her association with prominent figures like the captain, Winn's decorous account obeys the rules of polite society and defuses the popular anxiety that an emigrant ship is no place for a woman.

In an effort to dispel the stigmas associated with emigrant ships, as Winn does above, some FMCES emigrants report disposing of their fittings upon arrival in Australia or New Zealand by simply throwing them overboard. Although such an act seems counterintuitive given the importance of the cabin fittings in the performance of portable domesticity, it is nonetheless consistent with a series of efforts made by the governesses to conceal the fact that they traveled second class. Arriving in the colony with nothing but their luggage, as the first-class passengers would have done, the FMCES emigrants were able to leave behind any unpleasant reminders of past hardships and to begin their new lives in the Antipodes with a clean slate. The disposal of the fittings in the colony further reaffirms the idea that class status is linked, not only to material and economic realities, but also to powerful imaginings and performances.

Related to such performances was the governesses' engagement in strategic amnesia, a mode of forgetting that enabled them to preserve an illusion of class distinction irrespective of the realities of their circumstances at home in Britain, aboard ship, or in the colonies.[16] In some cases, for instance, the freedom and independence of the voyage, what one emigrant calls "the delightful solitude on the magnificent ocean" (Book 1, 307), appears to have overshadowed or colored the harsher realities of life at sea. Many emigrants recall their passages as particularly exhilarating experiences, regardless of physical discomforts. Cecille Nagelle writes: "I think the Sea air has done me much good, I am reaping the benefit of it now; I never felt better" (Clarke 42). Other emigrants describe favorable conditions and good weather despite newspaper accounts of the same voyages that report dangerous storms, extreme weather conditions, and food shortages. On the other hand, one unhappy traveler reports a mutiny aboard her ship that was never mentioned in the account of a fellow passenger (Clarke 29). Such instances of strategic amnesia may be attributed in part to the fact that these are retrospective accounts, often written months after the emigrants had arrived in Australia and New Zealand and subsequently experienced the numerous hardships and discomforts associated with adapting to a new way of life. But in many cases the experience aboard an emigrant ship appears to have been enjoyable precisely because it suspended the inevitable, creating a liminal space where the dismal reality of life in Britain could be forgotten and where hope for the future could be nourished: "The voyage was a very pleasant one and I need hardly tell you that I was very sorry when it came to an end, and I found myself for the first time in my life at the mercy of strangers" (Clarke 47). Ellen Ollard's letter displays a characteristic regret that is infused with fears about the future difficulties associated with her displacement.

Once on shore in Australia and New Zealand, as Patricia Clarke asserts, "the governesses faced not a temporary three to four months' adaptation to life aboard ship, but, in most cases, a lifetime in strange and challenging surroundings where their livelihood was by no means as assured as they had hoped or expected" (48). Accordingly, many FMCES emigrants expressed ambivalence about colonial life and customs even as they begrudgingly adopted colonial ways. Rosa Phayne, a governess who lamented her decision to emigrate and never successfully adapted to her new surroundings, violently resisted converting to an Australian way of life: "I hate Australia and the Australians, I shall [be] with them but never of them" (Clarke 111). Maria Barrow's reaction is more tempered and there-fore more typical, yet it still reflects a deliberate resistance to assimilation and an accompanying sense of alienation: "I can't quite make up my mind about the Colony whether to like it or not. . . . We have had fine weather ever since I have been here and it is very pleasant, still I miss the fresh-ness of some of our fine days in dear old England, everything is so dried up, and certainly the birds don't sing and the flowers (generally) don't smell" (Clarke 63). Despite the fine weather, for Barrow the experience of displacement is so jarring that even nature is impenetrable to her inter-pretations; its laws are not universal. However, other FMCES emigrants, particularly those who found a home either with family members or in permanent situations, were able to circumvent such feelings of alienation by engaging in a form of strategic amnesia that enabled them to minimize the contrasts between Britain and Australia or New Zealand. Emigrant guides and catalogs frequently describe Australia and New Zealand as the most "English-like" of all the colonies, a sentiment reinforced in some of the governesses' letters.[17] Isabella McGillivray, who traveled with three of her sisters to her brother's Australian home, explains that "[w]e have met with very great kindness here and things are so like home, that we do not feel in a foreign land in the least" (Book 1, 45). Fanny Giles performs a sim-ilar erasure when she writes that "everything about me seems so English that I cannot yet realize being so far from my native land" (Book 1, 153).

Whether they enjoyed their new homes or not, most of the govern-esses went to great lengths to convince their friends and families at home that their class status, and even their identities, had remained unchanged by their colonial experiences. In many cases, the governesses enlisted the help of the FMCES in maintaining secrecy regarding their debts or their impoverished circumstances in the colonies (xii), a practice that is consis-tent with what Robert Hughes has called a "national pact of silence" about Australia's vexed colonial history.[18] For instance, Laura Jones, a govern-ess who lived in a hut in the bush among dissenters and had to take up needlework when she lost a situation, requests that Lewin conceal her difficulties from her friends and relations in Britain: "I have not written to any of my friends at home as I disliked telling them of my circumstances, but I will write soon now and may ask a favour: that you will not answer any enquiries that may be made respecting me—I will write and tell them as much as I wish them to know" (Clarke 120). Jones' request that Lewin maintain silence regarding her temporary social descent (she subsequently obtained a position teaching at a boarding school and repaid her debt in full), suggests the empowerment that comes from gaining control over one's own narrative. The ability to do so was a hard-earned freedom that Jones, among others, privileged highly.

In Australia and New Zealand, where the rigid social distinctions upheld in Britain were no longer enforced, the project of self-maintenance gradually led many of the FMCES emigrants to expand their notions of success to include an ideal of female individualism. For those who were successful and who adapted to colonial life despite initial setbacks, the freedom and independence they experienced often compensated for being away from home. Louisa Geoghegan, whose letters reflect a gradual reconciliation with displacement, exhibits a characteristic amnesia that suggests how her ideals have been transformed:

> I am now so reconciled to Australia that I was surprised to see by your letter that I had apparently been disappointed at first. At times I feel it is rather dull work never to go beyond the garden or Croquet ground, but then I remember I can rake or hoe in the garden as I please and the freedom to please oneself more than compensates for monotony. (Clarke 105)

The ideal of "pleas[ing] oneself" is consistent with Rye's rhetoric of female agency and the drive to decide one's own fate. For Geoghegan and others who were flexible enough to adapt to—rather than be affronted by—a new set of social codes and standards, bush life, which Geoghegan calls "a strange mixture of roughing and refinement" (Clarke 103), was empowering. This "strange mixture" provided the governesses with access to a new role: that of the colonial woman, a figure who could combine gentility with a measure of practicality and independence.

Ironically, the performances of portable domesticity that enabled the FMCES emigrants to maintain their class affiliations aboard emigrant ships served to free them from class constraints once they arrived in Australia and New Zealand. Colonial governesses were often expected to perform a range of household chores not ordinarily required of an English governess.

While some FMCES emigrants had difficulty accepting such responsibilities because they regarded them as a degradation in status, the more resilient women attempted to adapt themselves to their new environments, as in the case of Mary Wilson, who writes from New Zealand that "I am getting more reconciled to colonial life in many ways, it is so different from home, but I endeavor to suit myself to the people and the place" (Book 1, 375). Still others found such work liberating because it enabled them to enjoy a degree of independence that was otherwise unprecedented. Nancy Barlow, who opened her own school in Australia, explained that "I am getting quite a Colonial woman, and fear I should not easily fit into English ideas again—can scrub a floor with anyone, and bake my own bread and many other things that an English Governess and Schoolmistress would be horrified at" (Clarke 69). The subtext beneath Barlow's celebration of her new identity is the recognition that she is unfitting herself for English life. In fact, the governesses who were part of a superfluous class in Britain shared the dilemma of the convicts who were transported to Australia in the first half of the century; like them, these women could be socially redeemed in the colony, but they could not transport their new identities back home.[19]

Although the FMCES emigrants describe a range of responses to the psychic experience of emigration, the majority of the letters testify to the success of Rye and Lewin's society in granting a class-differentiated access into colonialism. Most FMCES emigrants were eventually able to repay the debts they incurred in Britain to make their passages over, but some subsequently struggled to save enough money to return home. Miss Ireland writes, "I have indeed been an unfortunate girl and as soon as I have paid my debts and saved enough money for my passage I shall come back to dear Old England" (Book 1, 68–9). Although some emigrants optimistically planned to return, few probably did so. More often, the governesses resigned themselves to their forced migration, as the following letter from Gertrude Gooch suggests:

> I am certain it will be a long while before I see the Old Country again, perhaps never. I love it as ever, but I can earn more money here and I expect always [will] find something to do. There are enough of us at home. I often think of you, our old Ship, the Voyage and many other things and cannot believe I am 17,000 miles away from Old England. (Clarke 57)

Gooch's letter reveals an interesting tension between a nostalgia for the nation that enables her to memorialize England and a sense of reproach against the domestic politics that failed to provide for her. Her affiliation with a collective yet disenfranchised "us" alludes to a fracture in the horizontal comradeship of the imagined community caused by the marginalization imposed upon "superfluous" women by virtue of their gender and class. Across this rift, which became an ocean, the FMCES emigrants performed a balancing act that exposed the instabilities inherent in their colonial identities, and in the nation they left behind.

BRIDGING THE GAP BETWEEN COLONY AND HOME

In addition to emigrant letters, the Victorians produced numerous autobiographical and fictional accounts of emigration that explore the single middle-class woman's status at the margins of the nation. One such account is the memoir of Ellen Clacy, a single, middle-class woman who traveled to Australia with her brother, got married, and returned to Britain, where she subsequently wrote a best-seller entitled *A Lady's Visit to the Gold Diggings of Australia 1852–53*. Clacy's autobiographical account reifies the energizing myths of emigration and of the gold rush, affirming Australia's abundant prospects for economic success and for marriage. However, like Rye and Lewin and the women depicted in "Alarming Prospect," Clacy relies upon a familiar idiom of self-determination and class distinction; she encourages healthy, self-reliant women to emigrate, insisting that in Australia, where men greatly outnumber women, "we may be pretty sure of having our own way" (151). Like the FMCES emigrants, Clacy employs rhetorical strategies in her memoir that are calculated to protect her middle-class "respectability," even in the most primitive conditions in the bush. She peppers her narrative with French and Italian phrases, excuses her use of "colonialisms," and insists on representing the truth as she hears or witnesses it. In addition, she minimizes the significance of displacement by repeatedly insisting that she has remained untainted by her colonial encounters.

Yet like the governesses, Clacy is in fact transformed in positive ways by her emigration to Australia. Such a transformation is evident on the title page alone, which includes the paradoxical designation "Written on the Spot by Mrs. Charles Clacy." Although her memoir was written after her return to Britain as a married woman, Clacy locates the act of authorship in Australia at the site of imperial adventure, "on the Spot," at a point when she could not yet have written as Mrs. Charles Clacy. Yet she nonetheless relies on the authority of her new signature, for it is her married name which signifies her successful assimilation back into British life. At the same time, the slippage from single female emigrant to writer and wife is representative of a larger transformation: the renovation of Clacy's superfluous status within the nation, not only through marriage, but also through her newly acquired authority with regard to colonial matters.

Clacy's ability to return home after her wedding is only one sign of her privileged position as a female emigrant. Unlike the FMCES emigrants who traveled alone or the diggers' wives who resigned themselves to "quietly settling down to this rough and primitive style of living, if not without a murmur, at least to all appearance with the determination to laugh and bear it" (Clacy 56), Clacy travels in the protection of men with the freedom to come and go as she pleases. Her presence at the gold diggings invokes the portability of English domesticity, where "[in] some tents the soft influence of our sex is pleasingly apparent" (56). Here the division of labor is based on an egalitarian mode that Clacy prefers; the men are eager to make puddings while Clacy takes an active role in their digging party. Yet her job in the gold excavation is nonetheless particularly domestic: "Tin-dish-washing is difficult to describe. It requires a watchful eye and a skillful hand; it is the most mysterious department of the gold-digging business" (64). Consistent with a false idea that women's work occurs without labor, Clacy renders her task "mysterious" and yet essential (like the work of domesticity, which must be constantly performed as if by invisible agency).

Clacy's penultimate role in the narrative is also performed imperceptibly when her party is attacked by bushrangers intending to rob them of their gold. Clacy escapes and is unmolested, as is their fortune, for she carries the traveling money and the gold receipts concealed inside the lining of her dress. This "strange treasury" (108), as she refers to it, is crucial, for it suggests the inviolability of the female middle-class body and also disrupts the prerogative to male ownership (both of land and of British women's bodies). In addition, it recasts "superfluous" women as valuable national resources, quite literally worth their weight in gold. As she sails into the English harbor upon her return home, Clacy is greeted by the sound of church bells that signify this new-found respectability. In concluding her narrative with this symbolic gesture she advertises her successful assimilation back into English life, an ending that was nonetheless rarely represented in fact or fiction.

EMIGRATION, PERFORMANCE, AND THE FAILURE OF COLONIALISM

Such a seamless reconciliation between home and colony is more problematic in Anthony Trollope's gold rush novel, *John Caldigate,* which depicts the emigration of a widowed middle-class woman who fails to perform adequately the strategies of self-maintenance that are so important to Clacy and to the FMCES emigrants. In the novel, as in the FMCES letters, class distinctions affect the success of such a project, but issues of gender often override those of class. For Trollope, the female emigrant serves as a locus for anxieties about class and colonial reformation that are bound up with popular stereotypes about Australia as a place where individuals could rise in social status through the discovery of gold or through the agency of matrimonial colonization. Discrediting the popular opinion that "anything done in the wilds of Australia ought not 'to count' here at home in England" (399), Trollope challenges such stereotypes in *John Caldigate* by generating a plot in which none of his emigrants is able to return home unscathed after experiencing the "uncivilized" influences of colonial life. However, whereas the eponymous hero is gradually reassimilated into British life through the resolution of the domestic marriage plot, Trollope's female emigrant, Euphemia Smith, is not. Although Mrs. Smith engages in performances of portable domesticity and strategic amnesia aboard ship, her respectability is questioned because she simultaneously flaunts other expectations associated with her gender and sexuality. When she continues to violate such gender roles in Australia, the independence and empowerment she consequently gains are represented, not as positive outcroppings of colonial freedom (as they are in the governesses' letters), but as a dangerous challenge to the status quo in Britain. Such a challenge culminates in Mrs. Smith's refusal to accept a marginalized place in relation to her home nation when she returns to Britain and accuses John Caldigate of bigamy. This accusation in turn highlights the inequalities created by class and gender privilege within the nation and undermines the success of a colonial project designed to reform emigrants and unite the empire.

In Trollope's novel, as in the FMCES letters, portable domesticity plays an important role in maintaining class distinctions aboard ship. Trollope describes the experience on the outward-bound *Goldfinder* as a dramatic departure from everyday life insofar as no work is required and passengers may do just as they please. Yet his emphasis on its utter distinctiveness is partly ironic, for despite their unbounded freedom, passengers are quick to reproduce the social structure of the nation:

> There is no peculiar life more thoroughly apart from life in general, more unlike our usual life, more completely a life of itself, governed by its own rules and having its own roughnesses and amenities, than life on board ship. What tender friendship it produces, and what bitter

enmities! How completely the society has formed itself into separate sets after the three or four first days! How thoroughly it is acknowledged that this is the aristocratic set, and that the plebian! How determined are the aristocrats to admit no intrusion, and how anxious are the plebians to intrude! (38)

The rapidity with which social demarcations get consolidated aboard ship reveals the profound impact of class performatives on the life of the nation. By replicating aspects of their lives at home, the passengers reinstate the social structure of Britain; the first-class passengers are distinguished by their idleness and fashionable attire, the second-class passengers by their industry in reading or sewing, and the steerage passengers by their invisibility. Dining, dancing, and socializing become indices of class status aboard the *Goldfinder*.

Within this restrictive social economy, Euphemia Smith is ambivalently positioned as an impoverished gentlewoman who travels second class, but who nonetheless holds herself superior to the majority of her fellow passengers. A widow with a mysterious past, Mrs. Smith is subjected to the scrutiny (and often scorn) of the first- and second-class passengers, many of whom assume that she is emigrating with the stereotypical motive of "husband hunting." She attracts the notice in particular of John Caldigate and his friend, Dick Shand, because of an obvious discrepancy between her physical appearance and her manner; they are intrigued to discover that "[s]he talks a great deal better than her gown" (40). Once the voyage is underway, Mrs. Smith engages in portable domesticity by donning her best clothes and improving her formerly shabby appearance, thereby performing upward mobility. She also participates in leisure pursuits such as reading and sewing that suggest her affiliation with the middle classes. By deliberately "forgetting" her former poverty during the voyage out, Mrs. Smith exhibits the type of strategic amnesia that enabled the FMCES emigrants temporarily to suspend the uncertainties associated with their past and future lives. Like some of them, she asserts that she would like life on ship "if it led to nothing else" (41). After she becomes involved in a shipboard romance with Caldigate, she laments that the journey must inevitably end:

So we have come to the end of it. . . . To the end of all that is pleasant and easy and safe. Don't you remember my telling you how I dreaded the finish? Here I have been fairly comfortable, and have in many respects enjoyed it. I have had you to talk to; and there has been a flavour of old days about it. What shall I be doing this time to-morrow? (70)

Mirroring the FMCES letters, Mrs. Smith's words underscore the role of strategic amnesia in evoking feelings of nostalgia for the past. In this case, such nostalgia is linked to the "old days," presumably prior to Mrs. Smith's marriage when she still had hopes for her future. While the passage temporarily allows for the renewal of such hope, Mrs. Smith's question also invokes the fear and uncertainty that many of the FMCES emigrants experienced at the end of the voyage when they had to begin their new lives far from home and alone.

Despite the similarities between Mrs. Smith's performances aboard ship and those of the FMCES governesses, Mrs. Smith's respectability is called into question during the voyage because even as she conforms to some middle-class standards of behavior, she simultaneously transgresses other boundaries related to gender and sexuality. The extent to which is she is eventually shunned by other passengers whereas Caldigate and Shand are well received illustrates that "[w]omen are defined by their sexuality while men remain gender neutral and are defined by class" (Davidoff and Hall 29). One of Mrs. Smith's transgressions has to do with her vigorous defense of her independence, since she travels without the assistance of an organization like the FMCES and eschews any protection she might gain through fellowship with other female passengers. When she revels in the self-sufficiency made possible by life at sea, Mrs. Smith ironically echoes the discourse of rights that the FMCES governesses employ as a means of preserving their status: "here I have a proud feeling of having paid my way. To have settled in advance for your dinner for six weeks to come is a magnificent thing. If I get too tired of it I can throw myself overboard. You can't even do that in London without the police being down upon you" (41). Mrs. Smith's words resonate with Rye's imperative for middle-class female emigrants to "decide their own fate," but whereas the self-determination Rye advocates is framed as heroism, in Trollope's novel it is a potentially dangerous form of empowerment that results in Mrs. Smith's ostracism from her fellow passengers, and later, from her fellow Britons. The passage above explicitly links self-determination to suicide, and through her refusal to capitulate to conventional expectations of her behavior as a widowed woman, Mrs. Smith in effect commits a social death aboard ship. Although she boards the *Goldfinder* under the guardianship of a family to whom she is vaguely connected, she shuns their protection when their interference in her affairs threatens her liberty. Likewise, she alienates most of her fellow travelers by deliberately avoiding female company and instead associating exclusively with Caldigate and Shand, the only gentlemen who travel second-class. The romance that subsequently ensues seals Mrs. Smith's fate as an outcast,

underscoring the link between class and sexuality that is evident in the
FMCES rhetoric about fallen women.

Once she arrives in Australia, Mrs. Smith fails to restore her respectability because she continues to violate expectations associated with gender and sexuality as well as class. Unlike the FMCES governesses, who
preserve their status by maintaining secrecy when they must resort to lower-class forms of work, Mrs. Smith refuses to participate in the "national
pact of silence" that might protect her class distinction and her virtue.
Instead, she readily adopts various class positions and personas in Australia, taking on a variety of name variants, not to protect her identity, but to
suit the requirements of a given role. When Caldigate questions her about
posters advertising her performances on stage as Mademoiselle Cettini,
for instance, Mrs. Smith justifies her efforts at self-promotion by explaining that she is merely catering to the demands of her audience: "You have
got to inculcate into the minds of the people an idea that a pure young
girl is going to jump about for their diversion. They know it isn't so. But
there must be a flavour of the idea. It isn't nice, but one has to live" (113).
Disregarding Caldigate's qualms about her chosen profession, Mrs. Smith
prioritizes her ability to earn a living even when doing so compromises
her status. As a result, she enacts the governesses' collective nightmare
as she relinquishes her identity in the colony, as is evidenced later in the
novel when she calls herself Mrs. Caldigate while living with the hero at
the diggings and Euphemia Cettini while prospecting for gold. Troped
as a foreigner and often referred to as an Australian woman, Mrs. Smith
metaphorically loses all ties to Britain. By the time she returns home, her
identity has become so problematic that she cannot sign a legal document
because of "a difficulty about the name" (378).

By contrast to Mrs. Smith, the FMCES emigrants maintained their
identities in the colony by adapting to new domestic roles that enabled
them to retain an affiliation with the colonial middle and upper classes. But
Mrs. Smith, who transgresses numerous boundaries when she becomes a
gold prospector, understands even prior to this penultimate transgression
that she is no longer a "productive" citizen of the nation. She explains to
Caldigate that

> [t]hings do come back to men. . . . You have a resurrection;—I mean
> here upon earth. We never have. Though we live as long as you, the
> pleasure-seeking years of our lives are much shorter. We burst out into
> full flowering early in our spring, but long before the summer is over, we
> are no more than huddled leaves and thick stalks. (46)

The metaphors of seasonal change in this passage invoke what is now called the biological clock and the imperative to female reproduction, figured here and in the rhetoric of matrimonial colonization as an essential aspect of nation-building. The FMCES emigrants resolved the contradiction that as single women they were necessarily outside the nation (both in a literal and a figurative sense) by assuming domestic roles as governesses in other people's families.[20] While they experienced freedom from many of the conventional expectations associated with class and gender, such freedoms rarely extended far beyond the limits of their domestic roles. Mrs. Smith, on the other hand, is doubly marginalized by virtue of her exclusion both from the domestic family and from the nation.

The burden of such gendered exclusion is evident when comparing the divergent fates of Trollope's male and female emigrants. Although none of the emigrants escapes the colonial encounter unscathed, Caldigate and Shand fare well by contrast to Mrs. Smith. Caldigate's body bears the signs of his Australian emigration when he returns to Britain "much darker in colour, having been, as it seemed, bronzed through and through by colonial suns and colonial labour" (126).[21] A gentleman by birth, Caldigate's reputation is threatened by the charge of bigamy, levied by Mrs. Smith and substantiated by others, that follows him back from Australia. However, after a lengthy ordeal he is publicly exonerated and assimilated back into British life. Likewise, Shand, Caldigate's partner at the diggings, is stigmatized when he returns to Britain with a darkened complexion, wearing the sturdy yellow trousers that are the typical uniform of the Australian convict. Shand's appearance coupled with his "bush manners" together brand him irredeemable, rendering him wholly unfit for life in Britain. As a result, he returns to Australia after contributing to Caldigate's exoneration, but not without a small capital from his friend that ensures his success in the colony as a partner on a sugar estate.

For Euphemia Smith no such recuperation is possible, either in Britain or in Australia. While the dissolution of identity that Caldigate and Shand experience in the colony is figured through their darkened complexions, for Mrs. Smith the marker of colonial contact is a sexualized, gender-specific trope: the loss of beauty. In London she appears before Caldigate wearing a veil (suggestive both of the impenetrability of the female body and of all that must be disguised or hidden) that effectively conceals the nature of her social descent. When Caldigate requests that she remove it, the spectacle of beauty which the veil is traditionally assumed to conceal is conspicuously absent:

But there she stood, looking at him, and to be looked at,—but without a word. During the whole interview she never once opened her lips.

She had lost all her comeliness. It was now nearly seven years since they two had been on the Goldfinder together, and then he had found her very attractive. There was no attraction now. . . . Since those days she had become a slave to gold,—and such slavery is hardly compatible with good looks in a woman. There she stood,—ready to listen to him, ready to take his money, but determined not to utter a word. (377)

In the above passage the idiom of slavery and the nexus of exchange (both of money and of the gaze) invoke the metaphors of prostitution, underscoring Mrs. Smith's submission as a pawn between men and highlighting the link between class and sexuality. Malek Alloula argues that within the harem the veil signifies an enclosure of private space, but also an injunction against trespassing that extends it into the public arena. Although she is not physically veiled at her own perjury trial, Mrs. Smith manifests this injunction through a similar stoicism by again refusing to speak and by maintaining an inscrutable countenance that frustrates the gaze of the courtroom spectators.[22] Like the FMCES emigrants, she uses silence as a means of empowerment, but in this case, such silence is represented as a form of defiance that signifies Mrs. Smith's resistance to her own marginalization.

This resistance has implications that extend, not just to Caldigate and his family, but to the nation. The legal plot that comprises the latter half of Trollope's novel and culminates in the return of all three emigrants—John Caldigate, Dick Shand, and Euphemia Smith—revolves around a discrepancy regarding Mrs. Smith's textual identity: her proper name. The damning piece of evidence in Caldigate's bigamy trial is an envelope addressed to "Mrs. Caldigate" and written in his own hand. Unlike the FMCES letters that straddle the gap between home and colony, this epistolary fragment was never supposed to reach Britain. The testimony provided by the envelope undermines the stability of the empire and exemplifies what Deirdre David calls "a pattern of counterintrusion by subaltern figures" (20), a reversal of the power dynamics of imperialism wherein the mother country is infiltrated by the colony. Because names in Britain form the basis for the system of primogeniture that maintains firm social demarcations, the name on the envelope threatens the foundations of the family, and by extension the nation, by questioning the legitimacy of Caldigate's marriage to Hester Bolton, her name, and his son's rightful inheritance. While this crisis is ultimately resolved through the discovery of the envelope's false postmark and

Mrs. Smith's perjury, it is nonetheless cause for alarm. As Homi K. Bhabha suggests, it is precisely such "scraps, patches, and rags of daily life" that keep the fabric of the nation intact ("DissemiNation" 297).

In *John Caldigate*, evidence of corruption in the lives of middle-class emigrants like Euphemia Smith suggests that the practices ensuring self-maintenance described in the FMCES letters are not being performed in Australia. The fate of Mrs. Smith and her Australian partner, Thomas Crinkett—incarceration for three years with hard labor—insinuates that Britain had come full circle since the establishment of a convict colony at Botany Bay. By making literal Mrs. Smith's superfluous position in relation to the nation through her marginalization within the confines of a prison, Trollope implies that emigration, like transportation, had failed to stabilize the empire or to reform convicts and settlers. The strategic amnesia that enables the FMCES emigrants to memorialize Britain without censure is absent in Trollope's account of female emigration. Writing in the late Victorian period with the benefit of his own personal experience in Australia,[23] Trollope reproaches the nation for failing to take care of its superfluous classes.

Unlike the more optimistic accounts in the FMCES letters, Trollope's rendering of female emigration in *John Caldigate* actualizes the "Alarming Prospect" with which I began this chapter. The fate of his female emigrant suggests that class and gender inequalities do more than destabilize the nation; they threaten to undermine the very foundations of the British imperial project. While the governesses' letters testify to the renovating power of the colonial to make new identities available to middle-class British women who are willing to adapt to less rigid social standards in Australia and New Zealand, they simultaneously acknowledge the impossibility of transporting those identities back to Britain. Unlike Mrs. Smith, who places a claim on the nation through her legal accusations against John Caldigate, many of the governesses readily accepted an increasingly marginalized position in relation to Britain in exchange for colonial freedom and independence. But Mrs. Smith is unwilling to make such a bargain, and her return home signifies a protest against her exclusion from the privileges associated with national identity and allegiance. Although Trollope's novel and the FMCES letters differ in their assessments of the success of the project of self-maintenance, both suggest that the rift caused by class and gender inequality within the nation is widened in the context of emigration, thereby creating a space for potentially empowering and often threatening forms of female self-assertion and independence.

PORTABLE DOMESTICITY AND PARTIAL TRUTHS

In *Imagining the Middle Class*, Dror Wahrman isolates the Reform Act of
1832 as a pivotal moment in the consolidation of the "middle class" in
Victorian Britain, arguing that at this point the centrality of this social
constituency was proclaimed not only as "the core of the 'public,'" but also
as "the epitome of hearth and home, at the core of the 'private'" (381). The
importance of this historical shift has been fruitfully examined by Wahrman, John Tosh, Leonore Davidoff, and Catherine Hall, among others,
to identify the specific ways in which British national identity historically
came to be bound up with middle-class ideologies and practices, and in
particular, with domesticity. While Wahrman's work has demonstrated
how ideologies associated with the middle class were reflected and constructed through political language, studies by both Tosh and Davidoff
and Hall have reconceptualized conventional accounts of class by illustrating the pivotal role that gender played in shaping middle-class life.
Likewise, these studies have exemplified the extent to which domesticity
transcended class boundaries to become linked with wider definitions of
English national identity. Tosh explains that domesticity became "the goal
of the conventional good life without distinction of class, subscribed to by
all but the bohemian and the very poor. Domesticity not only defined people's material ambitions, but also filled their symbolic world in a new way"
(4). Similarly, Davidoff and Hall's influential study, *Family Fortunes*, demonstrates how domestic culture became essential to the national character
of the English (28), with the family playing a pivotal role in securing the
health of the state: "the family was to provide a secure basis for national
stability. Men did not have the time; they were occupied in the world of
business and politics. Women had both the time, the moral capacity, and
the influence to exercise real power in the domestic world. It was their
responsibility to re-create society from below" (183). Given this responsibility, middle-class women played a unique role in the construction of
English national identity by imposing a moral order that both defined
appropriate gender relations and demarcated who belonged within the
nation (Davidoff and Hall 450).

If, as these historical accounts of class, gender, and nation have pos-
tulated, domesticity was foundational to the health and stability of the
nation, then female emigration offered the promise of effectively trans-
planting British domestic values through Australian colonial settlement.
By marrying British men in the colonies, bearing children, and furthering
the progress of settlement, female emigrants had the potential to shore up
British national identity and the empire itself through "the breeding and

ideological tasks of reproducing 'the nation'" (Stasiulis and Yuval-Davis 14). Yet, as we have seen in the real and fictional accounts of the governesses, Mrs. Clacy, and Trollope's Mrs. Smith, this idealized promise was never realized. Indeed, the wholesale transplantation of domestic values was never possible; such transfer was always partial and incomplete.

Although the accounts in this chapter suggest that some emigrants clung to their British roots with a remarkable degree of tenacity, these emigrants nonetheless could not withstand the gradual transformation of their settler identities once in the colonies. Indeed, as Davia Stasiulis and Nira Yuval-Davis have claimed, despite the fact that white settlers resisted integration with indigenous populations and clung to their European origins, "[t]his sense of identification with the 'mother country,' has not . . . mitigated the unevenness and fragility of settler identities, which were often forged in defence against metropolitan contempt" (20–21). Such "unevenness and fragility" is evident to differing degrees in all of the accounts of white settlement examined in this chapter. From the governesses' diffidence in adapting to new standards of domestic life in the colony; to Mrs. Clacy's strategic attempts to advertise the success of her new identity as a married woman and a returned emigrant; to Mrs. Smith's seeming defiance against the British standards that would stereotype her as a colonial woman, we see the push and pull between metropole and colony made manifest.

This ambivalence among colonial settlers toward the British imperial metropole is, according to Annie E. Coombes, one of the central features of settler colonialism in nations such as Australia, Aotearoa New Zealand, Canada, and South Africa (3), whose common histories as British colonies and later dominions generated a tension between the need for strong imperial ties and the exercise of freedom through self-governance (1). While this chapter has focused on the complexities of portable domesticity in the context of the voyage out and colonial settlement, the recurring possibility of returning to Britain highlights the complex vacillation between Britain and Australia that settlers continually negotiated. Each of the three accounts in this chapter raises the prospect of colonial return and the concomitant issue of how well emigrant or settler identities might translate *back* to Britain.

The fate of Trollope's returned emigrants in *John Caldigate* highlights particularly well the perils inherent in such colonial return as well as the ambivalence with which Britons viewed the practice of "top-dress[ing] the English acres with a little Australian gold" (217). Literally referring to the practice of applying manure to the surface of the soil as a fertilizer, "top-dressing" offers a rich metaphor for considering the implications of return, questions of portability, and the vexed relationship between Britain and Australia. Trollope's metaphor evokes the agricultural richness of the Australian continent and its valuable natural resources, while also encoding a critique of imperial exploitation by referencing the seeming nonchalance with which Britain attempted to achieve the wholesale transplantation of people and of natural resources. Just as the female emigrants examined here could not transmit and preserve British domestic values and practices wholesale in colonial Australia, Trollope implies that returned emigrants from Australia cannot simply transport themselves or "a little Australian gold" back to Britain without repercussions. These consequences are explored in detail in the next chapter, further illuminating the processes wherein domestic security—both national concerns and the primacy of the home—is imperiled by returned emigrants and colonials who threaten the peace and prosperity of "English acres."

Chapter Three

The Fraudulent Family

*Emigration, Colonial Return,
and the Sensational Crimes of Empire*

A fascinating nineteenth-century color cartoon vividly dramatizes an
unwelcome effect of British colonial emigration—a phenomenon
frequently referred to as "reverse colonization," in which natives of the
colonies "return" to the mother country. Entitled, "Probable Effects of
Over [*sic*] Female Emigration, or <u>Importing</u> the Fair Sex from the Savage
Islands in Consequence of <u>Exporting</u> all our own to Australia!!!!!," the
cartoon depicts a group of Aboriginal women from "the Savage Islands"
(presumably Australia and New Zealand) standing on the dock of a British seaport, displaying broad smiles for the benefit of a group of British
gentlemen who stand opposite them with wide-eyed expressions suggestive of their shock and horror (Figure 3.1). Although the women display
the trappings of Victorian femininity through their dress—one woman in
particular carries a parasol while two others wear prominent bustles—
they are stereotypically racialized in accordance with nineteenth-century
conceptions of blackness. Coupled with their dark skin, large lips, and
wide grins, their racial difference is signaled by the large gold earrings
and nose rings that many of the women wear and by the golden hoo-
kah one woman holds out as an offering. The latter gesture, as well as
the excited or coy expressions on the women's faces, suggest that they
are willing participants in a match-making exchange with the British
gentlemen that is being brokered by a European man in the center of
the image. Dressed in colonial garb, the broker casually leans back and
smokes as he points towards one of the Aboriginal women. The "Probable
Effects" mentioned in the cartoon's title thus begin with the infiltration

FIGURE 3.1. "Probable Effects of Over [sic] Female Emigration, or Importing the Fair Sex from the Savage Islands in Consequence of Exporting all our own to Australia!!!!" Courtesy of Bodleian Library, University of Oxford, John Johnson Collection, Emigration Large Folio.

of Britain by "savages" in the form of hyper-sexualized and racialized Aboriginal women *and* the returning colonist who acts as intermediary; the effects of this infiltration, the cartoon hints, will quickly evolve to include miscegenation.

Illustrating the spectacle generated by the return of "colonials" to Britain's shores, this color cartoon suggests that such return is an inevitable by-product of British colonial practices, and of emigration in particular. The growing horror with which these new arrivals are viewed by the British men suggests that colonial return is a deeply unnerving and threatening possibility, largely because it disrupts the traditional power dynamics implicit in the relationship between colonizer and colonized. Such a disruption is dramatized in this image both through the literal "invasion" of British space by native peoples, and through an obvious lack of agency on the part of the Britons as they engage in the brokering that is in process. Rather than being in control of this exchange, most of the British gentlemen pictured in the foreground of the cartoon are clearly unwilling participants who are nonetheless implicated in a situation that seems to parody the colonial slave trade, a practice that was abolished throughout the British colonies in 1833.[1] Their mere presence on the docks thus involves them in what could be viewed metaphorically as a criminal act involving the assertion of colonialist power. A further indication of such complicity, and of the potential ensnaring of British men in such crimes, is evidenced by the presence of a British gentleman who appears to be acting in concert with the colonial broker; this man stands at the edge of the dock with pen and paper in hand and appears to be making notations about the Aboriginal women as they disembark from the ship below.

While the upper-class men in the foreground of the image gaze at the colonial women with apparent horror and disdain, still more gentlemen clamor down a staircase and onto the docks in order to get a glimpse at these new arrivals, who are evidently also a source of intrigue when considered from a distance. One man in this group even raises a cane or umbrella as if he is trying to beat his way through the crowd. Another looks out toward sea with a telescope, as if hoping to determine amid the chaos whether more such women are on the way. The movement of these British gentlemen en masse down the staircase signals their symbolic degeneration and loss of agency as they become unwittingly caught up in the scene below, and as their responses upon actually seeing the women shift from intrigue to horror. Even further off in the distance, a group of soldiers run in single file past the Union Jack, presumably hurrying toward the spectacle created by the disembarking ship. Their presence in the background alludes to the alarming possibility that while the upper-class men stand ready to discourage and even rebuke this infiltration by colonial natives, these men from the lower classes, in this case, soldiers who are often stereotypically viewed as sexually profligate, may willingly participate in the match-making process at hand.

In a clever visual parallel, the cartoon depicts the arriving Aboriginal women who instigate this threat moving up a staircase and onto the docks in direct contrast to the British men who move down the staircase on the opposite side. Ironically referred to in the title as "the Fair Sex from the Savage Islands," these Aboriginal women are symbolically uplifted to the status of "ladies" as they arrive on British shores and engage in a parody of Victorian womanhood. In a further disruption of the power dynamics associated with the relationship between colonizer and colonized, these robust Aboriginal women challenge the primacy of the male gaze and visually overpower the crowd of cowering British men. While they are clearly depicted as a source of spectacle themselves, these women do not turn shyly away from the gaze of the gaping gentlemen—they too are actively looking. One woman in particular stands out in this regard; she wears a bright red and gold dress that distinguishes her from the group, and she stands proudly with her hands on her hips, as if surveying *her* options for a future mate.

Ironically, the disruption of colonial power dynamics evident in the scenario described above takes place through the importation of otherness into the Victorian family, here through the vehicle of conventional match-making. Although Victorian proponents like William R. Greg viewed colonial emigration as a way to resolve rather than create problems within both the Victorian family and the British nation by redressing a troubling imbalance between the sexes and reducing the numbers of "superfluous women" at home, the cartoon relies on the language of commerce to parody such schemes by suggesting that for each British export, a single woman, there will be a parallel import, a colonial one. The cartoon reinforces this idea through the symmetrical placement of equal groups of women and men separated by a match-maker in between, an arrangement that suggests the likelihood of a one-to-one exchange, perhaps regardless of one party's obvious reluctance. Along with its suggestion of pairings between British men and Aboriginal women posing in conventionally feminine ways, the cartoon also insinuates the possibility of reproduction. Among the "Probable Effects" alluded to in the title then, are not just the return of colonials to the mother country and the resulting disruption of colonial power dynamics, or even the threat of sexual and racial ambiguity implicit in the presence of colonial women, but also the seemingly inevitable mixing of British and Aboriginal cultures through invasion, contact, intermarriage, and miscegenation.

Whereas the cartoon "Alarming Prospect" discussed in the previous chapter dwells on the implications of sending single British women off into the empire, "Probable Effects" provides a mirror image in its depiction of colonial women arriving into the metropolis. Through its highly sensationalized portrait, "Probable Effects" illustrates how the British nation is threatened—via the family romance—by the unsettling integration of colonial life and culture through the "return" of native peoples to the mother country. As Deirdre David astutely notes, such instances of return in empire writing are often troped through images of invasion that dramatize how "in an ironic reversal of the pattern of British invasion and subjugation of lands and peoples throughout the Victorian period, the colonized begin to invade the imperial center" (3). As the cartoon implies, the British family itself is at stake in this process, no small matter considering the ideological weight of British domesticity at mid-century. As John Tosh and others have noted, determining who belonged within the Victorian family also had critical ramifications for the British nation, since Victorian political thinkers held "that the authority relations of the household were a microcosm of the state: disorder in one boded ill for the stability of the other" (3).[2] Yet while the influence of reverse colonization has typically been understood in terms of the return of the colonized or postcolonial subject to the colonizer's country,[3] less attention has been given to the kinds of colonial return we see in Trollope's *John Caldigate* and in many other Victorian plots in which British emigrants come home from the colonies, oftentimes with a substantial fortune. In many such fictional accounts, which Patrick Brantlinger aptly labels "a sociological 'return of the repressed'" (120–21), similar anxieties about the disruption of colonial power dynamics and cross-cultural threats to the family arise in more subtle yet interesting ways.

I opened *Antipodal England* by considering the resilience and portability of the Victorian family in the context of colonial emigration. I described how the family functions in emigrant guides and in pro-emigration rhetoric as a disciplinary unit capable of shoring up the nation-state by promoting a system of national colonization that allows for safe passage and successful settlement. However, as the letters of the FMCES emigrants suggest, such portability typically operates in only one direction, since it is complicated by the mere prospect of an emigrant's return. To extend my analysis of such complications, this chapter focuses on two contemporaneous and wildly popular accounts of colonial return from Australia to Britain, one a fictional account and one based on a notorious legal case.

By focusing on the return of British emigrants rather than on natives of the colonies, these accounts illustrate that the anxieties informing "Probable Effects" continued to hold sway through the 1860s and 1870s, and consistently called British identity at home into question along racial and economic lines.

The analysis that follows traces the figure of the returning emigrant from Mary Elizabeth Braddon's 1862 best-selling sensation novel, *Lady Audley's Secret*, to the public scandal surrounding an actual emigrant's homecoming that first generated attention in 1867 and subsequently led to the sensational and much publicized trials of the Tichborne Claimant that took place in London between 1871 and 1874. Although these two accounts differ significantly, they resonate in surprising ways, with colonial emigration in particular being of central importance to both accounts of fraud and crime within the Victorian family. By examining these accounts as an instance of life imitating art, I demonstrate that conventions of genre help to articulate the central tension of these texts: both *Lady Audley's Secret* and the Tichborne romance draw on the structure and emotional impact of sensation fiction to dramatize and heighten anxieties about the intertwining of familial and national concerns in the context of colonialism. They do so by showing how emigration—and more specifically, return—undermines the British family, and by extension, the nation, by importing the fluidity associated with colonial identity into the supposedly stable British home. The figure of the returning emigrant upsets and thus exposes the tenuous stability of familial relationships, suggesting that crimes and confusion, including bigamy, desertion, fraud, and doubt remain skeletons in the closets of many a British household.

In *Lady Audley's Secret*, questions of identity revolve largely around the novel's heroine, a figure who, like the Tichborne Claimant, inhabits a series of identities, in this case as Helen Talboys, Lucy Graham, and later Lucy, Lady Audley. Most criticism of Braddon's novel has accordingly focused on the terrifying concerns about female duplicity and madness raised by the heroine, or more recently, on questions of identity that are specifically linked to masculinity and profession through the detective figure, Robert Audley.[4] Yet this body of criticism does not tell the whole story of the novel's investments in questions of gender and identity, and it overlooks the significant, albeit marginalized character of George Talboys. The discussion that follows focuses almost exclusively on this figure and on how his emigration and return generate a familial crisis that raises issues of selfhood and national belonging that, while not as obviously threatening as Lady Audley's own masquerade or that of the Tichborne Claimant, contribute to the novel's sensational heightening of anxieties about identity, particularly in the context of British colonialism. While Talboys—unlike Lady Audley—does not engage in criminal behavior that is subject to punishment by law, he does desert his wife and child to pursue a fortune at the Australian gold diggings. This desertion creates a rupture in his domestic life that has reverberating effects, creating the opening for his wife's act of bigamy and generating a crisis of identity for Talboys that results in his own inability to reassimilate fully into his family, but also his nation. In this respect, his fate prefigures that of the Tichborne Claimant.

As is the case with George Talboys' story, "[t]he pathos of Tichborne was based on homecoming. It was a story rooted in homesickness" (McWilliam 262). The Tichborne story revolves around two trials involving a British emigrant who returned from Australia in 1867 and attempted unsuccessfully to impersonate a deceased Baronet, Sir Roger Charles Doughty Tichborne, in order to inherit his fortune. During the resulting legal proceedings—a civil trial for the possession of the estates and a criminal trial in which the Claimant was charged with perjury—the courts struggled to sort out the Claimant's multiple identities, knowing only that he had adopted several names while living in Australia, including Thomas Castro, Arthur Orton, and Sir Roger Tichborne. As with Braddon's *Lady Audley's Secret*, this story of spectacular class mobility, in this case about a man seemingly transformed from a poor butcher in Australia to a baronet in Britain, was wildly popular. The ongoing saga of the Tichborne Claimant's fate received widespread attention over a span of many years,[5] generating a plethora of articles, ballads, etchings, and grassroots publications, such as the *Tichborne Gazette*, a periodical authored by the Claimant's defense lawyer after the criminal trial to champion his client during his seven-year prison sentence for perjury. The fervor associated with the case garnered the Claimant broad popular support, particularly among working-class people, even after the case was non-suited in the civil trial. In fact, discussing the Claimant's story seems to have become a kind of national obsession, with the case taking on the character of a romance (Roe 36). Writing in the months prior to the conclusion of the criminal trial, the *Graphic* tellingly describes the resolution of the Tichborne case as a matter of national importance: "the gentlemen of the jury . . . *are expected to do for the nation* what we are afraid we should never be able to do for ourselves—viz., arrive at a satisfactory and conclusive verdict upon one of the most bewildering questions of identity which have ever been submitted to human judgment" ("Topics" Feb. 14, 1874, italics mine). With its roots in the family romance, the Claimant's story quickly took on dimensions that were larger-than-life, placing the identity of this singular individual at the center of what became a national debate.[6]

In her recent discussion of Victorian female emigration, Rita S. Kranidis contends that Victorian texts are often "dominated and structured by the issues that surface within them only as marginal concerns" (*The Victorian Spinster* 18). Indeed, representations of emigration and return are rarely given central prominence in the plots of Victorian novels; instead, emigrants like George Talboys often occupy marginal roles, appearing from or disappearing into the colonies at timely moments and in ways that work to further plots or to provide resolutions that might not otherwise have been possible. During the saga involving the Tichborne Claimant, however, issues that are marginalized in *Lady Audley's Secret* and other novelistic accounts of emigration were brought into the mainstream of Victorian culture through the sensational coverage of the trials and the attention to questions of identity and national belonging that they raised. While the intense public fascination with Tichborne clearly stemmed in part from salacious detail and the evidence of criminal behavior within a well-known and wealthy family, David Wayne Thomas' recent work persuasively shows how "the Tichborne sensation" gained popularity because it "indexed large-scale concerns of its own moment" (85). While recent scholarship on Tichborne by Thomas, Michael Roe, and Rohan McWilliam has focused variously on the ways in which the case tapped into contemporary cultural concerns, especially regarding class, my intent is to focus on how the Tichborne sensation speaks to pervasive cultural anxieties about emigration and the possibility of colonial return. Such anxiety was heightened in the case of Australian emigration, both because of that colony's vexed history as a convict settlement and because of the unique opportunities for social mobility created by the Australian gold rush.

COLONIAL RETURN AND CRIME
IN AN AUSTRALIAN CONTEXT

Propaganda about Australian emigration often features the fantasy that men without fortune or profession, especially middle-class men and second sons, can reap the benefits of the gold rush or the rich farmland and then go back home to the mother country in possession of a large fortune. In Anthony Trollope's *Harry Heathcote of Gangoil*, the titular hero's wife, Mary Heathcote, hopefully speculates that she and her settler family will live out this fantasy. Envisioning a future time when her baby son will have grown up, she tentatively asks her husband a question that equates social mobility with return: "By that time, Harry, you will have got rich, and we shall all be in England—shan't we?" (9). Although Trollope does not represent such an outcome and the historical record offers contradictory evidence regarding the likelihood of such a homecoming for British emigrants, the myth of return was nonetheless a powerful and pervasive ideal.

Charles Hursthouse, author of *Emigration. Where to Go and Who Should Go. New Zealand & Australia (as Emigration Fields) in contrast with Canada and the United States*, urges emigration, brightly insisting that return presents few obstacles for middle-class men:

> if it turned out that any of them did not like the life, they would return
> for good; they would have tried the thing at comparatively insignificant
> cost of time and money—they would only be a year or so older in age,
> but many years older in good, useful experience and expansion of ideas;
> and they would now be better satisfied, more inclined to make the best
> of anything offering in England. (94)

Hursthouse's comments suggest that gender, class, and age play key roles in determining who can return, especially since saving money to pay for a passage back home was often a substantial impediment. Whereas middle-class men, according to Hursthouse, can easily spare the time and expense involved, this was certainly not the case for middle-class women, as I have demonstrated in the previous chapter. By contrast to Hursthouse though, J. S. Tait, author of an emigration guide for the middle classes, frames emigration as a permanent act, explaining that "[n]o mistake in life is so fatal as an error in emigration. A return is scarcely possible. Where an emigrant goes there he must stay, whatever the conditions" (2). Regardless of this contradictory advice or the obstacles involved, evidence suggests that compared to Scotland, Ireland, and other parts of Europe, England and Wales had an unusually high rate of return: "of the 4,675,100 who left England and Wales between 1853 and 1900 only about 2,250,000 were permanent migrants" (Woods 310).

Yet those emigrants who did return to Britain were likely to receive an ambivalent welcome at best, since the Victorians upheld a double standard with respect to the advantages to be gained through emigration. While the potential for social mobility, whether through economic success or marriage, often featured prominently in propaganda about Australia, such mobility was valued only if it did not reinfiltrate established British social systems; Greater Britain was not meant to facilitate colonial advancement in the imperial metropolis itself. According to the logic of imperialist progress, "emigrants must not return, after all, and the horizon must be expanded outward in a linear progression, broadening the scope of the empire" (Kranidis, *The Victorian Spinster* 126).

While emigrants to Australia often left their home country in order to effect a transformation in their social standing, their later reinsertion into the local economy in Britain troubled long-standing political and economic practices such as primogeniture and inheritance. Such a disruption is famously illustrated in Charles Dickens's 1862 novel, *Great Expectations*, which was serialized in the same year as *Lady Audley's Secret*. Dickens's novel, published five years after the abolition of the sentence of transportation,[7] explores the consequences of this practice by detailing Abel Magwitch's return to Britain and the deleterious consequences it has for Pip and his family. As Coral Lansbury notes, the optimistic picture of Australian reformation that Dickens paints in *David Copperfield* is substantially darkened in his later representation of the convict's return from Australia: "Superficially, Magwitch had been reformed in New South Wales—he was at least a man of property on his return to England—but Magwitch dies in prison, a convict to the last" (149). *Great Expectations* highlights the danger inherent in the social mobility that enables Magwitch to lead a kind of double life when the returned convict explains to Pip the means through which this doubling occurs: "'it was a recompense to me, look 'ee here, to know in secret that I was making a gentleman. . . . If I ain't a gentleman, nor yet ain't got no learning, I'm the owner of such'" (300). While Magwitch's success in Australia is phenomenal, the logic of imperialism dictates that such upward mobility is good for the empire *only* if successful colonists, and especially ex-convicts, keep their distance from Britain. As Edward Said aptly notes, "[t]he prohibition placed on Magwitch's return is not only penal but imperial: subjects can be taken to places like Australia, but they cannot be allowed a 'return' to metropolitan space, which, as all Dickens's fiction testifies, is meticulously charted, spoken for, inhabited by a hierarchy of metropolitan personages" (xvi).[8] Magwitch's transgression, then, resides not in the fact that he gains access to wealth, but that he also seeks the corollary status that accrues to wealth at home in Britain by creating his protégé, Pip. Significantly, it is not until Magwitch physically reappears in Britain that his secret is unveiled, making visible the challenge he and Pip present to the existing class system and to the traditions of primogeniture and inheritance. At the same moment, sensationalism enters the otherwise realist plot, hinting by generic convention that the convict's return is already associated with scandal, intrigue, and anxiety in the public imagination.

While Dickens's representation of the dangers associated with transportation in *Great Expectations* indelibly connected emigration and crime in the Victorian popular imagination, the increasing interest after mid-century in middle-class emigration and colonial settlement for all classes helped to reform the image of Australian emigration. However, despite gradual changes in popular attitudes, the linkage between emigration and crime forged through convict transportation continued to evoke anxieties about imperialism even after that practice was abolished in 1857 and then phased out over the next decade. After mid-century, when free settlers, as opposed to convicts, began to populate Australia and other settlement colonies in greater numbers, new anxieties about imperialism and crime began to surface in Victorian literature and culture, this time centered around problems that developed in conjunction with colonial return, including bigamy, desertion, and fraud.

The atmosphere in which such anxieties were nurtured was one of rapid social mobility and shifting identities in the Antipodes. Such mobility certainly contributed to facilitating the kinds of deception and fraud perpetrated by the Tichborne Claimant, which allowed him to embody two personas at once, as both butcher from Wagga Wagga, Australia and titled gentleman from Hampshire, England. James Hammerton notes that "[f]or young emigrants the act of emigration itself could trigger social mobility, and this of course was a constant theme in emigration propaganda" ("'Out of Their Natural Station'" 152). This theme is evident in an emigration guide that makes the claim that "[i]n the mere money balance, a man in England with a clear £500 a-year is just nobody; but a man in New Zealand with this income would just be himself and somebody else too" (Hursthouse 91). Read metaphorically, the doubleness and upward mobility this passage describes is suggestive of status accrued through economic success, but read more literally, the addition of "somebody else too" might also signal a new status accrued through marriage and the acquisition of a wife.

Indeed, colonial marriage was a form of upward mobility that—like economic success—contributed to the creation of an atmosphere wherein shifting identities were the norm and not the exception. The popularity of "diggers' weddings" (Clacy, *A Lady's Visit* 23), or unions abruptly forged at the Australian gold fields, contributes to the laissez-faire attitude toward marriage that is cultivated in the colonies. In her memoir of the Australian gold rush, Ellen Clacy satirizes such attitudes, explaining that "[a]lthough railroads are as yet unknown in Australia, everything goes on at railway speed; and a marriage concocted one day is frequently solemnized the next" (*A Lady's Visit* 46). The levity attached to marriage in a colony where "bridal veils, white kid gloves, and, above all, orange blossoms are generally most difficult to procure at any price" (*A Lady's Visit* 23), helps to account for the haziness surrounding Euphemia Smith's marriage at the diggings and her subsequent accusations of bigamy in Trollope's *John Caldigate*. Despite the fact that John Caldigate eventually receives the Queen's pardon following his conviction, the evidence associated both with the bigamy trial and with his reprieve is highly ambiguous. Furthermore, such evidence instigates a crisis of identity that afflicts both Caldigate and Smith, creating family problems that get magnified on a national scale, as in the Tichborne trials, through the intervention of the law.

This intertwining of familial and national concerns through bigamy and fraud becomes within the framework of this particular cultural milieu an almost inevitable corollary to imperial expansion. The prevalence of such crimes in Australia is highlighted in Catherine Helen Spence's *Clara Morison*, when the heroine is warned against the risks a single woman faces in the Antipodes: "Girls should be very careful who they marry in a place like this, for there are many men who have a wife in each of these colonies, besides one in England" (1: 204).[9] While Spence represents bigamy here as a crime perpetrated in the colonies with deliberation and forethought, a column in an 1874 edition of the *Graphic* identifies "innocent bigamy" as a growing crisis created by the conditions of colonial emigration. The column describes several cases involving individuals who remarried after their spouses were presumed to have perished in the colonies or been lost at sea, only subsequently to discover that their spouses were living and that they themselves were bigamists:

> Bigamy is one of those offences which may imply consummate villainy, or may be undeserving of the mildest punishment known to the law. With the blacker phase of this offence every one is familiar, and none would wish, so long as monogamy exists, to see a jot of its penalty abated. Of what may be termed innocent bigamy, some curious instances have recently been reported, and the several stories demand a few moments of consideration. ("Topics" Feb. 21, 1874)

Perceived here as a novel problem associated with the expansion of the British empire, the paradox of "innocent bigamy" raises new questions about the types of crimes that might be committed in colonial contexts, and about whether all such crimes are deserving of punishment under British law. Given such preoccupations with bigamy, whether "innocent" or not, it should come as no surprise that this phenomenon is everywhere evident in the Victorian novel in the second half of the century, when mobility was occurring at unprecedented rates.

One of the most famous representations of the linkage between bigamy, fraud, and imperialism in the Victorian novel prefigures Braddon's novel and others from the 1860s—Charlotte Brontë's 1847 novel, *Jane Eyre*.

Although Jane escapes from the threat of bigamy when her suitor's secret is revealed, the novel questions the extent to which Rochester is accountable for his attempts to deceive Jane and his wife, Bertha Mason.[10] Rochester's confession of guilt is coupled by a plea that Jane (and the reader) judge him compassionately: "Bigamy is an ugly word!—I meant, however, to be a big-amist: but fate has outmanoeuvred me; or Providence has checked me. . . . You shall see what sort of a being I was cheated into espousing, and judge whether or not I had a right to break the compact, and seek sympathy with something at least human" (Brontë 326). Although Jane attempts to escape complicity in this crime of empire, her involvement in the novel's bigamy plot illustrates the extent to which colonialism infiltrates the British fam-ily, in this case, through parallel images of invasion involving "the arrival of fortune-seeking Rochester in creole Jamaica and the counterarrival by his wife in the isolation of the rural midlands" (David 9). These instances of invasion directly affect Jane despite her departure from Thornfield, leading to a predictable pattern wherein her own identity is compromised. Immediately after she leaves Rochester, Jane adopts an alias which initiates a masquerade that is not discovered until St. John Rivers learns her real name and she subsequently recognizes her true desires respecting Roches-ter. Jane Eyre escapes the "ugly word" and the fate of bigamy, but Brontë's novel helped to usher in a spate of bigamy novels in the 1860s, including *Lady Audley's Secret*.[11]

In Braddon's novel, the titular heroine, like Rochester, similarly ratio-nalizes her bigamous second marriage by insisting "I have a right to think that [George Talboys] is dead, or that he wishes me to believe him dead, and his shadow shall not stand between me and prosperity" (354). Yet whereas Rochester's crime is at least partially pardoned within the logic of the plot, Lady Audley is severely punished for her transgression when she is exiled to a *maison de santé* in a chapter suggestively titled "Buried Alive." In this way, she becomes a parallel figure to Bertha Mason Rochester, also imprisoned for the good of her health. By contrast, Rochester, like John Caldigate, is free to remarry Jane after Bertha's death, and like Caldigate, he is tentatively reassimilated into the domestic realm. The similarity of these two instances suggests that the most important question in these cases is not simply whether bigamy is innocent or not, but who gets vic-timized by this fraud. When the victim is a woman and a "colonial," like Bertha Mason or Euphemia Smith (who is troped as a colonial woman and a foreigner once she arrives in Australia), the crimes of empire can pre-sumably be overlooked. On the other hand, as we will see in the case of *Lady Audley's Secret* and the Tichborne Claimant, when the victim of fraud occupies a privileged position in terms of gender or class (when he is a man or a member of the aristocracy), such crimes create a sensationalized response that has reverberating effects that are less than forgiving.

IDENTITY AND THE OTHER END OF THE WORLD

In Braddon's *Lady Audley's Secret*, as in *John Caldigate*, the hero returns to Britain complete with a fortune gleaned at the gold diggings, with the intention to settle down into an idealized domestic life. In each case, bigamy disrupts these intentions and raises questions about the protagonist's identity. Just as Caldigate dreams of Hester Bolton while in the wilds of Australia, George Talboys is sustained throughout his trials at the diggings by the memory of his beloved wife: "I clung to the memory of my darling, and the trust that I had in her love and truth, as the one keystone that kept the fabric of my past life together—the one star that lit the thick black darkness of the future" (21). George's domestic life, and his relationship with his wife in particular, is figured here as central to his own self-definition. This is consistent with John Tosh's recent claim that domesticity was a critical component of masculine identity for most of the nineteenth century, since "home was widely held to be a man's place, not only in the sense of being his possession and fiefdom, but also as the place where his deepest needs were met" (1). Initially lacking a home of his own and mortified by the birth of a son who would be "heir to his father's poverty" (19), George sets his sights on Australia in hopes that he might succeed in gaining the means to provide for his family. At the diggings, he envisions his wife as the embodiment of portable domesticity, "under [his] wretched canvas tent, sitting by [his] side, with her boy in her arms" (22). Yet his own failure to engage in strategies of self-maintenance that would allow him to retain his ties to the domestic life he reverences causes him to lose his family, and subsequently, the means of his self-definition. Although he is in Australia for three and a half years, George never sends a letter home, (a strategy I have previously shown to be quite crucial for the women who emigrated under the auspices of the Female Middle Class Emigration Society), and his wife accordingly presumes herself deserted.

The dissolution of identity that George experiences at the Australian gold diggings becomes evident in a moment of alarming self-recognition that he describes to a fellow passenger aboard the homeward bound *Argus*: "I was in the centre of riot, drunkenness, and debauchery; but the purifying influence of my love kept me safe from all. Thin and gaunt, the half-starved shadow of what I once had been, I saw myself one day in a broken bit of looking-glass, and was frightened of my own face" (21). Unlike the governesses I discuss in the previous chapter, whose shipboard mirrors serve to reflect back the evidence of their success-ful self-maintenance, George's mirror reveals an alarming transformation that is symbolic of the extent to which his identity has been compro-mised by his experiences in the Antipodes. Despite his assumption that his love renders him impervious to the influences that surround him, the mirror indicates that George is indeed altered. Likewise, his sudden departure from England and his failure to write home create a window of opportunity for his wife to change as well; in the interim between his departure and return, Helen Talboys famously "sink[s] her identity" by transforming herself into Lucy Graham and then into Lucy Audley (271). Although George experiences self-reproach regarding "the recollection of that desertion which must have seemed so cruel to her who waited and watched at home!" (241), his remorse comes too late, and he returns to Britain oblivious to the fact that his prospects for a domestic reunion have already been blighted.

The superficial transformation through which George becomes a "shadow of what [he] once had been" is an important and persistent trope in Victorian representations of emigration, which often thematize the identity crises brought on by displacement in purely physical terms. In *A Tramp to the Diggings: Being Notes of a Ramble in Australia and New Zealand in 1852*, John Shaw, M.D., describes the inevitable physical effects of emigra-tion that he has witnessed during his travels in the Antipodes. Not sur-prisingly, the characteristic feature Shaw identifies, consistent with what George sees when he looks at his own reflection, is the wasting away of a healthy English complexion:

> In society the native Australian (of course I mean the whites, not the aborigines,) is a most agreeable person. . . . Both men and women, how-ever, lose that healthy look which is ever characteristic of an English face; the colour goes, and the cheek shrinks, with the skin either wrin-kled or loose, and assumes a coarse or sun-burnt aspect. (226–7)

The bodily transformation Shaw describes is a familiar marker of colo-nial contact in the Victorian novel. The trope of darkened or yellowed skin is most frequently evoked to signify exposure to colonial conditions that are perceived to be both physically and psychologically demanding. Such exposure becomes a kind of taint that is associated in the novel with fears of both class and racial degradation; as Carolyn Vellenga Berman puts it, "[m]elting like butter in the tropical sun, colonial whites blurred the national borders of Great(er) Britain" (32).[12] Here, Shaw is careful to avoid such blurring by subsequently identifying causal agents that bring on the bodily degeneration he describes (excessive drinking and smoking) and by differentiating between white settlers and Aborigines. But the remarkable slippage whereby the former become "native Australians" suggests not only the violence associated with colonial settlement but also the physical and psychic transformations emigrants had to undergo in making the transition from home to colony.

Through such transformations, the violence of displacement and colonial contact gets written on the emigrant body as a characteristically "English face" is supplanted by a racialized one. Such a substitution visually signals the kind of identity crisis that often follows in the wake of an emigrant's return to Britain, and like the cartoon "Probable Effects," it evokes the most threatening aspects of the colonial encounter—miscegenation and the mingling of two cultures. Examples from the Victorian novel abound; to name just the most relevant instances here, Trollope's John Caldigate and Dick Shand wear characteristically colonial complexions when they return, as does George Talboys, whose skin is described as "dark bronze" in color when he arrives in London (36). However, George also speaks to his friend Robert Audley of physical manifestations of the psychic pain associated with emigration that are not always visible to the unknowing observer:

> Do you know, Bob . . . that when some of our fellows were wounded in India, they came home bringing bullets inside them. They did not talk of them, and they were stout and hearty, and looked as well, perhaps, as you or I; but every change in the weather, however slight, brought back the old agony of their wounds as sharp as ever they had felt it on the battle-field. I've had my wound, Bob; I carry the bullet still, and I shall carry it into my coffin. (49)

Likening his grief and self-reproach over his wife's death and his own abandonment of her to a physical wound that never heals, George aligns his own colonial experience and its consequences with that of British soldiers who were presumably wounded in battle during the Indian Mutiny. Unlike the obvious changes in complexion that make apparent the transformations wrought by emigration, the hidden wounds George invokes here highlight an important disjunction between reality and appearance that is far more subversive.[13] The bullet he carries stands in for the secrets associated with colonialism that the Victorians sought to repress, secrets involving crime and bigamy (embodied in the return of fictional emigrants like Abel Magwitch, Bertha Mason, and Euphemia Smith), as well as violence (signified here by oblique reference to the Indian Mutiny). The implied disjunction in this passage between imperial expansion and the realities of colonial violence parallels the disjunction between the knowable and the unknowable aspects of an individual's identity.

Similar ambiguities about the wounds of displacement are highlighted by the presence aboard the *Argus* of Miss Morley, a 35-year-old governess who is on her way home to marry a man to whom she has been engaged for fifteen years. Given that she travels first class and carries with her a savings accrued in Australia, it is evident that Miss Morley has achieved some measure of financial success and social mobility in the colony. Yet she returns without the optimism that George Talboys, with his £20,000 fortune, initially enjoys. In an echo of the paradigm wherein female passengers lament the ending of the voyage out and the future uncertainties it brings, Miss Morley dreads the moment in which she will finally arrive in Britain. Imagining a litany of problems that could result from the ways in which both she and her fiancé have changed during the lengthy interval between her departure for Australia and her return home, she cannot envision her future marriage or her reassimilation into normative British life. Ten days before the *Argus* is expected to reach land, the governess expresses her fears to her friend and fellow passenger, George Talboys: "I wonder, looking back, to think how hopeful I was when the vessel sailed . . . but for this last month of the voyage, day by day, and hour by hour, my heart sinks, and my hopeful fancies fade away, and I dread the end as much as if I *knew* that I was going to England to attend a funeral" (17). Miss Morley's dread highlights the gendering of colonial redemption, especially when read in conjunction with George Talboys's optimism. It also helps to account for Helen Talboys's decision to adopt a fraudulent identity in Britain rather than to seek a new beginning through female emigration, an avenue she briefly contemplates but subsequently discounts because of precisely the kind of uncertainties about her fate that Miss Morley experiences. Although Miss Morley assures George that her story is "an exceptional case," the testimony of the FMCES governesses and the fate of Euphemia Smith suggest otherwise. When George defensively informs his companion that "your terrors have nothing to do with me" (18), he ironically underscores his own complicity in upholding the gendered double standard that allows him to desert his wife and expect nonetheless to find her waiting at home unchanged.

As evidence of his miscalculation, however, the dissolution of George's identity is emphasized in descriptions of his position aboard the *Argus*, where "nobody knew who or what he was, or where he came from, but every body liked him" (14). The extent to which he has changed in the interim between his departure and his return is signaled by his status aboard ship: he travels out to Australia in steerage, but returns a first-class passenger. Yet rather than frame this upward mobility in a positive light, Braddon pointedly undermines her hero's success, critiquing his abandonment of Helen Talboys "in the pursuit of a fortune which she never lived to share" (47). The penalty George pays for this infidelity is his inability to reassimilate, figured through the sense of rootlessness that causes him to endure a series of successive displacements that follow on the heels of his Australian emigration. Immediately after he arrives in London and learns of his wife's death, George vows to Robert Audley that he will leave Britain again, recognizing that reassimilation will be impossible: "I shall set sail in the very next vessel that leaves Liverpool for Australia. I shall be better in the diggings or the backwoods than ever I could be here. I'm broken for a civilised life from this hour, Bob" (45). Because his sense of self-worth is tied to his domestic role as a provider for his family, it is not surprising that the supposed death of his wife intensifies his crisis of identity. Yet his misfortune is figured here as a "domestic" failure in a dual sense, with the implication that in leaving again he fails not only his family, but also his nation.

Before he emigrates for a second time, George's identity crisis intensifies, and as a result, he asks his friend Robert to be his son's guardian. Although George continues to provide for his son financially, his efforts to ingratiate himself with little Georgey falter, signaling his failure adequately to fulfill his parental role: "He always went loaded with toys and sweetmeats to give to the child; but, for all this, Georgey would not become very familiar with his papa, and the young man's heart sickened as he began to fancy that even his child was lost to him" (49–50). George's sense of loss in connection with his son is indicative of George's exiled position outside of the family, and it intensifies the identity crisis that leads up to his second disappearance. This crucial event occurs after Lady Audley attempts to efface George's identity as she has effaced her own by watching him "sink with one horrible cry into the black mouth of the well" (394). When he miraculously gets out alive, thanks to his experience in the Australian mines, he is wholly unrecognizable, and according to Robert Audley, "lost . . . as suddenly and unaccountably as if a trap-door had opened in the solid earth, and let him through to the Antipodes!" (151). Mr. Marks, who looks after George in his dazed state, taxes his mother to remember their unusual guest: "Do you remember my bringin' home a gentleman . . . as was wet through the skin, and was covered with mud and slush, and green slime and black muck . . . and was such a objeck that nobody would ha' knowed him? . . . and didn't know where he was, or who he was" (419). Having left behind all that might define him, including the Army, his wife and son, and his friend, Robert, George is "gone mad or stupid-like" (419), a condition that echoes Lady Audley's supposed madness in the face of her own crisis of identity.

Despite his determination to return to Australia, however, George never carries out this resolution, opting instead to board a ship bound for America. His choice of destination is important since it suggests the extent to which his national identity is compromised by his initial displacement. In nineteenth-century emigration guides, the United States is often represented as a problematic destination, insofar as this locale threatens the British emigrant's sense of national allegiance. Emigrants are often figured in the rhetoric of such guides as valuable cultural capital; by extension, emigration to the United States signifies the waste of capital, as the following tract advocating emigration to Canada, a settler colony like Australia, makes clear:

> Year after year we have gone on giving the bone and sinew of our people
> to increase the strength of a rival confederation, not always animated
> by the best or kindest feelings towards our country. The United States
> have thriven with unexampled rapidity on the hosts of sturdy labourers
> who have swarmed over to their ports, to escape from the poverty and
> destitution which awaited them in the battle of life at home [in Britain].
> (*Tracts: Canada: The Land of Hope* 3)

Whereas emigration to the settler colonies presumably strengthens the bonds of empire by directing emigrant labor toward the settlement of Britain's colonial possessions and the expansion of the empire, emigration to the United States weakens these bonds and allows the cultural capital of emigrant labor to be permanently lost.

Given these contemporary associations, we might read George's subsequent emigration to America as an emblem of his weakened allegiances to Britain. His decision to exchange his berth on the *Victoria Regia*, an emigrant ship bound for Melbourne and aptly named for Britain's queen, for one bound for New York might be read as a second desertion, this time of queen and country. In addition to suggesting George's rootlessness—he no longer belongs in Britain *or* in Australia—this change of plans signifies the apex of an identity crisis that culminates in his sudden and mysterious disappearance. The fact that he travels under an alias, Thomas Brown, makes him impossible to trace and renders Robert's advertisements in the *Times* fruitless.

As I have indicated earlier, Kranidis argues that the colonies function in Victorian discourse as entities of "relative value" that are constantly redefined to suit the ideological and material needs of the mother country (*The Victorian Spinster* 59). George's emigration, and the empire more broadly construed, function in *Lady Audley's Secret* as the catalysts that trigger the novel's sensationalism and help to harbor its secrets—Lady Audley's crimes of impersonation, bigamy, and the attempted murder of George Talboys, among others. While Harcourt Talboys's act of disinheriting his son George when the latter marries beneath his station also helps to instigate the events that unfold in the novel's opening chapters, it is the act of emigration that has decisive consequences, both for Talboys and for his wife, Helen. The problems associated with the failure of the system of primogeniture to treat George fairly underscore an omnipresent anxiety about the fractures that exist in the British family that are subsequently exacerbated by the act of emigration. Ironically, while emigration and empire help to widen such fractures, they are also imagined as the means through which the familial problems caused by the novel's secrets might be resolved. As one Victorian reviewer sarcastically notes of Braddon's oeuvre, "[i]t is a peculiarity of Miss Braddon's heroes and heroines that they are always ready to abandon wife, children, and home, and to proceed at a moment's notice either to Australia or America" (Rae 103). As the site for escape or for exile, for brashly seeking fortunes or for quietly sinking into obscurity, these distant locales exert a kind of invisible agency in the plot of *Lady Audley's Secret*. Contrast, for example, the differences between George's motivations each time he emigrates. The first time, he goes to Australia filled with expectations, "to try [his] fortune in a new world" (21). When he emigrates to America, by contrast, he goes "a broken-hearted man, to seek some corner of the earth in which [he] may live and die unknown and forgotten" (421), completely severing his ties to his family and nation.

Although George Talboys is the only major character who emigrates, almost all the others contemplate following in his footsteps at one point or another, including Lady Audley, Robert Audley, Clara Talboys, and Alicia Audley. Going "to the end of the world" (363), whether on a mission to find George Talboys or as a means of facilitating Sir Michael Audley's recovery, is imagined both as a means of escape and as a means of displacing or resolving the problems brought on by the novel's secrets. Lady Audley, for instance, contemplates disappearing as George did, but as I have suggested, her anxieties about doing so underscore the difficulties attached to female emigration: "But where could I go? What would become of me?. . . . What could I do?" (316). Likewise, Clara Talboys alludes to the envious mobility men possess when she asserts that "[i]f I were a man, I would go to Australia, and find [George], and bring him back" (439).

Robert, on the other hand, who does have access to such mobility, conceives of emigration as a means of escaping the growing chain of evidence regarding his friend's disappearance once he realizes where it will lead him: to Lady Audley. Torn between his desire for justice and his love and pride respecting his uncle, Robert contemplates a prospect that merely substitutes one form of allegiance, familial, over another, national: "If I *could* let the matter rest; if—if I could leave England for ever, and purposely fly from the possibility of ever coming across another clue to the secret, I would do it—I would gladly, thankfully do it—but I *cannot!*" (172). The impossibility of evading what he perceives to be the stronger claim upon him, his commitment to justice, compels Robert to substitute Lady Audley's exile for his escape; "let [her] go away," Robert warns Mr. Maldon, "[she] shall not be pursued" (173). Ultimately, this is exactly how Robert resolves the problem of Lady Audley's guilt and his own complicity in its revelation. Fearing the spectacle that must attend upon a murder trial, Robert single-handedly punishes Lady Audley by displacing her into the realm of the foreign. Exile figures here as the ultimate punitive measure and closural device, as the bigamist, whose crimes are nurtured in part through the conditions of colonialism, is removed from Britain, and thus restrained from committing further harm. It is almost as if the novel suggests that Lady Audley loses her identity as soon as she is transported off British shores (and subsequently renamed by Robert Audley), and indeed, that her punishment is the loss of the identity she has struggled so hard to secure. It is only after the remote possibility of Lady Audley's return from abroad is nullified through her death that Braddon insinuates the possibility of George Talboys's tentative reassimilation into the Victorian family.

RECENTERING THE FAMILY CIRCLE

In 1862, the understanding that the family was subject to assault and fracture through the reverberating effects of colonial expansion is made evident not only in *Lady Audley's Secret*, but also in Dickens's humorous depiction of Mr. Wemmick's castle in *Great Expectations*. Wemmick's home in Walworth, "got hold of a bit at a time" is described as "a freehold" that allows him to capitalize on the benefits of what he calls "portable property" (194). Like Mr. Peggotty's boathouse, Wemmick's castle is represented as an idyllic, insular, and delightfully quirky home. Yet it is also highly functional, working to protect the privacy of Wemmick's personal life and the sacredness of his family. Fortified by a moat and a working drawbridge, the design of the castle offers Wemmick a way to "cut off the communication" and thereby protect against the encroachments of the world beyond the family (192). Wemmick's intense protection of his home is indicative of the family's vulnerability to outside forces, and especially to the novel threats generated by imperial expansion and the phenomenon of return, whether by natives, convicts, or emigrants. In dramatic opposition to Braddon's Audley Court, a place whose "broad outer moat was dry and grass-grown" (3) hence leaving it open to such threats, Dickens's suburban castle suggests the need for a staunch defense of the middle-class values of privacy and seclusion. Such values are prized in both novels over against the sensationalism generated by return,[14] particularly in the representations of Wemmick's castle in *Great Expectations* and the fairy cottage on the Thames in *Lady Audley's Secret.*

Helena Michie argues that the configuration of the family circle that closes Braddon's novel "reestablishes middle-class life and middle-class morality at the expense of the two extremes" (*Sororophobia* 71). Indeed, after exchanging his bachelorhood for middle-class marriage, Robert Audley fulfills his "dream of a fairy cottage . . . where, amid a little forest of foliage, there is a fantastical dwelling-place of rustic woodwork, whose latticed windows look out upon the river" (445). Rather than marrying his cousin, Alicia, and sustaining the aristocratic lifestyle associated with Audley Court, Robert elects not to make the kind of advantageous "bargain" that Sir Michael and Lady Audley make when they marry (11). Instead, he chooses Clara and marries for love. He also becomes industrious in his professional life, and when we last see him in this capacity he is prosecuting a breach of promise suit, having presumably become a staunch defender of the institution of marriage. Although he is accused by Harcourt Talboys of having "paltered with the laws of [his] country" in his supposedly lenient treatment of Lady Audley (434), Robert's work as a barrister neatly resolves the previous conflicts he has had between his personal, familial obligations and his professional ones. Likewise, it suggests a mounting defense of the family circle over against the sensational crimes of empire that have shaken both the Talboys and the Audley families.

Anne Cvetkovich argues that the novel's happy ending is undercut, however, by the fact that "[i]n *Lady Audley's Secret*, the family is not a refuge from problems that occur elsewhere, but a suddenly healed instance of an institution that has been riddled by conflict throughout the narrative" (53). However, I contend that the domestic idyll represented in the final chapter is not merely a "healed instance" or a repetition of the familial models represented in the rest of the novel, but rather, that it represents a departure to a new style of domesticity. In other words, I suggest that the fairy cottage on the Thames, with its extended portable family, is convincing precisely because it stands in opposition to other forms of failed domesticity in the novel. As in *David Copperfield*, where Mr. Peggotty's boathouse is represented as an idyllic home precisely because it is atypical, the fairy cottage in *Lady Audley's Secret* is equally successful because it is not bound by the rigid conventions or expectations that govern other homes and families in the novel. According to middle-class Victorian ideals, "[i]f companionate marriage and the raising of children were to flourish, so went the common wisdom, they needed not only space but seclusion. The 'family circle' beloved of the didactic writers was intimate and inward-looking" (Tosh 28). Robert and Clara's retreat certainly embodies this ideal of seclusion and intimacy—echoing the sheltered trio of husband, wife, and child idealized in *The Last of England*—but their family circle is simultaneously capacious enough to embrace extended family members. In addition to offering a place for George Talboys, Robert and Clara's home is a haven for their frequent guests, including Georgey, Sir Michael Audley, Alicia Audley, and Sir Harry Towers.

By contrast to this portable family, instances of failed domesticity in Braddon's novel are evident across class lines; Audley Court and Squire Talboys's home in Dorsetshire offer aristocratic examples, while Captain Maldon's home at Southampton and the Marks's Castle Inn offer examples from among the lower classes.[15] Framed in the opening and closing chapters by descriptions of two homes, Audley Court and the fairy cottage, *Lady Audley's Secret* invites the reader to generate comparisons between the different domestic modes. These comparisons, in turn, highlight the excessiveness of Britain's domestic ideals, which are constantly undermined by the presence of single women, like the deserted Helen Talboys, and disavowed or second sons, like George Talboys, for whom the family cannot (or will not) provide. Not coincidentally, such individuals are the same ones who are depicted in Victorian emigration propaganda as the ideal candidates for emigration to the colonies, which becomes the means whereby the problems they represent can be repressed, but only temporarily in the event of colonial return. Unable to sustain the pressures created by such contradictions in domestic ideology, *Lady Audley's Secret* reveals the fractures inherent in the Victorian family and offers an alternative possibility in the fairy cottage on the Thames.

George Talboys's relation to this domestic idyll as a third party to the marriage of his sister and his dear friend has been the subject of much critical commentary, which has focused primarily on the homoerotic dynamics that inform this triangulated relationship, wherein Clara appears merely to be a pawn between the two men.[16] Indeed, George attributes his return home from America as well as his rootlessness to his longing for the fellowship he shared with Robert, a longing which is mediated through another woman, in this case Helen Talboys: "I might have made plenty of friends had I pleased, but I carried the old bullet in my breast; and what sympathy could I have with men who knew nothing of my grief? I yearned for the strong grasp of your hand, Bob; the friendly touch of the hand which had guided me through the darkest passage of my life" (444). George's ambiguous position within this domestic idyll contributes to Braddon's efforts to reconfigure the family circle for strategic purposes.

Yet it is important to note that George Talboys is absorbed into the middle-class idyll not through the marriage plot, which is ultimately the means for John Caldigate's reassimilation, but through the agency of portable domesticity. Exchanging his journeys aboard emigrant ships for the "slender wherries" in which he and Robert traverse the Thames (445), George is accommodated into the British family as an avuncular figure whose homosocial relation to the marriage plot is simultaneously liberating and threatening. In her study of the place of uncles in Victorian literature, Eileen Cleere argues that "a model of the extended family—especially and most significantly a model of the avunculate—was often implemented by Victorian writers to highlight the inadequacies of paternalistic and affective family paradigms" ("*The Shape of Uncles*" 14).[17] While George's position as an adjunct to the family certainly serves this purpose, it is also important to note, as Cleere suggests, that the trope of the avunculate is not strictly benign. In terms of affective ties, George's place in the family is problematic insofar as the homosocial bond he shares with Robert threatens to undermine the ties between husband and wife. Although the narrator alludes to the possibility that George might himself one day remarry, indicating that "*it is not quite impossible that he may by-and-by find some one who will be able to console him for the past*" (446, italics mine), this tentative, almost hyperbolic formulation makes the prospect seem unlikely. From an economic standpoint, George's status as a gentleman of fortune leaves him independent of Robert and Clara's family, so that he may remain indefinitely at its margins as neither dependent nor provider. His liminality within the homosocial triad thus enables him to defer his own marriage plot, leaving him in a titillating position that underscores his conditional reassimiliation into the Victorian family and the continuing strain of the hidden wounds inflicted by his colonial encounters.[18]

SENSATION FICTION AND THE CASE
OF THE TICHBORNE CLAIMANT

The fictional story of George Talboys's conditional return to Britain is echoed in the sensational account of the Tichborne Claimant, and recent scholarship by Thomas and McWilliam has identified strong links in the Tichborne case between law and literature. Thomas writes that "supporters and detractors alike appear to have treated the Claimant as an object of narrative fascination and fitful identification, and thus he was a kind of literary object, a foil for reflections on social or ethical agency" (82). Likewise, McWilliam asserts, "[l]egal and literary London were never far apart, as the novel aspired to much the same function as the courtroom" (36). Given these linkages, it is not surprising that many of the anxieties about colonial return that are embedded in Braddon's novel get reworked in this contemporaneous public sensation.

The Claimant's story begins on Christmas day in 1866 when an Australian emigrant arrived in London claiming to be Roger Charles Doughty Tichborne, Baronet and heir to the Tichborne estates. One of England's oldest families, with estates dating back to the time before William the Conqueror, the Tichborne family of Hampshire had recently mourned the death of Roger's father, Sir James Tichborne. Until the emigrant's arrival, the family had believed that Roger, the eldest son, had been lost at sea off the coast of South America in 1854. Only Lady Tichborne, Roger's mother, maintained the hope that her son might have survived the wreck of the emigrant ship, *Bella*.

Eager to believe the rumors that circulated in England in 1854 and again in 1857 that there had been survivors from the wreck who had been taken to Australia, Lady Tichborne placed advertisements for her son in the *Times* in 1863 in English, French, and Spanish. When these failed to yield any results, she decided in May of 1865 to hire a detective at a Missing Friends' Office in Sydney to look for her son. The advertisements that Arthur Cubitt subsequently placed in local newspapers caught the attention of an Australian attorney, William Gibbes, who approached Thomas Castro, a butcher whom he suspected of being Tichborne. Gibbes's suspicions were based on the fact that his client, Castro, had made passing references to having property in England and to having survived a shipwreck, and also that he smoked a pipe carved with the initials R. C. T. Despite Castro's initial reluctance to come forward, Gibbes, who may have been motivated by the advertisement's promise of a liberal reward, convinced his client to write to Lady Tichborne and identify himself. This correspondence initiated what would become a long struggle to prove that

Castro was Roger Tichborne, and thereafter he became famous under an illustrious title—the Tichborne Claimant.

In the first of many poorly written letters to Lady Tichborne, the Claimant alludes to identifying features that would prove to his mother that he was indeed her lost son. He writes: "Mr. Gibbs suggest to me as essential That I should recall to your Memory things which can be only known to you and me to convince you of my Identity. I don't thing [*sic*] it needful, my dear Mother, although I send them Namely the Brown Mark on my side And the Card Case at Brighton" (qtd. in Woodruff 44–5). Ironically, although Lady Tichborne had no recollection of the latter detail and only vague recollections of the former, evidence from family servants suggests that Roger was born with a birthmark on his side. Yet Lady Tichborne was convinced that this man was her son, not by this mark, but by a photograph sent by Gibbes and by the handwriting and the general tenor of the Claimant's letter. As a result, she eventually sent the passage money so that the Claimant and his family could return to Europe to meet her face to face. In the meantime, the Claimant was recognized by two ex-servants of the Tichborne family who were living in Sydney, Andrew Bogle, who returned to England with the Claimant, and Michael Guilfoyle, a gardener who later withdrew his recognition.

In the days following his return to England, the Claimant went to Paris and met with Lady Tichborne, who immediately claimed him as her lost son, Roger. This recognition carried the weighty backing of maternal instinct, and as such, it was a crucial component in garnering popular support for the Claimant's story. Additionally, it allowed the Claimant to assume Sir Roger's identity without significant contestation for more than a year until Lady Tichborne's sudden death in 1868. Her death before the trials had begun meant that she never witnessed the evidence stacked against the Claimant, and there is compelling reason to believe she willfully disregarded evidence that cast doubts on the identity of the man she believed to be her son. In *A Literary and Pictorial Record of the Great Tichborne Case*, the *Graphic* outlines a fairly typical view among the Claimant's detractors of Lady Tichborne as someone whose "impulsive self-willed but essentially weak and visionary character" allowed her to overlook many inconsistencies in her early correspondence and initial meeting with the Claimant—including a tenuous physical resemblance—because a "fixed idea" had long possessed her that her son was still alive. Because of this, the *Graphic* argues, she was predisposed to believe the Claimant's story, and even unwittingly aided his imposture by providing a wealth of information about her son Roger in the 1863 advertisements.

After Lady Tichborne's recognition in the weeks subsequent to his return to Britain, the Claimant was repudiated by various members of Roger Tichborne's extended family, all of whom believed him to be an imposter. Additionally, Vincent Gosford, who had been Tichborne's steward and confidential agent, failed to recognize him upon his arrival in Britain. Yet the Claimant would eventually acquire 85 witnesses who could attest to his identity as Roger Tichborne, including the family solicitor, family servants, various Hampshire residents including tenants of the estate, and fellow soldiers from his regiment.[19] The confusion instigated by these conflicting testimonials resulted in two trials of unprecedented length, one a civil action for the possession of the Tichborne estates that ran from 10 May 1871 to 6 March 1872, and the second a criminal trial that ran from 23 April 1873 to 28 February 1874 wherein the Claimant was charged with perjury. While the prosecution in the first trial insisted that the Claimant was an imposter driven by greed, the defense argued that the family members who disavowed Roger did so not because he was an imposter, but because his return after having led a humble lifestyle in Australia humiliated the family and threatened their own pecuniary interests, including the legacy of the presumptive heir, the infant son of Roger's younger brother, Sir Alfred Tichborne. For a period of roughly seven years from the Claimant's arrival in London until the end of the criminal trial, these contradictions captured the popular imagination. It was not until February 1874, in an ironic echo of convict transportation, that he was finally found guilty of perjury and sentenced to fourteen years penal servitude.

Evidence suggests that the genre of sensation fiction may have influenced the elaborate nature of the Tichborne Claimant's imposture. As Michael Roe notes, "[c]ontemporaries often referred to the case as 'romance,' both the *Times* and the *Saturday Review* later suggesting that the Claimant himself had been encouraged in his fantasy by indulgence in novel-reading" (36). Indeed, investigators responsible for gathering evidence about the Claimant's life in Australia discovered a memorandum in a pocket-book that he had carried while living in Wagga Wagga. The memorandum contained an aphorism the Claimant had paraphrased from the companion novel to *Lady Audley's Secret*, Braddon's *Aurora Floyd*. Known as "the famous entry" and signed R. C. Tichborne Bart, this text was frequently invoked by the Claimant's opponents, who argued that it laid bare his motivations for imposture. It read: "some men has plenty/money and no brains/and some men has/plenty brains and no money/surely men with plenty/money and no brain/where made for men with plenty brains and no money" (qtd. in Woodruff 188).[20] The presence of this novelistic fragment among the Claimant's belongings was taken as support for the prosecution's theory that the Claimant was Arthur Orton, a butcher's son who had emigrated from Wapping, England to Wagga Wagga, Australia and subsequently perpetrated the imposture of Sir Roger Tichborne.[21] The Claimant's supporters, on the other hand, rallied around the aphorism's implicit critique of economic inequalities as they are codified within the British traditions of primogeniture and inheritance, making supporters all the more eager to back the Claimant in his pursuit of justice and fair play.[22]

In addition to influencing the Claimant himself, the structure and emotional impact of sensation fiction likely affected the ways in which the Tichborne trials imported a range of anxieties about fraud within the family into the national imaginary. For a readership conditioned throughout the 1860s to enjoy best-selling stories of crime and duplicity, the Tichborne trials presented what sometimes seemed like a parallel form of entertainment. One noteworthy anecdote demonstrating this interlinking of fiction with reality involves the judge in the criminal trial, Chief Justice Sir Alexander Cockburn, who related in court that he had greedily devoured a copy of *Aurora Floyd*, which Braddon had sent to him so that he could verify the aphorism, during evenings when he should have been preparing for the trial. Likewise, at the end of the trial, Cockburn's lengthy summation, which comprised a broad overview of the case, was published in a form akin to a novel (McWilliam 105). Finally, the popularity of a serialized edition of the criminal trial that appeared between 1875–1880 (which McWilliam calls "the most remarkable piece of Tichborniana") testifies to the popularity of the trial account as a viable genre (203). McWilliam argues that the simultaneous popularity of newspaper trial accounts and serialized fiction is no coincidence:

> Both forms created communities. Readers found a new identity, based on fascination with the narratives contained in novels and newspapers, that linked them to other individuals and helped constitute the imagined community called 'public opinion.' Just as the Sensation Novel turned its readers into detectives requiring them to guess the dark secrets at the heart of the tale . . . *cause célèbres* required that readers of the press should consider the evidence and become anonymous members of the jury. (35–36)

As detectives and jurors, Tichborne readers were drawn into the sensationalism of the trials in ways that paralleled their novel-reading practices.

If "sensationalism derives its power from rendering concrete or visible what would otherwise be hidden" (Cvetkovich 50), then the trials garnered the rapt attention of the public in part by promising to make visible the secret evidence of the Claimant's true identity, which was presumed to reside in his body. Given the contradictory nature of witness testimony—from the many friends, family, and acquaintances who could not agree on whether or not the Claimant was Sir Roger—and the often bewildering gap between the Claimant's detailed knowledge of some aspects of Roger Tichborne's life and his sheer ignorance of others,[23] it was extraordinarily difficult to establish the Claimant's identity through personal testimonies and affidavits alone. Hence the obsession with the Claimant's physical body, which became the centerpiece of the trial and possibly "the most heavily discussed body of the Victorian age" (McWilliam 197). Beginning with the "Brown Mark" that the Claimant invokes in his first letter to Lady Tichborne in an attempt to prove that he is her lost son, numerous forms of physical, bodily evidence, from tattoos to scars to ears to hands to locks of hair, were presented in an effort to establish a definitive identity for the Claimant. An 1874 illustration from the *True Briton*, a newspaper written in opposition to the supposed impostor, offers a visual comparison of the differences between the ears of Sir Roger Tichborne and those of the Claimant (Figure 3.2), dramatizing the degree to which such physical evidence became a source of public obsession.

The absence or presence of a physical resemblance between Sir Roger Tichborne and the Claimant was of primary importance among the forms of bodily evidence, and the most obvious site of visual incoherence in this respect was the discrepancy between the Claimant's size and stature and that of Roger Tichborne. While Tichborne possessed a delicate, slight build, the Claimant weighed approximately twenty-six stone (over 300 pounds) at the height of the trials (McWilliam 200), a fact that was famously caricatured by *Vanity Fair* in their "Men of the Day" series (Figure 3.3). While scholars have accounted for the public fascination with the Claimant's increasing corpulence by explaining that it represented an eschewal of self-discipline and respectability (Thomas 88) or a celebration of wealth, liberty, and fun that could be alternately liberating or threatening (McWilliam 200), this aspect of the Claimant's physicality was also intimately tied to colonial stereotypes and to his history in the Australian bush. For instance, a nurse reportedly overheard Lady Tichborne remark "that her son was very thin and that people must have been savages in Australia to have made him so rough" (Woodruff 154). Evidence of stereotypes about such "savagery" is equally apparent in a contemporary ballad that parodies the perceived excesses of colonial life:

THE

TRUE BRITON

THE AVOWED ENEMY AND ANTIDOTE TO

Dr. Kenealy's "Englishman."

No. 6.   SATURDAY, MAY 30TH, 1874.   PRICE 1D.

THE EARS OF SIR ROGER AND THE CLAIMANT.

Enlarged by the Lense from the Genuine Portraits.

(SEE REVIEW OF "A CRUCIAL TEST.")

The Claimant's Left Ear.

Sir R. Tichborne's Right Ear.

Sir R. Tichborne's Left Ear.

FIGURE 3.2. "The Ears of Sir Roger and the Claimant," *True Briton* (1874). Courtesy of Bodleian Library, University of Oxford, John Johnson Collection, Tichborne Case Box 1.

When Roger was young he was very thin, about
    As fat as a match sir,
But now he weighs over twenty stone, well made
    before and behind, sir;
Kangaroo soup and parrot pie, Australian soups
    and jellies,
They are the things that blow you out, and fatten
    up your bellies. ("Would you be surprised to Hear?")

Like the explanations of the Claimant's obesity, the ingestion of colonial foodstuffs as described here seems both liberating and dangerous; as such, the Claimant's corpulent body speaks at once to the metamorphic potential of colonial experience *and* the possibility that insatiable, even criminal colonials may return eager to "fatten [their] bellies" at Britain's expense.

While the Claimant's imposing presence in the courtroom offered compelling visual evidence of a troubling discrepancy, additional factors contributed to the seeming incoherence of the physical evidence. One such factor was a perceived discrepancy between the Claimant's aristocratic dress and the less than polished quality of his written and verbal communication. Like Braddon's novel, which derives its sensational effects in part through the contradiction between Lady Audley's appearance as an angelic, infantilized woman and her behavior as sinister social climber, the trial centered around a similarly sensational discrepancy between the Claimant's appearance as an aristocrat and his "rough" speech and behavior. Additionally, his conspicuous body also ironically impeded the efforts to uncover his identity. Prior to the civil trial, his ill health prevented him from returning to Australia, where he was expected to meet with witnesses and gather evidence. Likewise, his frequent illnesses, presumably brought on by a combination of excesses that included obesity, alcoholism, and venereal disease (Roe 39), frequently disrupted the progress of the trials. As in *Lady Audley's Secret* when Robert loses George's trail by failing to recognize his friend in a description of an outbound emigrant with his arm bound in a sling, the Claimant's unruly body added to the incoherence and the sensationalism of the trials.

The most provocative of the bodily proofs used to link the Claimant to Roger Tichborne was an infamous "malformation," a genital abnormality described as a recessed or retracted penis, which some speculated Tichborne had from birth.[24] The Tichbornes' physician, Dr. Lipscomb, the first to describe this feature after an examination of the Claimant, reported that the Claimant's "penis and testicles are small; the former so much retracted (when not excited) that it rests upon the upper part

FIGURE 3.3. Men of the Day, No. 25, "Sir Roger Doughty Tichborne, Bart.? Baronet or Butcher," *Vanity Fair* (1871). Courtesy of Bodleian Library, University of Oxford, John Johnson Collection, Tichborne Case Box 2.

of the scrotum like a bud" (qtd. in McWilliam 199). This abnormality was never brought into evidence in the civil trial, probably because the Claimant's lawyers believed it worked against him since the Claimant had children. However, although a second physician confirmed the presence of the Claimant's abnormality and gave evidence in the criminal trial, this testimony was of little value from a legal perspective because it was difficult to prove conclusively that Roger also possessed the "malformation." Regardless of its insignificance in court, however, "[t]he 'malformation' tested the limits of Victorian speech" (McWilliam 200), and in so doing, it contributed in a voyeuristic way to the sensationalism of the trials and to the question of how identity could and could not be made visible.[25] A single stanza from a contemporary ballad humorously accentuates such voyeurism by insinuating that Lady Tichborne's recognition of her son was based upon her own inspection of the Claimant's abnormality: "She swore to her child, the rightful heir/How she knew will make you stare,/ She stript him of course, she'd not neglect it,/She found the strawberry where she left it" (qtd. in Roe 38). Another ballad centered on the Claimant's body parodies the court proceedings in the criminal trial, which included clearing the courtroom for days to allow for a discussion of testimony related to the "malformation": "Now Lawyer Gab he wanted to know, if the/Judge had any objection,/To have Sir Roger stripped in Court for medical/Inspection,/They found a mark upon his breast, his belly had/grown bigger,/And then they twig'd his roundabout, and admir'd/ his noble figure" ("Would you be surprised to hear?").

The act of stripping alluded to in these ballads illustrates the impulse behind sensationalism to reveal what is ordinarily hidden and to locate sensation within the body. As D. A. Miller's renowned argument suggests, sensation fiction is a corporeal genre that impacts on the reader's central nervous system to create dramatic adrenaline effects. Such effects are elicited in two especially titillating scenes from *Lady Audley's Secret* in which Phoebe and Luke, and later Robert and George, steal into the heroine's dressing-room. Figured as acts of penetration, these intrusions, which involve navigating a secret passage and opening a hidden drawer, culminate in both cases in a metaphorical stripping of Lady Audley's absent body. In the first instance, the discovery of Lady Audley's "hidden relics" (30), the baby shoe and the lock of hair, reveal the secret of her former pregnancy and ultimately provide the means for reducing her identity to the body, locating it in the taint of hereditary madness that is presumably triggered by her motherhood. In the second, Lady Audley's absent body is evoked when "the whole of her glittering toilette apparatus lay about on the marble dressing-table. . . . Two or three handsome dresses lay in a heap upon the ground, and the open doors of a wardrobe revealed the treasures within" (69). Like the voyeurism implied by the scenes of Lady Tichborne's recognition or the courtroom inspection, these passages from the novel are alluring both for what they can and cannot reveal.

The titillation created by the mystery surrounding the Tichborne "malformation" was accentuated by sexual secrets involving Roger Tichborne's first cousin, Katherine Doughty, that were disclosed during the trials and that uncomfortably exposed the aristocratic female body to plain view, as in the examples we have seen from *Lady Audley's Secret*. Central among these secrets was the existence of a mysterious sealed packet that Roger Tichborne reputedly had given to his steward, Gosford, before leaving for South America. The influence of sensation fiction is perhaps at work in the Claimant's daring account of the contents of the sealed packet. Prior to his departure in 1853, Roger had hoped to marry his cousin, Katherine Doughty, but was rebuffed by her parents, who opposed the union but who agreed to reconsider his proposal after three years had elapsed. Gosford claimed that the sealed packet indicated Roger's resolution to construct a chapel at Tichborne dedicated to the Virgin Mary if the marriage eventually did take place. The Claimant, however, unaware of Gosford's testimony, gave contradictory evidence attesting to the packet's contents, indicating that it contained information about his seduction of Katherine Doughty, her possible pregnancy, and a secret marriage which had supposedly taken place prior to his emigration.

The fact that the revelation of these sexual relations came to light while Katherine Doughty, now Lady Radcliffe, was present in the courtroom reinforces the notion of the trials as public spectacle. Likewise, because these secrets directly implicated a second member of the Tichborne family circle in the scandal, their effects further underscore the way that rifts in the British family reverberate out to the nation as a whole, in this case by undermining the reputation of a well-known and respected wife and mother and threatening the paternity of her first child. Braddon clearly outlines the dynamics of a similar nexus of familial and national concerns in *Lady Audley's Secret* when she dramatizes Robert Audley's crisis of conscience in deciding whether or not to prosecute his Aunt's crimes and thereby risk destroying both his Uncle and the family's honor. Ultimately, the threat Lady Audley represents is contained only by protecting the family through the repression of her secrets and exiling her outside of the nation's borders.

By contrast, the revelation of secrets regarding the contents of the sealed packet intensified the status of the Tichborne trial as public spectacle. Katherine Doughty had become engaged to Percival Pickford Radcliffe, an aristocrat from Yorkshire, even before the news of the *Bella* and Roger's death reached Tichborne (Woodruff 32). Like George Talboys's initial return to Britain or his uncomfortable presence as an adjunct to his sister's marriage at the end of *Lady Audley's Secret*, the Claimant's testimony regarding the sealed packet introduced an unwelcome third party into Lady Radcliffe's marriage. If his explanations were true, they implicated her in a seduction. But perhaps more damaging was the unstated implication that if they were true, and if the Claimant was Roger Tichborne, then Lady Radcliffe, like Lady Audley, was guilty of bigamy, and not of the "innocent" kind described in the *Graphic*. Douglas Woodruff asserts that the Claimant's admission regarding the sealed packet was "the fuse of a time-bomb" that would eventually destroy him: "It was to entangle the questions of his identity with the honour of a highly-respected wife and mother, well known in country society and, until she died in 1906, no one could write about this part of the case without making it plain that merely to report it was a painful necessity" (96). As I suggested above, in the context of bigamy, the status of the victim matters a great deal. The insinuation that the respectable Lady Radcliffe might have duped her aristocratic husband, not to mention the other members of her elite social circle, was regarded as the Claimant's most heinous perjury. In summing up the verdict in the criminal trial, the judge spoke angrily of his nefarious attempts to pass as Roger Tichborne, but the criticism shifted to a hyperbolic register when he turned to the Claimant's attempts to "blast the reputation of Lady Radcliffe" (qtd. in Woodruff 369). By contrast, it is interesting to note that although the Claimant subsequently committed bigamy after he was released from prison in 1884, "[n]o one seems to have worried that two women both claimed to be not only Lady Tichborne but the legal wife of the Claimant" (Woodruff 443).[26]

While the evidence regarding the body—especially pertaining to the mysterious sealed packet and the illicit love affair between cousins— seemed to come straight out of British sensation fiction, other elements of the trials were derived from "the romance of the bush," or the propagandistic myths about Australia as a rough, independent society where traditional British standards of class and gender did not apply. As McWilliam notes, one of the many images of the Claimant was "that of an Englishman who had been changed by life in the colonies," someone who had disappeared into the empire, "a place where white men could become degenerate and abandon their allegedly civilised norms of behaviour" (193–194). The colonial magistrate and titular hero of Trollope's *Harry Heathcote of Gangoil* speaks to the renegade nature of colonial life when he questions his neighbor's deviance from the unspoken codes that govern colonial life and bush justice: "What did this man know of the Australian bush, that he should dare to talk of this or that as being wrong because it was un-English? In England there were police to guard men's property. Here, out in the Australian forests, a man must guard his own or lose it" (43). This renegade code of justice, which also allows for John Caldigate's reprieve, suggests that British standards of behavior and propriety are not valid in the bush, where independence, masculinity, and self-preservation inevitably win out. Within the context of this social code, birth is still an important feature of identity, but the markers of social class are far more fluid. Despite the fact that Harry Heathcote, for example, is "rough to look at," the narrator contends that "by all who understood Australian life he would have been taken to be a gentleman" (4).

The Claimant's defense capitalized on such fluidity by emphasizing the roughness and mysteriousness of bush life, thereby contributing to the incoherence of the Australian evidence and providing an explanation of how Roger Tichborne could have been radically transformed from a baronet to a butcher in the wilds of the colonies. The Claimant's reticence to speak about this aspect of his past contributed to this incoherence and triggered intimations that he or Arthur Orton might have been involved in a murder in Australia. Regardless of whether this was true or not, the defense portrayed the Claimant as a figure not unlike Lady Audley who embodied multiple identities, in this case as "an archetypical outback worker: station-hand, gold-digger, rouseabout, mailman, with a whiff of bushrangery and violence" (Roe 37). A contemporary ballad entitled "The Yarn of the Claimant" (written in the style of Coleridge's "The Rime of the Ancient Mariner") also illustrates how the duplicity associated with colonial life and its freedoms shaped the Claimant's fate, as the following stanzas make evident:

> Oh, I am a knight and a soldier brave,
>   And a butcher, burley and big,
> And a shipwrecked crew, and a stockman too,
>   And a man up to every rig . . .
> When the ship reached port, as money ran short,
>   A butcher I then became;
> In the bush I ranged, for my nature seemed changed,
>   And I also changed my name.—
> Then he twitched his face, with a queer grimace—
>   I'm a butcher, burley and big,
> What I've had to endure, 'tis no wonder, sure,
>   I'm a man up to every rig.

The ballad emphasizes the Claimant's malleability in performing multiple roles, a necessity created by the conditions of colonial life that is potentially very threatening to conventional definitions of identity. As described above, the Claimant's transformations are not merely superficial, since they entail a change in the Claimant's very "nature." Evidence of the dangers inherent in such change is apparent in a stanza describing how the Claimant survived the shipwreck of the *Bella* by engaging in cannibalism—"And none ever knew, I had eaten the crew,/Who escaped from the sinking wreck." Here, the ballad dramatizes anxieties about colonial contact such as those portrayed in "Probable Effects" by associating colonial life with practices deemed to be savage and horrific.

While this imagined transgression parodies anxieties about racial otherness and emigration, a contemporaneous account of Roger Tichborne's travels as an emigrant offer a troubling portrait of the way racial difference and criminal behavior are linked through emigration. According to *A Literary and Pictorial Record of the Tichborne Case*, when Roger Tichborne left South America and embarked on the *Bella*, the fateful ship that was later lost at sea, he did so as an illegal stowaway. At the time of his departure, the ship's captain, and presumably the baronet himself, feared that because he lacked a passport and had a complexion "reddened and darkened" through exposure to colonial sun, he might be mistaken for a runaway slave (12). As a result, Roger hid in the ship's lazaretto (a storage space also used to quarantine those with infectious diseases) during the final inspection, emerging only after the ship was safely out at sea. Regardless of whether the *Graphic's* story is true or not, it illustrates a pervasive Victorian concern with the potential loss of British identity in the wilds of the colonies, here presented, as in "Probable Effects," through the figure of the racial Other.

This example from the *Graphic* suggests that if British identity is not secure, colonial contact could render it transformed beyond recognition, thus undermining the stability of individual families and the structure of the empire. One distinctive feature of Australian life mentioned in the ballad above and repeatedly highlighted during the trials was "one of the great relevant truths about Australian life—that people altered their names at convenience" (Woodruff 154). The legacy of convict transportation contributed to an unspoken code that implicitly allowed such alterations of identity to go unremarked in the colony. Woodruff explains that "[i]t was a free-and-easy society in which men drifted in and out of occupation, and many of them were not at all anxious to have all their movements traced. . . . More so than in most places, it was bad form to ask personal questions or to show any undue curiosity" (161). Precisely because the practice of adopting false names was such a common and unquestioned feature of Australian life, the evidence out of Australia was often inconclusive. Like Trollope's Euphemia Smith, whose adoption of numerous aliases in Australia renders her unable to sign a legal document, the Claimant's use of several name variants—including Thomas Castro, Alfred Smith, Arthur Orton, Tom Morgan, and Roger Tichborne—leaves him no identity in the eyes of the law. Thus, references to the Claimant in the court records are never singular; when he is indicted in the civil trial, he is referred to as Thomas Castro, *alias* Arthur Orton, *alias* Sir Roger Charles Doughty Tichborne.

Of course, this form of identity confusion was also a characteristic feature of sensation fiction in the 1860s, and it contributes to the sensational denouement of *Lady Audley's Secret* wherein the heroine's multiple identities are revealed. Yet while such duplicity is accepted as commonplace in Australia, it is regarded in Britain as a criminal offense, as both the outcome of the novel and the outcome of the trial suggest. After Robert discovers the labels on the discarded bonnet-box that link Lucy Graham to Helen Talboys, he penetrates Lady Audley's motivations, describing for her benefit the processes underlying her attempted self-transformation: "'What do people generally do when they wish to begin a new existence—to start for a second time in the race of life, free from the encumbrances that had fettered their first journey? *They change their names*, Lady Audley'" (271). While Robert chooses not to prosecute Lady Audley's crimes in order to protect his uncle and the Audley name, the questions of identity and fraud raised here and in the Tichborne case were a troubling locus of anxiety for the Victorians, particularly because both accounts of colonial return implicated well-known and elite families—whether fictional or actual—in the sensational crimes of empire. As if to illustrate the need for protection against such threats in the aftermath of the Tichborne case, Britain passed the False Personations Act in July 1874, making it a crime carrying a maximum sentence of penal servitude for life to engage in imposture.

THE REVERBERATING EFFECTS OF COLONIAL RETURN

Contrary to popular expectations, the sensationalism associated with the Tichborne case did not end with the resolution of the second trial or with the passage of the False Personations Act. The *Graphic* regretfully reports that the fervor associated with the case continued to resonate in the weeks following the Claimant's incarceration:

> Now that the Claimant, after the most protracted trial on record, has been found guilty of the crimes imputed to him, it might have been

hoped that both the subject and the prisoner would have been suffered to sink into obscurity, and that the public would seek recreation
in fresher topics of excitement. Instead of this, the gigantic investigation seems likely to be followed by a series of minor episodes. ("Topics"
March 14, 1874)

These "minor episodes" had reverberating effects in Britain throughout the next two decades. After the Claimant's release from prison in
1884, he initiated a campaign of public speaking that took him, perhaps
not coincidentally, to New York and back. This temporary displacement,
like George Talboys's departure for America, signals the Claimant's tentative assimilation into the Victorian family even after serving his sentence.
Around the same time, rumors that had trickled back from Australia about
an asylum inmate named William Cresswell came to a head, briefly reviv-
ing public speculation about the identity of the rightful Tichborne heir.
Cresswell was alternately reputed to be Arthur Orton and Roger Tichborne, and persuasive evidence was gathered in favor of the former supposition. Eventually, however, an Australian commission finally refuted
the rumors, relying, among other things, on the fact that Cresswell had
no genital abnormality and thus could not be Arthur Orton (Roe 160).
Remarkably, in 1885, the Claimant published a confession indicating that
he was Orton, and in keeping with the sensational history of his case, he
retracted it shortly thereafter.

In a passage from *Australia and New Zealand* often cited in discussions of the Tichborne case, Trollope suggests that public opinion in the
colonies ran in the Claimant's favor, not because he was personally well
liked, but because "there was a pleasurable excitement in the idea that
such a man should return home from the wild reckless life of the Australian Bush and turn out to be an English Baronet" (412). The "pleasurable
excitement" evoked by the trials and their rehearsal of a familiar colonial
fantasy is coterminous both with the sense of intrigue illustrated in the
color cartoon with which I opened this chapter and with the excitement
gained through reading sensation fiction. In the cartoon, the anticipation
evinced by the British gentlemen and soldiers who clamor down to the
dock to see the new arrivals is quickly transformed into horror and complicity as they become engaged in the scene below, which ominously con-
flates match-making with slave trading. Through this entanglement of the
family in imperialist crimes, which also occurs in Braddon's novel and
the Tichborne trials, we are reminded of the ways in which the crimes of
empire can infiltrate the British family and by extension, the nation, creating a profound sense of anxiety and unease.

In each of the instances of colonial return discussed in this chapter, the titillating pleasure Trollope describes is inevitably tied to an uneasiness about the integrity of the family and the nation that was grounded in the material reality that Britons were beginning to populate various parts of the globe at growing rates, until at the height of empire in the 1890s, one in four persons in the world was a British subject (Arnstein, "Victoria" 836). Like the return of George Talboys to Britain, which sets in motion Braddon's intertwining and sensational plots, the Claimant's return from Australia foregrounds anxieties about emigration and identity that raise troubling questions about the possibility of uniting British subjects across such vast distances. These questions had extended reverberations in part because, as the Victorians had witnessed in fictional form in *Lady Audley's Secret*, rather than signaling an end, the emigrant's return marked the beginning of a complex and often much longer story about British self-definition.

Chapter Four

"Verily the Antipodes of Home"

Narrating Domesticity in the Bush

*I*n "A Bush Fire," a short story that appeared in the collection entitled *Lights and Shadows of Australian Life* (1854), Mrs. Charles Clacy describes her heroine, Julia, a young British woman who exchanges her social status as "the 'all-but-belle' of giddy, fashionable C—" for the role of "housekeeper to a squatter's establishment in the colonies" (168). After she is abandoned by her fiancé, a British officer in India who opts to marry for wealth and title, Julia undergoes a series of rapid self-transformations: she emigrates to Australia to join her brother, nearly loses her life in a bush fire, and subsequently marries her brother's partner after he rescues her from the blaze. Through this speedy resolution of her heroine's marriage plot, Clacy offers a romanticized image of female emigration that is consistent with British propaganda emphasizing the ready availability of husbands for single women in Australia.[1]

Yet despite Clacy's acquiescence to the imperatives of the romance plot, "A Bush Fire" simultaneously undercuts other romantic conventions through its portrayal of Julia as a resourceful and adaptable heroine:

> She had early learnt one great lesson—to conquer herself; and, instead of wandering beneath the gum-trees like a forsaken maiden in romance, she exerted all her energies to impart to her brother's home that air of comfort which a true Englishwoman disseminates wherever she goes. There was always something to be done, and she entered into the rough life with a hearty good will, and at length found herself absolutely enjoying it. (173)

Julia's ability to accommodate herself to "the rough life" of the Australian bush is attributed exclusively to her ability to make domesticity portable; her capacity to recreate domestic comfort "wherever she goes" is represented in Clacy's short story as a powerful source of female agency. That such agency is linked to privileges associated with class and nationality is implicit in the idealized and exclusive categorization of the "true Englishwoman." For Julia, "go[ing] about in a gingham dress superintending butter-making, mutton-picking, and innumerable other bush amusements" is enjoyable both because these are novel occupations and because her participation in them is limited to a supervisory role (168).

I begin this chapter with Clacy's short story rather than a visual image (as I have done in previous chapters) in part because it aptly represents the intersection of several concerns that will be the focus of this chapter: portable domesticity, colonial marriage, and feminist agency. Yet, perhaps more importantly, the story serves as a tangible illustration of how domestic fiction was transported to and transformed in the Australian bush, in ways that helped to forestall the threats associated with colonial return that I have detailed in the previous chapter. In deliberately invoking and then rewriting an earlier romance tradition, "A Bush Fire" partakes in the project of redefining domestic fiction *and* domesticity within a colonial context, as the careful enumeration of Julia's domestic duties in the bush suggests. As such, this story and others like it provided a model of successful settlement, thereby reducing the likelihood that emigrants would return home and consequently disrupt the intended progress associated with imperial expansion. To further explore the scope and stakes of this project, I turn again to the figure of the emigrant governess and briefly, to one of the most well-loved domestic novels in the British tradition, *Jane Eyre*.

PORTABLE FICTIONS

In a seldom-discussed passage that occurs late in Charlotte Brontë's *Jane Eyre*, the innkeeper living near Thornfield Hall unwittingly reveals to Jane that he believes she is complicit in Rochester's downfall: "I knew him from a boy, you see: and for my part, I have often wished that Miss Eyre had been sunk in the sea before she came to Thornfield Hall" (475). The innkeeper's evident disdain for Jane and his wish that she had drowned in lieu of coming to Thornfield reflect a well-documented Victorian anxiety about the subversive potential of the governess to destroy the integrity of the British family.[2] Additionally, the innkeeper's allusion to Jane's imagined drowning suggests an impulse to move the threat the governess represented (as well as the domestic conflicts she created) off of Britain's shores, which most often meant the colonies. Such an impulse is worthy of further consideration, since it recurs in *Jane Eyre* on at least three other occasions.

From very early on in course of Jane Eyre's journey, emigration is imagined as a potential solution to the problem of the heroine's dependency. As a young girl living at Gateshead, Jane is attuned to the dangers associated with colonial displacement when she imagines that the elves she has read about in fairy tales "were all gone out of England to some savage country" (28). The first instance when emigration becomes a possibility for Jane occurs when John Eyre writes a letter to Mrs. Reed, intimating that he wishes to adopt Jane and have her join him in Madeira;[3] the second occurs when Rochester claims to have found Jane a position as a governess to a family with five daughters in Connacht, a remote region in the west of Ireland;[4] and the third occurs when St. John Rivers urges Jane to emigrate with him to India as his wife and fellow missionary. Of course, Jane Eyre never emigrates, but her successive displacements from one British family or institution to another are powerful reminders of the precariousness of her situation as well as her cultural instability as a figure who has no home within the British nation. Perhaps because of this liminality, Brontë can resolve the problem of Jane's dependency only through the device of Jane's colonial inheritance, an outcome that signals the author's ambivalence about the relationship between domestic life in Britain and imperial practices abroad.[5]

While critics of *Jane Eyre* have fruitfully debated the complex ways in which domesticity and imperialism intersect in the figure of Bertha Mason Rochester,[6] few have remarked on how Jane Eyre is herself a locus of anxieties about female emigration and empire. As the examples above suggest, however, Brontë seemingly could not narrate the story of the governess without addressing the cultural imperative to banish her heroine from Britain. Her fascination with and resistance to her heroine's emigration provides a valuable context for understanding Catherine Helen Spence's *Clara Morison: A Tale of South Australia During the Gold Fever*, a novel that dramatizes a fate that, despite being a historical reality for single, middle-class women, is rarely represented in British governess novels.[7] Originally published in London in 1854, the novel was not reprinted until 1971 and has only recently begun to receive critical attention as the work that Australian writer Miles Franklin calls "our most interesting and in some ways our most valuable early novel" (qtd. in Magarey v). Running contrary to the popular tradition of novels that celebrate "the romance of the bush," a tradition that flourished in the 1890s and located Australian nationality in the ideals of masculinity and mateship, Spence's novel explores Australian life through attention to the domestic lives of a group of colonial settlers in South Australia, including her emigrant heroine. By focusing on the anxieties *Clara Morison* shares with its predecessor, *Jane Eyre*, I explore the consequences of transporting the governess—and the domestic values she was charged to protect—to colonial Australia. Likewise, I examine what this pairing reveals about how the domestic novel as a genre was modified and transformed within this specific colonial context.

For more than a decade, critics of Victorian literature and culture have been interested in the British governess as a figure who highlights a range of cultural anxieties related to domesticity, class, and gender. In her well-known analysis of *Jane Eyre* and the debates surrounding female education and employment in the Victorian era, Mary Poovey identifies challenges to prevailing domestic ideologies that are posed by the governess' shared alliances with both middle-class and working-class women, while Helena Michie ably explores issues of corporeal liminality in the nineteenth-century governess novel.[8] Like her British counterpart, the colonial governess occupied a liminal position by virtue of her class status, but her liminality was even more pronounced, in part because she made visible to the British the class and gender inequalities that necessitated her emigration. As Rita S. Kranidis has noted, the industry of female emigration exposed the paradox that although middle-class women held an exalted position in Victorian domestic ideology, those who were unmarried were ironically urged to emigrate in order to escape a life of misery in Britain. According to Kranidis, single women thus functioned in pro-emigration rhetoric as entities of "relative value" that could be constantly redefined to suit Britain's ideological or material needs (*The Victorian Spinster* 59). This liminality was further amplified in the colonies, where the colonial governess was truly "a threshold creature," precariously positioned not only by virtue of class, but also by virtue of education and race: "Graced with an education, she did not have the opportunity to use it. Racially a member of the white elite, she was in reality a member of the serving class. She was protected by racial privilege but not by economic security" (McClintock 277). The difficulty of finding work in burgeoning colonies where families often could not afford the services of the educated classes sometimes necessitated shifts in station for emigrant governesses who were subsequently forced to obtain work as domestic servants or as needlewomen.[9] In addition, colonial governesses were uncomfortably aligned in terms of the work they did with indigenous peoples who were members of the serving classes. Because of such alliances, these women challenged the boundaries associated not only with class and gender, but also with race and nationality. While such liminality was in many ways problematic, it also ironically allowed for a degree of flexibility and freedom from social conventions that would rarely have been available to governesses at home in Britain.

Poised at the junction of so many paradoxes, the colonial governess not surprisingly became a source of contention within Victorian debates about the emigration of single women to the British colonies, particularly those debates centered on the work of the Female Middle Class Emigration Society. The formation of the FMCES marked the beginning of a campaign that would span several decades and ultimately facilitate the emigration of just over three hundred single, middle-class women to the British colonies. Yet the records of the FMCES—including Rye's letters to the British press, letters from the colonies written by emigrant governesses, and the society's annual reports—all indicate that the organization was plagued from its inception by inconsistencies with respect to its purposes and its success-es.[10] These inconsistencies suggest that as a site of rhetorical instability, the colonial governess embodied the potential both to maintain and transform British domestic ideologies associated with gender and nationality.

In *Clara Morison*, Catherine Helen Spence explores this potential through the story of a young Scottish emigrant who hopes to find work in Australia as a governess. Like her heroine, Spence was also an Austra-lian immigrant; she left Scotland for the colony in 1839 and subsequently remained in Australia for the duration of her life, where she established a reputation as a novelist, a journalist, and a public speaker.[11] Spence's first novel, *Clara Morison*, was published less than a decade after *Jane Eyre*, and it depicts the story of the protagonist's journey from governess to domestic servant to genteel wife, a progression made possible through an extended marriage plot that hinges on the hero and heroine's shared love of British literature. Throughout this progression, Clara Morison's identity in the colony is continually inflected by her class, gender, and nationality. Yet rather than read this liminality as a liability, as critics have typically done when discussing the governess in Britain,[12] I argue that her shifting iden-tity is powerfully transformative, because it simultaneously enables her to transport domestic values and practices to Australia while adapting them to a new colonial lifestyle. The potential of such "portable domesticity" is dramatized in *Clara Morison* on two levels: thematically, by examining the role of British literature in enabling Clara to maintain her ties to Britain despite her displacement; and metatextually, by rewriting the domestic novel and adapting its conventions to a new, postcolonial setting. While I identify portable domesticity as a source of agency both for the heroine and for the novel, I am also attentive to how it is inextricably imbricated in cultural imperialism and specifically in the displacement of indigenous populations, a problematic that *Clara Morison* shares with *Jane Eyre*.

UNEASY IDENTIFICATIONS

An analysis of the correspondence of the Female Middle Class Emigration Society reveals how the governess' liminality can be interpreted both as a liability and as source of flexibility that could lead to transformation. As I have indicated earlier, the FMCES was founded in 1862, a year during which the problems associated with Britain's escalating population of "superfluous women" were hotly debated in the press. From the outset, Rye and Lewin had different ideas about how best to run the FMCES. Rye envisioned a two-tier system of female emigration that would cater both to well-trained governesses and to lower middle-class women. Because she was less preoccupied than Lewin with the feminist implications of their work, Rye was unconcerned with whether marriage or domestic service were inevitable by-products of emigration. She insisted that "[i]f these women of mine work, it will be well; if they marry, it will be well; whichever happens, good must arise for the colonies, for our countrywomen, and for commerce" (*Times*, April 29, 1862). Lewin, however, resented the popular association between female emigration and "husband-hunting," a motive that was often ascribed to female emigrants because of the disproportionate number of single men in the colonies (particularly in Australia around the time of the gold rush). Lewin consequently rejected the propaganda promoting "matrimonial colonization," or the emigration of women for the explicit purpose of providing colonial settlers with wives and mothers. Whether Lewin's objections centered around her desire to promote female independence or from her anxieties about who comprised the marriage pool is unclear. However, when Rye left the FMCES in 1865 to focus her efforts on juvenile emigration from Britain to Canada, Lewin took over as Honorary Secretary and thereafter limited the scope of the society's work by catering exclusively to middle-class women who were seeking professional careers as governesses in the colonies.[13]

The difficulties the founders of the FMCES had in determining which middle-class women to assist through emigration is indicative of the governess' liminal status, even within the middle classes. To complicate matters further, the original propaganda published by the FMCES often deliberately neglected to distinguish between lower-middle class women who were experienced as domestic servants and educated middle-class women who were qualified to be governesses. As a result, such propaganda often overstated the opportunities for governesses in the colonies. A typical exaggeration is evident in *Clara Morison* when one of the characters insists that "Governesses of every kind are so much wanted [in Australia], that I have heard of people going in quest of them on board every newly-arrived ship, and engaging them before they put foot on shore" (1: 6). This idea that Australia could provide an outlet for one of Britain's growing domestic problems was challenged by colonial authorities who repeatedly insisted they had minimal need for the services of the educated classes. In addition, the perils associated with the emigration of single, middle-class women—lack of appropriate protection, the inevitable mixing of classes on board ship, fears about moral ruin, and the physical dangers of the journey at sea—were invoked by opponents in Britain as obstacles to female emigration. Despite these warnings and objections, and despite their own differences in defining the ideal female middle-class emigrant, Rye, and later Lewin, continued to help single, middle-class women to emigrate for over twenty years. Their work is remarkable because they persevered in advancing their cause by manipulating the very objections that threatened to sabotage their efforts.

For example, in a series of letters on the subject of female emigration written to the *Times* in 1862, Rye relies on a rhetoric that wavers according to her purposes, shifting from an emphasis on female agency to an emphasis on female victimization designed to spur reform. This rhetorical strategy is calculated to combat opposition against female emigration and to elicit support for the work of the FMCES by differentiating their "women of sterling worth" from lower-class female emigrants (*Times*, April 29, 1862). By strategically invoking the privileges associated with class and nationality, Rye endows her emigrants—whether domestic servants or governesses—with a sense of agency that is absent from the propaganda associated with the emigration of other "superfluous" populations, including prostitutes, convicts, the Irish, and the poor.[14]

In my earlier discussion, I argued that Rye utilizes a rhetoric of self-determination to foreground explicitly feminist and middle-class preoccupations with female empowerment and individuation. In the process, she endows her emigrants, frequently labeled distressed or "superfluous" women, with a powerful sense of agency and purpose. By rousing her emigrants to garner "the courage to march on and possess" the colonies (*Times*, April 29, 1862), Rye inserts these robust pioneers into a heroic discourse of colonialism commonly reserved for men and insists that they are destined to play a decisive role in colonizing the British empire. In so doing, she represents domestic settlement as military conquest, a conflation that echoes colonialist rhetorics and policies that blatantly disregard the consequences of such territorial expansion.[15]

Despite Rye's implicit confidence in the prospects of colonial success "for women who can take care of themselves, and intend to walk uprightly" (*Times*, May 29, 1863), she reverts to a rhetoric of victimization in another letter in which she describes her own experience as an escort to a group of single women who emigrated to New Zealand in the spring of 1863. After describing the successful placement of her female emigrants, Rye claims that "[o]f the voyage the less said the better," but she subsequently fills the better part of the column with explicit details regarding the horrors of being aboard the emigrant ship. Her descriptions of the voyage out reinforce sensationalist stereotypes about the sexual danger associated with the emigration of single women, and by extension, they confirm her opponents' fears that female emigration is neither safe nor respectable. Rye emphasizes that regardless of her supervision and that of the ship's captain, "no one man, however vigilant, can keep constant guard over 60 or 70 men, and we suffered sorrow of heart enough" (*Times*, May 29, 1863). This representative example demonstrates the vulnerability of Rye's female emigrants with respect to both class and sexuality, and it offers a dramatic departure from her earlier emphasis on agency.

Although such a rhetorical shift appears to be counter-intuitive, it actually serves a strategic purpose. As entities of "relative value," Rye's emigrants are continually redefined in her letters, not necessarily to suit the needs of the mother country, but to suit Rye's own objectives. By confirming the worst stereotypes about female emigration, Rye separates her organization from negative associations of emigration with prostitution and convict transportation; by emphasizing the respectability of her emigrants, she depicts them as helpless victims, rather than licentious participants in their own degradation. Through such strategic differentiations, Rye effectively subverts the stereotypes that would otherwise be so damaging to her work. At the same time, her rhetorical shifts from a discourse of female agency to one of victimization create a platform from which she launches a powerful call to reform the industry of female emigration and thereby to elevate the respectability of this option for single, middle-class women.

The letters written from the colonies by the FMCES emigrants frequently allude to the paradoxes evident in Rye's rhetoric, especially by calling attention to the extent of the society's misrepresentations. The emigrants' letters suggest that Rye and Lewin persistently conflated reality and myth by exaggerating the need for governesses in the colonies, the wages they could hope to earn, and the protection that would be offered to them through the FMCES colonial committees. And while the incentive to marriage was never deliberately promoted by the FMCES, one governess' letter is explicit in refuting all of these myths associated with female emigration: "It was a matter of surprise my getting an Engagement the same week I came, *teaching is not plentiful here* as we are led to believe in

England; salaries are not high; there are *numbers* of unmarried ladies; I think it is high time the *fables* about Australia were ended" (Clarke 145). Yet Rye and Lewin were all too eager to believe the myths and equally willing to disregard firsthand accounts from colonial authorities and unhappy emigrants alike. They clung to emigrant success stories, using these as the basis for their determined efforts.

The disappointments many of the FMCES emigrants faced when they reached Australia and discovered that the colony did not live up to the excessive expectations created by British propaganda forced them to adopt new definitions of emigrant success. As I have argued in chapter 2, the FMCES letters suggest that many governesses redefined success in the colony in terms of achievements that seem relatively moderate in comparison to colonial fantasies about the ready availability of husbands for marriageable women and the promises of the gold rush. Yet these defining achievements, which included the attainment of financial independence and the enjoyment of freedom from social convention, were significant when compared to what was possible for single women in Britain. The following excerpt from a letter written by Rosa Phayne, a governess who alternately berated and then guardedly resigned herself to Australian life, suggests a process of ongoing redefinition that is representative of these women's experiences:

> In Bush Life there is a great charm; lonely perhaps, some people would find it. I never have done so. I have seen more of life, of the springs of action in people, their ways and peculiarities than I ever did in my life before and I have traveled and seen much; perhaps it is because there is less reserve, less stiffness, less of the conventionalities of life, I like it. I am very happy with all this; I feel I am in the Colony, simply not of the people or with them beyond our own household. (Clarke 113–4).

The tension in this letter between resigned contentment and self-imposed alienation dramatizes vividly one governess' attempt to negotiate between the poles Rye represented in terms of power and vulnerability. By delineating a distinction between being "in the Colony" versus "of the people," Phayne fetishizes the boundary lines that Rye draws in relation to class privilege while also alluding to how domesticity functions to maintain racial boundaries by creating "a space of racial purity that the colonial housewife guards from contamination" (Sharpe 92). In this role, Phayne exemplifies an "ambivalence of emplacement" that is unique to the colonial settler by showing how her alienation is offset by the privileges of increased movement and freedom (Slemon 39). While such privileges fall short of the more dramatic fantasies of transformation associated with the governess, this is often not the case in British and Australian domestic fiction. In *Jane Eyre* and *Clara Morison* in particular, marriage in each novel marks the culmination of a series of transformations that each heroine undergoes before achieving social mobility.

LITERACY AND PORTABLE DOMESTICITY

The extent to which Clara Morison is transformed by her experience in Australia is evident late in the novel when she contemplates returning to Scotland and is dissuaded by her cousin, Gilbert Elliot, who makes the following irrefutable argument: "you cannot mean to leave the colony the same Clara Morison you came" (2: 242). Indeed, Clara's identity is challenged from the moment she arrives in Australia. After she is placated with exaggerated claims about her colonial prospects, the titular heroine, like many of the FMCES emigrants, is "thrown into the colony with no connexions that any one knew of, and with merely a letter-of-introduction passport into society" (1: 60). Clara's "passport," the letter she carries from her uncle to a gentleman who had emigrated from Scotland years earlier, is the only authentication of her identity in Australia. However, this document lacks the authority her uncle assumes it carries, insofar as the recipient of the letter, Mr. Campbell, can offer Clara neither assistance nor protection. He insists that Clara's letter is more or less worthless: "Everybody that can do nothing at home is sent out as quite good enough for the colonies, and generally with such a flaming high character, that we require to be cautious" (1: 30). Like the FMCES emigrants, Clara is deceived by misrepresentations in emigration propaganda.[16] While her letter is the credential that should ensure her success in finding remunerative work, it serves instead merely to highlight the fact that her story, indeed her very identity (tellingly represented through a textual object), will have to be rewritten.

The transformation that Gilbert invokes as evidence of Clara's attachment to the colony begins shortly after her arrival in Adelaide, when she is forced by economic necessity to undergo training as a domestic servant after failing to obtain a situation as a governess. The identity confusion caused by this change in station is evident when Clara must disguise her gentility in order to secure a position as Mrs. Bantam's servant: "Clara had dressed herself very plainly, in case Mrs. Bantam might wish to see her; so there was nothing to distinguish her from others except the propriety of her language; but that her Scotch accent prevented Mrs. Bantam from observing" (1: 88). In order to avoid the fate of her prospective employer's former servant, whose aspirations to gentility caused her to lose her place because she attempted "to unite in her own person the incompatible offices of lady and servant" (1: 231), Clara must hide her genteel origins. Like gentlemen who occasionally traveled second-class on the voyage out to Australia in order to practice assuming the roles they would soon adopt as miners, Clara performs a masquerade that is antithetical to the traditional model of class climbing. Her performance is successful both because of her superficial transformation (wearing the appropriate clothing) and because of her national marginality (speaking with a Scotch, rather than an English, accent).

Later in the novel, Clara performs a masquerade in reverse, pretending to be a governess while she is still working as a servant. After several months with Mrs. Bantam, Clara visits a friend whom she had met upon arrival in the colony. Mrs. Handy insists that Clara has retained her respectability in spite of her change in station: "though you are thinner, and have lost your colour, you are quite as lady-like as ever. I did not let my husband know you were at service; he fancies you are a governess, so give yourself a few airs, and he will believe it" (1: 150). Clara's ability to revert quickly to her former role testifies to the malleability of her colonial identity. At the end of the novel, when it is widely learned that "'Clara, second daughter of the late William Morison, Esq., of Edinburgh,' was the identical Clara who had been at Mrs. Bantam's" (1: 269), the extraordinary possibilities for class mobility in Australia are dramatically underscored.

Despite the seeming fluidity of class in the Antipodes, however, the reader is continually reminded throughout the novel that Clara is as genteel, and sometimes more genteel, than the individuals she must serve.[17] In the interval between Clara's entrance into domestic service and her marriage to a respectable sheep farmer, the signs of her gentility are always affiliated with her literacy. In *Australia and New Zealand*, Anthony Trollope writes: "I have been at many bush-houses . . . but at not one, as I think, in which I have not found a fair provision of books. . . . To have a Shakespeare is a point of honour with every man who owns a book at all,—whether he reads it or leaves it unread" (310). According to Trollope, the book, and not the act of reading, earns iconographic status in the Antipodes, where many emigrants attempted to transplant British domestic life to a colonial setting. However, in Spence's novel, the act of reading—and more specifically, how and what characters read—demarcates their class standing and their relationship to Britain.

In Australia, literacy thus serves as a form of what Pierre Bourdieu has termed "cultural capital," since it reaffirms Clara's class distinction and ultimately ensures her social mobility in the colonies. The marriage plot that makes this possible hinges specifically on the hero and heroine's shared "tastes," their love of British literature.[18] Both Clara and her future husband, Charles Reginald, retain strong ties to each other and to the British middle classes because they avidly consume and discuss the latest British literary works, and because they both frequently write letters home. As Leonore Davidoff and Catherine Hall have argued, reading and discussion were defining features of middle-class life in England that helped to consolidate "the family circle": "Reading was not only a form of instruction, self-discovery and self-definition, it was also a source of profound pleasure" (162). This is certainly the case in *Clara Morison*, where all of the heroine's familial relationships, including the one she develops with her future husband, are nurtured through reading and through conversations about books.

When Clara meets Reginald at a boarding-house in Adelaide, he initiates a conversation with her by likening the company at the dinner table to the residents of Mrs. Todgers's boarding-house in Charles Dickens's *Martin Chuzzlewit*. This allusion figuratively links Reginald and Clara back to their shared national origins in Britain, but it also transports Clara in a more literal sense, as her visceral response to an admonishment that Reginald is keeping her all to himself suggests: "Miss Morison blushed. She had forgotten the whole company; she had heard voices and laughter, but knew not what had been said, or who had been amused. She had even forgotten that Miss Waterstone was present; she had only felt happy, and was unconscious of anything else" (1: 35). In addition to rendering Clara oblivious to the entire company around her, her discussion with Reginald also temporarily transports Clara by reminding her of a happier period in her life when she had engaged her father in such conversations. The "little allusion to a book" that initiates their conversation, and indeed, their veiled courtship, has the power of transfixing Clara and Reginald (1: 33), a phenomenon that recurs throughout the novel. The fact that the allusion comes from a domestic novel by Dickens affirms that domesticity and the practices associated with it—in this case, courtship and marriage—are transplanted to the colonies in part through books.

During the period of her servitude, Clara's friendship with Reginald serves to distinguish her from other educated women who are presumably her betters with respect to class. When Clara must wait on Reginald as a servant during his visit to her employer, she elicits his complicity in keeping her identity a secret and thinks to herself: "I must wait on him here for a month . . . and never speak to him, and nobody must know that we have ever met. He said that our meeting formed a page of his life; truly it fills a page in mine, too" (1: 105). Represented through the idiom of books and reading, Clara and Reginald's relationship continues to progress despite her change in station because she retains her gentility through the medium of literacy.

Reading calibrates with character in other instances in *Clara Morison* as well. Clara is easily distinguished from her vulgar and flirtatious traveling companion, Miss Waterstone, by the latter's reading practices: "Of course Miss Waterstone had read all the current literature of the day . . . and considered herself, in her own phrase, *a well-read woman*; but whatever she read she made a point of forgetting, so that for those four months Clara had been debarred from her favourite topic of conversation" (1: 33–4). Miss Waterstone's shortcomings as a reader distinguish her from Clara, who does more than just read; she also remembers. By contrast, Miss Waterstone has either failed to read the books she claims to be conversant with, or she has not understood or retained any knowledge through her reading. Aboard the *Magnificent* en route from Britain to Australia, Miss Waterstone is a source of constant embarrassment to Clara, who loathes to be too closely associated with her cabinmate. Once in the colony, Miss Waterstone refuses to read newspapers, which often create the vital links between Britain and Australia that enable other characters to maintain their ties to their home nation. When the Great Exhibition arrives in London and several emigrants return home to see it, Miss Waterstone is content to hear about it third-hand, from people in the colony who have only read about it: "And after all, I suppose we will see all about it in the papers; though I do hate newspapers, and never read them when I can help it; and there's nobody now to make me read them against my will, which is a great comfort, isn't it, Clara?" (1: 59). Miss Waterstone's adamant resistance to reading here as well as her lack of interest in the Great Exhibition typifies her lack of imagination as well as her frivolity.

Miss Withering, who is an emigrant governess like Clara, is similarly judged according to her intellectual habits. Her reading is limited exclusively to an outdated history textbook that the narrator derisively refers to as "a book of chips" (1: 247). The superficial quality of Miss Withering's reading—the "chips" of history that inform her understanding of the world—underscores the triviality of her nature; her petty conversation and complaints, coupled with her constant attempts to undermine Clara's abilities as a servant, are exposed as desperate pretensions to gentility. In an effort to undercut Clara's intellectual authority over her, Miss Withering admonishes Mrs. Bantam to keep a tighter rein on Clara by insisting that "[t]here is nothing spoils a servant so much as a taste for reading. . . . The old plan was best, to have servants in their proper places; let them learn to wash and scour, bake and brew, and leave reading and writing to

their betters. 'A little learning is a dangerous thing'" (1: 101). Miss Withering's adherence to conventionally inflexible distinctions between the
stations, exposed in the language of cliché, signals her rigidity and demonstrates her failure to adapt successfully to her new surroundings.[19]

By contrast to Miss Withering's repeated invocation of "chips" like
the cliché above, Clara is distinguished by the originality of her thought
and expression. Despite prohibitions issued by Miss Withering and later
by Mrs. Bantam, Clara continues to read and write avidly throughout her
term of service. At one point, Mrs. Bantam requests that Clara not read in
her bedroom by repeating a cautionary tale about a former servant who
had inadvertently fallen asleep while reading and subsequently set fire to
her bed. While she is ostensibly concerned for Clara's safety, Mrs. Bantam
is also clearly anxious about the possibility of class transgression. Such
an anxiety was also common within the budding middle classes in Britain, where "there was a constant unease that 'literary domestics' might be
tempted beyond their station" (Davidoff and Hall 392). But Clara's persis-
tence in pursuing her reading and writing suggests that the preservation
of her class position depends upon the intellectual work that helps sustain
her. After painstakingly sewing a dress for herself, Clara recognizes that
while such work may enable her to "keep up appearances," it nonetheless
has devastating physical and mental effects on her: "It is right that I have
made this dress, but to make another in the same way would kill me, I
think. I had better go in rags than have my heartstrings torn up like this.
I must read, though I have no face to look up to when I lift my eyes from
the book; I must write, though nobody but myself shall read it" (1: 95).
Eschewing the ostentatious gentility of readers like Miss Waterstone and
Miss Withering, who enjoy parading their superficial knowledge, Clara
pursues her intellectual work without need of an audience.

One activity that Clara performs in private to dispel her loneliness
and reconnect herself to her home involves the recitation of her favorite
poetry. When the Bantams leave her alone in their home for a fortnight,
Clara attempts to recreate the domestic haven she had enjoyed as a young
girl in Scotland:

> Clara began to repeat what she called her 'household treasures,'—those
> pieces of poetry which she had learned in happier times, and which
> her father used to call for in the twilight, when he sat in his easy chair
> by the fire, and she was on a low stool at his feet. . . . Different as were
> her circumstances now, and different as the scene was on which her
> eyes rested, it was surprising how much better she felt in thus making
> her thoughts and memories audible to herself; poem after poem was

gone through in a low, distinct voice while her fingers mechanically endeavored to twine the hair, which she had properly braided on going to service, into the long ringlets she had worn at home. Her kitchen brightened as she stirred the fire and snuffed the candle at intervals; her spirits rose, and life seemed again endurable. (1: 127)

Clara's "household treasures" are the emblems of portable domesticity that enable her to retain an appropriate relation to the domestic realm, even while she is presumably degraded by working as a servant in the Bantam household. Yet the language used to describe these treasures— they are "pieces of poetry" that make "thoughts and memories audible"— also suggests their materiality. These prized possessions are markers of class status that are analogous to the portable domestic objects, including dishes, bedding, and mirrors, that are fetishized in the FMCES letters because of their importance in the creation of makeshift homes aboard emigrant ships. Yet while Clara's treasures need not be displayed for an audience, they nonetheless lead to a notable physical transformation. As she engages in the indulgent reverie brought on by the recitation of her poetry, Clara's fingers inadvertently twine the ringlets that signify her leisure and respectability. This act of unloosening her braids evinces Clara's freedom from the restraints that are imposed on her when she goes into service—restraints that include her promise of secrecy from Reginald and her disciplined attempts to master her household tasks.

Clara's ringlets are only one of several signs that foreshadow the restoration to a genteel station that culminates with her marriage to Reginald. Interestingly, although her poetry and occasional sermons inadvertently receive a public audience on several occasions, only Reginald discovers the secret of Clara's authorship, a sign of his intuitive affinity for her genteel nature. Other characters harbor suspicions about Clara, including Minnie Hodges, who is also a frequent guest of Mrs. Bantam. After Clara recites poetry to her, Minnie guesses that Clara is not what she seems: "I was much comforted the other night by the servant Clara . . . repeating poetry so softly and sweetly, that it really felt like a balm to my ears and nerves, after they had been irritated by Miss Withering's sharp, inquisitive, mischief-making voice. I cannot help thinking that Clara must be a lady, her accent is so beautiful" (1: 162). Here again, Clara's literacy and education set her apart from Miss Withering and serve as signs of her inherent gentility. Such adherence to middle-class values, as Carolyn Vellenga Berman argues, can function as a colonial heroine's "inner dowry" (85).

Given the importance of literacy and its relation to middle-class life, it is fitting that Clara's family ties—and her identity—are ultimately revealed

and consolidated in Australia through the sharing of books. Minnie's sus-
picion is confirmed when Clara discovers that the Elliots, a respectable
family of Scotch emigrants who live next door to the Bantams, are actually her blood relations. Shortly after she makes this discovery, Clara's
genteel origins are revealed, and she finds a home with these cousins. The
relationship she develops with them, like her relationship with Reginald,
is framed through acts of reading and intellectual exchange. Grace Elliot
explains to Clara the terms of their co-habitation: "You will tell us how
things are done at home . . . without insisting that everything colonial is
radically bad. You will read our books, and we shall read yours" (2: 4).[20]
Reading one another's books becomes a sign of mutual interdependence
and a marker of cultural exchange. In addition, the privileging of literacy
suggests one way in which British middle-class values were transplanted
to Australia.

    Yet while literacy is associated with inherent gentility in a colonial
space where social standards are in flux, literacy does not have the same
currency for the governess back home in Britain. In *Jane Eyre*, Jane's reading serves as a figure for traveling and for transcending the limitations
imposed by class; however, literacy alone does not constitute a viable form
of cultural capital.[21] Only after gaining economic capital in the form of
her colonial inheritance does Jane achieve social mobility, and it is at this
point, when she becomes a reader for the blinded Rochester, that her literacy also accrues value. This difference between what is possible for Clara
and Jane demonstrates how the governess' liminality serves as an asset
rather than a liability in a colonial setting where social mobility is less
rigidly circumscribed.

CLARA MORISON: A POSTCOLONIAL JANE EYRE

The dual alliances that Grace Elliot invokes when she describes Clara's
future reading practices signal Clara's unique status as a woman who is
charged both with maintaining home values and adapting to new ones.
The liminality of her position is dramatized most vividly in *Clara Morison*
when Miss Withering offers Clara one of her old gowns: "How Clara longed
to refuse it! But she swallowed down her proud heart, and heroically said,
'thank you,' determining to give it to the first black woman who might
come to chop wood" (1: 167). Miss Withering's gift emphasizes Clara's
subservient relation to the members of the colonial, white elite, regardless
of her education, while Clara's urgency to dispose of the gown by passing
it on to an acquaintance called Black Mary underscores the uncomfortable
alliance she shares with Aboriginal servants (1: 167). Her need to reinforce

her own superiority over these servants reflects the reality that "[i]n settler societies, the advancement of racially/ethnically dominant women
was predicated upon assumptions of the inferiority and backwardness of
indigenous and minority women" (Stasiulis and Yuval-Davis 16). These
uneasy identifications are foregrounded later in the novel when Clara is
left alone for a fortnight while her employers are away. Desperate for companionship, Clara bribes Black Mary by offering one of her own gowns in
exchange for a story about the Aboriginal woman's history (1: 212). While
Clara finds the story unsatisfactory,[22] the substitution of this oral history
for the British poems that formerly assuaged her homesickness dramatizes
how, in this process of adaptation, she remains poised between two literary traditions—one British and one Australian.

As the vehicle for the representation of Clara's liminal position, Spence's novel is itself between traditions. While Spence thematizes the ways
in which British literature serves as a means for emigrants to maintain
a sense of national identity, she also literally transports and transforms
the domestic novel as a genre, thereby helping to forge the beginnings
of a new literary history that is distinctively Australian. To explore how
she achieves this, I turn in this section to a reading of the endings of *Jane
Eyre* and *Clara Morison*, examining intertextual references that reveal how
Spence both drew on and departed from the conventions associated with
the domestic tradition and the governess novel in Britain.[23] I contend that,
like Clara's "household treasures," the novel's status as a material object
enables it to circulate in Britain and Australia as a repository of cultural
values that are undergoing redefinition in the colony.

Spence's indebtedness to the British domestic tradition is evident in
the numerous structural and thematic parallels between the plots of *Jane
Eyre* and *Clara Morison*.[24] In fact, Spence invokes Brontë's novel when Clara
enters into a debate with a group of men about who is more prepossessing,
Milton's or Elizabeth Barrett Browning's Eve: "You make us so absurdly
amiable, and so dazzlingly lovely, that we do not recognize ourselves at
all. . . . Is not Jane Eyre, who is neither handsome nor what is called
good, a much more interesting and natural character than you will find
in men's books?" (2: 59).[25] Clara's critique of representations of women in
male-authored texts serves as a meta-commentary that highlights Spence's investments in realistic portrayals of women, and more importantly,
inserts *Clara Morison* into a domestic tradition dominated by women writers in Britain.

For both Spence and Brontë, the representation of domesticity results
in a dialectic that is similar to the opposition between agency and victimization that I have delineated in Rye's rhetoric in the *Times*. True to the

principles of realism, each author represents the exertion and oppression associated with domestic work by dramatizing her heroine's struggle to discipline herself to accept such drudgery.[26] However, each author also simultaneously idealizes domesticity as a means of essentializing her heroine's "Britishness" and distinguishing the heroine from her colonial counterpart (represented through the figures of Black Mary and Bertha Mason). Despite this seeming idealization of the home nation, however, the Australian setting of *Clara Morison* is nonetheless valorized because it allows for crucial differences in what can be imagined for middle-class women within domesticity. On the sheep station that becomes Clara's home at the end of the novel, new models of domestic life evolve in adaptation to the architectural features of the Australian bush house. Clara's marriage, together with her sister's emigration, situates the portable family at the center of colonial life, an outcome that offers Clara a continued engagement in intellectual pursuits and in the pleasures of female companionship. Additionally, the suburban cottage that Clara's cousin, Margaret Elliot, shares with her brother represents an alternative model of colonial domesticity—and an alternative ending to the marriage plot—that includes a unique resolution for a single, independent woman.

Taringa, the Australian bush house that becomes Clara's home after marriage, is characterized by visibility and openness, whereas Jane's home at Ferndean is troped through images associated with decay and darkness. Rochester retreats to this manor house injured and blind after the destruction of Thornfield, and he endures a "dark, dreary, hopeless life" until Jane arrives (486). Like Thornfield—which Rochester alternately describes as an "insolent vault" and a "narrow stone hell" (338)—Ferndean becomes a prison cell or tomb. Appropriately, Jane's first question when she sees the manor house is "Can there be life here?" (479). Indeed, because of its location "deep buried in a wood" on an "insalubrious site" (478), Rochester had once deemed Ferndean an unfit location for Bertha's captivity. Given these multiple associations of the manor house with death and decay, Ferndean is an ambiguous site at best for Jane and Rochester's attempts at domestic regeneration. For this reason, critics who read the ending of *Jane Eyre* as an egalitarian solution to the anxieties about oppression that dominate the novel are nonetheless troubled by the ominous overtones associated with Rochester and Jane's retreat.[27]

Yet as in *Clara Morison*, domesticity in Brontë's novel becomes a regenerating force that is idealized as an explicitly British trait. Despite Ferndean's remote location, Jane's "aspirations after family ties and domestic happiness" at the novel's end equip her to transform Ferndean into a viable home (432). And while St. John persistently attempts to inspire Jane with what he considers loftier goals, domestic ambitions are privileged within the context of the novel's closure. As Susan L. Meyer has argued, "[c]reating a clean, healthy, middle-class environment stands as the novel's symbolic alternative to an involvement in oppression" (264). The act of "cleaning house" is thus freighted with symbolic meanings. Just prior to her arrival at Ferndean, Jane consolidates her newly discovered family ties by engaging in an act of domestic fervor: "to *clean down* Moor House from chamber to cellar" (435), recreating a home for her cousins that is "a model of bright modest snugness" (437). The hyperbolic nature of Jane's house-keeping, which suggestively culminates in an elaborate Christmas dinner (perhaps the test case for domestic competence), presumably prepares her for the domestic challenges Ferndean presents. Indeed, when she arrives at the manor house, Jane immediately takes control of domestic affairs and begins to restore order to the carelessly maintained household. Her insistence that Rochester share a meal with her (despite the fact that he has ceased to take supper) represents her first attempt to reinstate the essential rituals that structure domestic life in Britain (485).

This restoration to order is also coupled by Jane's efforts to "rehuman-ize" Rochester (484), who has begun to assume the mantle of insanity. The innkeeper tells Jane that after her departure Rochester "grew savage— quite savage on his disappointment: he never was a wild man, but he got dangerous after he lost her" (475). In her discussion of *Jane Eyre*, Meyer suggests that anxieties about oppression are centered around Jane Eyre prior to Bertha's entrance into the novel about a third of the way through. By the same token, I contend that after Bertha's death, such anxieties are displaced onto Rochester, who begins to take on features, like his seem-ing madness, that had typically been associated with his wife. In pas-sages evoking visual imagery previously linked with Bertha, Rochester is described as having a "cicatrized visage" and "shaggy black mane" (485– 6).[28] Jane likens Rochester's hair to eagles' feathers and his nails to birds' claws (484–5), and she repeatedly compares him to a caged, impotent eagle. Such analogies deliberately echo his own frequent descriptions of Bertha as an animal or beast. In a dramatic reversal, after he ceases to be Bertha's captor, Rochester, who has earlier compared both Bertha and Jane to caged birds, is imprinted by the "taint" of his colonialist enterprises and symbolically imprisoned through his isolation at Ferndean.

But if Rochester's connection to Bertha transforms him and leads him into madness, Jane has the power to restore his sanity. By placing a premium on "domestic endearments and household joys" as "the best things the world has" (436), Jane consolidates British middle-class values and succeeds—at least superficially—in covering over the colonial ties both she and Rochester share. Reflecting back on her life with Rochester at Ferndean, Jane as narrator idealizes the marriage and disregards any traces of their former inequality: "I know no weariness of my Edward's society: he knows none of mine. . . . All my confidence is bestowed on him, all his confidence is devoted to me; we are precisely suited in character—perfect concord is the result" (500). As a corollary to her efforts to maintain such domestic harmony, Jane also ensures that Adèle acquires "a sound English education" that effaces the traces of her foreignness and molds her into a "docile, good-tempered, and well-principled" young woman (499–500). While these accomplishments are valorized in the novel's closure, the fact that it ends with St. John's impending death in India indicates that Jane's efforts to shore up the domestic realm over against the empire are only partially successful, since news from the colonies continues to infiltrate the haven she has attempted to create. Likewise, while the narrator alludes to annual visits from Mary and Diana and their husbands, such infrequent companionship does not compensate for Jane's troubling isolation at Ferndean, a location that by Rochester's own omission is dangerously unhealthy.

In *Clara Morison*, Clara's marriage to Reginald involves similar investments in an idealized domesticity, but the novel also allows for Clara's continued participation in a larger community. In a parody of the domineering husband (perhaps even a parody of Rochester's controlling fantasies about his future with Jane),[29] Reginald describes the demands he will place on his wife:

> And now, loving you incomparably more and better than ever I loved [Julia], I feel that I shall be an exacting husband. I shall want a very great deal of your time and attention; I shall tell you every thought as it arises, without asking myself if it is likely to be agreeable to you; I shall insist on your going over old reading and thinking ground with me; I shall bore you with the price of wool, with the health of my sheep, and the conduct of my shepherds; and all because I love you so very much. (2: 265–6)

Having broken off his engagement with his English fiancée, a woman who had balked at the idea of relinquishing her social engagements and living in the remote Australian bush, Reginald explains how comparatively effortless his relationship with Clara will be. Although he envisions a future that involves the mundane routines of life on a sequestered sheep station, Reginald also describes an egalitarian relationship in which Clara's intellectual life will be supported. Interestingly, he does not distinguish between the home and the workplace, or between leisure and business. Instead, Reginald's description of his future with Clara suggests that their marriage will involve compromises between old and new practices; in the bush, reading and thinking about British literature will be coupled with the quotidian concerns and activities typical of life on a sheep station.

This absence of a distinction between what have typically been referred to as the "separate spheres" of Victorian culture is due in large part to the spatial arrangements of an Australian station house. As Diana Archibald has argued, station houses in the bush utilized spatial patterns unlike those found in a British town house or country home, thus necessitating new cultural practices and domestic routines. Australian bush houses were typically linear in layout, with three adjacent, enclosed rooms surrounded by a veranda on three sides. Speaking about the domestic arrangements at a bush house in Trollope's *Harry Heathcote of Gangoil*, Archibald identifies the ways in which this architecture required adaptations to alternate domestic paradigms:

> The house at Gangoil itself poses certain impediments to the establishment of British-style domesticity. . . . The compartmentalization of activities into separate rooms in the London home is impossible in the bush. The veranda, instead, serves as sitting room, receiving room, library, and smoking room. The ladies and gentlemen do not separate after dinner; all go out together to the veranda, where it is not quite as hot and stuffy as the indoor parlor where they eat meals. . . . On the veranda also, women's work and men's work mingle: Mary's sewing machine shares the same space as Harry's business papers. Furthermore, there is no nursery at Gangoil. Children and adults live together. ("Angel in the Bush" 234–5)

Representing a new model for structuring domesticity, the bush house allows for a more egalitarian and unified conception of family life. At Trollope's Gangoil, the hero's wife enjoys the company of her husband, her children, and her sister. Likewise, after moving to Taringa, Clara gains the companionship not only of her husband, but also of her sister, who emigrates from Scotland to join them. And because the veranda functions as a communal space where men and women intermingle and where work and leisure are inseparable, the camaraderie Reginald describes when he envisions his life with Clara—which includes sharing intellectual and commercial concerns—seems possible within this new domestic space.

Despite its remote location in the bush, Taringa is represented as "a palace of a sheep-station" that is prosperous and vibrant. When Margaret visits Taringa shortly after Clara's marriage, she discovers that "whitewash and paper-hangings had quite divested Taringa of the gloomy appearance Reginald used to ascribe to it. It was really a cheerful, pretty place; the garden was thriving, and under Mrs. Duncanson's able management, the sheep-station began to look like a comfortable farm-house, for the domestic animals were her pride and her pleasure" (2: 271). The cheery interiors, the garden, and the domestic animals that Clara and her Scottish servant introduce into Taringa contribute to the project of "whitewashing" that transforms the stereotypically remote and uncivilized bush house into a home that resembles those found in the British countryside. Although Reginald's station house displayed many of the trappings of middle-class domesticity even before Clara's arrival, including "[b]ooks, pictures, fire-irons . . . a pretty cat and two handsome dogs for company" (2: 249), Clara's efforts make the home more appealing and comfortable, adaptations that mark the success of portable domesticity.

While Taringa is figured as an idealized colonial space, other models of middle-class domesticity are also depicted in the novel, including the all-female household created by the conditions of the gold rush that Clara briefly shares with her cousins as well as the suburban cottage that Margaret Elliot shares with her brother, Gilbert. The former is a transient and utopian space that mirrors Moor House in *Jane Eyre*, but the latter is a more progressive model that suggests how freedom from social conventions and stigmas creates liberating possibilities for women in the Australian colonies. Margaret and Gilbert's home in Adelaide is a haven where the siblings can pursue the study of law together. For Margaret, the cottage serves the purposes Virginia Woolf would later ascribe to "a room of one's own," insofar as it provides her with the financial security and the space necessary to pursue the work that fulfills her. Margaret, who has declined several offers of marriage, is contented to live as a single woman and to forsake the security and convenience of marriage in favor of independence and intellectual freedom. The narrator's description of Margaret's complacency with her single state allows for a liberating alternative to the marriage plot that is rarely possible in the British domestic novel: "So, after spending some weeks with those happy married people . . . Margaret settled herself down with her brother in their cottage, and studied with all the energy of her active nature; without ever fancying that such a home was in store for herself, or that she ever could be anything but an independent old maid" (2: 271–2). Rather than elaborating on the domestic interiors of the cottage, Spence focuses on the intellectual work Margaret does there, deliberately shifting the locus of attention from the traditional domestic roles of women and wives to a focus on female middle-class professionalism.

Unlike Jane Eyre, who achieves independence only within the ambivalent confines of Ferndean, Margaret Eliot's scope seems wider—along with the privileges of physical and intellectual independence she retains the comfort of having her friends and relations nearby.

Roughly fifty years after the publication of *Clara Morison*, Ellen Joyce, a professional woman and an advocate for female emigration, was able to assert that the British colonies were "little more secluded than the Yorkshire village from which Charlotte Brontë flooded the reading world of the fifties" (qtd. in Hammerton, "'Out of Their Natural Station'" 150). Although one FMCES emigrant claimed in a letter to Lewin that Australia and its people were "verily the Antipodes of home" (Clarke 114), the transplantation of the domestic novel to colonial Australia suggests that the relationship between Britain and Australia was more synergistic than oppositional. Spence's postcolonial rewriting of the domestic novel indicates how this transformation in the way Britons regarded the settlement colonies by the end of the nineteenth century might have taken place. *Clara Morison* is fascinating for its dramatization of how domestic narratives circulated in various ways in Australia, thereby influencing how emigrant settlers negotiated the tensions between retaining their ties to Britain and creating a unique set of domestic ideals and practices in the Australian bush.

Conclusion

Portable Domesticity
and Strategic Amnesia

*I*n her recent collection on settler colonialism in Australia, Canada, Aotearoa New Zealand, and South Africa, Annie E. Coombes emphasizes the importance of settler/indigenous relations in shaping the future directions of these nation-states:

> the colonisers' dealings with indigenous peoples—through resistance, containment, appropriation, assimilation, miscegenation or attempted destruction—is the historical factor which has ultimately shaped the cultural and political character of the new nations, mediating in highly significant ways their shared colonial roots/routes. (1–2)

Evidence of such dealings between colonizers and indigenous peoples has been remarkably rare within the various texts analyzed throughout this study, appearing—like emigration—only as a marginal subject. However, as Coombes suggests, the history of such encounters is of crucial importance for any understanding of Australia's colonial past or its future. This history is obscured in part because Australia was founded on the myth of unoccupied land—"the legal fiction of *terra nullius*"—which enabled colonial settlers to deny indigenous peoples the rights to their own land as well as the rights and privileges attached to citizenship within the new nation-state (Pettman 70). This attempt at the erasure of an indigenous presence within Australia has had resonating effects up to the present day.

Careful analysis of one colonial depiction of settler/indigeneous encounter will offer a useful index for examining the construction of this myth as well as stakes involved in its perpetuation. This depiction, the front

HETHERINGTON'S

USEFUL

Handbook for Intending Emigrants.

LIFE AT SEA

AND THE

IMMIGRANTS

PROSPECTS

AUSTRALIA

AND NEW ZEALAND

Advice to Intending
Emigrants.
Life at Sea.
Western Australia.
South Australia.
New Zealand.
Queensland.
New South Wales.
Tasmania.
Victoria.

Resources, Advantages and Attractions, Soil, Climate, Products,
Trade and Wages.

PUBLISHED AT THE OFFICE OF

"DOMESTIC HELP at Home & Abroad."

LONDON:—HETHERINGTON, 334, STRAND, W.C.

FIGURE 5. Frederick Wallace Hetherington, *Hetherington's Useful Handbook for Intending Emigrants. Life at Sea and the Immigrant's Prospects in Australia and New Zealand* (1884). © The British Library Board. All Rights Reserved 20/12/2007, 10491.g.6.

cover of *Hetherington's Useful Handbook for Intending Emigrants: Life at Sea and the Immigrant's Prospects in Australia and New Zealand* (Figure 5), stages what appears to be a friendly encounter between two male colonial settlers and an Aboriginal man. This seemingly casual, neighborly exchange occurs in the midst of various signposts of stability and settlement, including ships in the bay, men working in the fields, and a well-made bush home in the background. Within this domestic context, and surrounded by two women, a small boy, and a baby, the Aboriginal man in this image is assimilated into a familiar family circle, one that echoes the emigrant family in *The Last of England* with which I began this study.

Gillian Whitlock refers to the racial policies attached to settler colonialism as "an organising grammar that was at the heart of a *civilising mission* that repeatedly represented invasion in terms of benevolence" (28). In keeping with that "organizing grammar," the picture of settlement proffered on Hetherington's handbook is a far cry from the realities of colonization and the violent cultural clashes that frequently erupted between white settlers and Aborigines. Instead, the illustration insinuates that portable domesticity contributes to the British imperial mission by aiding in the conversion and "civilization" of Aboriginal people. As such, it presents a compelling, although unrealistic view of the Australian frontier not as the wild, untamed land of popular mythology, but as an orderly, disciplined landscape made safe and secure by the forces of colonization and settlement.

Even within this seemingly benevolent depiction of domestic assimilation, however, there are lingering signs of colonial violence that simultaneously point to the limits of portable domesticity and of colonial "progress" more generally. One such sign is the prominent spear-like implement that the Aboriginal man holds. This tool bisects the image into symmetrical halves, creating an artificial separation between white and black worlds that is further reinforced by a slice of fencing evident in the bottom left corner of the picture. This visual division reinforces conventional boundaries between colonizer and colonized that have otherwise been blurred through the use of domestic iconography, creating the illusion of a mirror image in which the Aboriginal family is, to rearticulate Homi K. Bhabha's famous phrase, "*[a]lmost the same but not white*" (*The Location of Culture* 89). Thus, even as the illustration hints at the assimilation of Australian Aborigines into a decidedly English domestic ideal, suggesting the permeability of native culture within this colonial space, it also subtly insists upon the fixity of certain racial and cultural barriers, and in so doing, dramatizes a sustaining tension in Anglo-Australian culture between the conversion fantasy that domesticity would civilize the Aborigines and the concurrent drive simply to displace indigenous bodies and culture by carving out defined geographical and spatial boundaries.

As this illustration makes clear, British domestic ideology was manipulated in Australia in the service of a collective myth that united white European settlers over against indigenous peoples. This strategic segregation ensured that when the disparate cultures of the British empire came together via emigration, they did so not primarily through invasion or force, nor through marriage and miscegenation (although these effects also occurred), but rather, through a controlled and managed mingling exemplified in part by the policies of forced assimilation that are alluded to in this image. The typical marginalization of an Aboriginal voice or presence in accounts that document nineteenth-century literature and culture in colonial Australia inadvertently reveals how difference was managed and contained both during and in the aftermath of colonial settlement, in turn illuminating how what had to be repressed or forgotten has nonetheless continued to resonate in postcolonial Australia up to the present day.

Such absences are telling, and they illustrate the effectiveness of a policy of "strategic amnesia" that enabled colonial settlers relentlessly to police the domestic realm while simultaneously overlooking the pernicious consequences of such policy for Australia's Aboriginal peoples (Anderson x). A cultural collusion between Britons at home in England (who turned a blind eye to disturbing reports they received about that state of "Aboriginal affairs") and white settlers in Australia (who disregarded indigenous peoples' rights) allowed for and in no small measure abetted the genocide of Aborigines and their culture so that colonization and settlement could proceed unhindered. As Jan Jindy Pettman explains, indigenous Australians "were excluded psychologically and culturally in an extraordinary exercise in forgetfulness, so that Australian history could be taught in terms of 'discovery' by Captain Cook and heroic British explorers mapping a fierce and empty land" (70). The strategic silences and erasures that enabled this myth to be sustained and that shrouded acts of genocide in secrecy contributed to the processes wherein Victorian ideas of domesticity, race, and culture were carried over into the twentieth century.

STRATEGIC AMNESIA AND THE CASE
OF THE STOLEN GENERATIONS

The reverberating legacies of nineteenth-century colonial settlement in Australia have come to light very publicly since May 1995, when a National Inquiry into the Separation of Aboriginal and Torres Strait

Islander Children from Their Families was established in order to examine the claims of what have become known as Australia's Stolen Generations.[1] This label represents the tens of thousands of indigenous children who, over the course of a century, were forcibly removed from their homes and placed in the custody of white institutions or foster families in an attempt to enforce assimilation into Anglo culture.[2] The Human Rights and Equal Opportunity Commission that examined their experiences controversially concluded that Australia's state and local governments had, for at least seventy years, engaged in a systematic policy of genocide with respect to Australia's indigenous people by removing children from their families and culture without consent and thereby creating the Stolen Generations.[3] Under the auspices of "protection" and bettering the childcare, education, and domestic practices of indigenous peoples, Aboriginal homes were destroyed and relationships sundered. The Stolen Generations were lost not only to their families, but to the cultural inheritance from which they were forcibly divorced.

The fact that such a policy began in the nineteenth century during the period of colonial settlement that this study examines suggests how portable domesticity, in addition to being an important resource for British emigrants struggling to maintain their ties to home while negotiating geographical and cultural displacements, contributed in the name of the civilizing mission to the forced displacement and dispossession of Aboriginal peoples and their culture. The Commission's 1997 report, "Bringing Them Home: Report of the National Inquiry into the Separation of Aboriginal and Torres Strait Islander Children from Their Families April 1997," concludes that the practice of removing Aboriginal children from their families without parental consent began as early as "the very first days of the European occupation of Australia" ("Bringing Them Home," The Report, chapter 2). Historian Henry Reynolds explains that during this period "any European on or near the frontier, quite regardless of their own circumstances, could acquire and maintain a personal servant" (qtd. in "Bringing Them Home," The Report, chapter 2). The colonial practice of widespread child abduction highlights the race-based economic disparities at work in Australia during this period, underscoring the fact that the lifestyle predicated on portable domesticity that many emigrants strove to achieve necessarily depended on the economic exploitation of indigenous people. During the colonial period, the actions of both renegade individuals and missionary or government representatives colluded to secure both the necessary labor to tame the landscape and the necessary training to "civilize" the people. It therefore served the interests of both the individual and the state to shroud these dehumanizing practices in the strategic amnesia that

glorified imperial progress—both economic and otherwise—while erasing its more pernicious by-products.

The logic undergirding the civilizing mission became increasingly
codified in the early years of the twentieth century as the motivations
and mechanisms for child removal became more systematic and sophis-
ticated. In *A Rape of the Soul So Profound*, historian Peter Read outlines
the resultant shift in policy that emphasized the conversion of Aboriginal
children from "a potential menace" into "a positive asset" (Read 23). Such a
conversion was predicated on the assumption that sustained contact with
white culture—in the form of raising and training children in boarding
schools, missions, and other institutions as well as in white families—
could improve the home life, education, and future opportunities available
to indigenous children.[4] Reynolds explains that "[s]o powerful was this
conviction and so deeply entrenched in European thinking that many of
those involved in removing children were genuinely convinced that the
project was a humane one enlivened by good intentions, regardless of how
distressing the execution might be" (163). Although some Aboriginal children were well treated after removal, particularly within adoptive families, the personal testimonies of adults who had experienced removal as
children suggest that even in the best of circumstances, this practice had
devastating, long-lasting psychological consequences both for individuals
and for the collective indigenous culture.[5] Even today, "[t]he material and
lived experiences of First Nations and indigenous peoples in . . . Australia continue to be shaped by extraordinarily high rates of poverty, death,
unemployment, youth suicide, substance and sexual abuse, domestic violence and family breakdown" (Whitlock 25).

For nearly a generation after the policies that facilitated Aboriginal
child removal ended, this history and its consequences remained a part of
the collective amnesia that allowed Australia's colonial past to be shrouded
in a rhetoric of benevolence and progress. Yet although the public testimonies surrounding forcible child removal did not come to light until the
1990s, historians emphasize a long history of indigenous resistance to such
practices (Whitlock 30). As Whitlock notes, "[t]elling in this context, then,
is not new, though the public acknowledgement of this history of struggle *is* a recent development. It is the harnessing of traumatic memories of
separation to a politics of reconciliation that produced in the 1990s the
threshold for speaking and hearing about child removal" (31–32). Yet the
process of reconciliation remains incomplete, particularly because Australian Aborigines have achieved less recognition of their claims than First
Nations or indigenous groups in other countries (Stasiulis and Yuval-Davis
25). In the aftermath of the publication of the "Bringing Them Home"

report, for example, debates raged in the popular and academic presses about the validity of the claims made on behalf of the Stolen Generations. Scholars who support the report's controversial findings of genocide have been accused of subscribing to what is termed a "black-armband version of history" that deliberately exaggerates the "less attractive" aspects of Australia's past (Reynolds 5). Nonetheless, in a historic breakthrough in relations between indigenous and white Australians, Australia's Prime Minister, Kevin Rudd, recently delivered a national apology for past wrongs against Australia's indigenous peoples that many perceived as long overdue. In his speech before Parliament in February 2008, Rudd acknowledged and apologized for the injustices and sufferings that led to the creation of Australia's Stolen Generations and pledged to work toward improving the lives of Australia's Aborigines and Torres Strait Islanders. However, while Rudd's apology was symbolically very significant from a historical and cultural perspective, the Prime Minister stopped short of offering to provide financial reparations on behalf of the government to members of the Stolen Generations, an issue that remains contentious. The reverberations of these controversies and the evidence of ongoing discrimination against indigenous children point to the lingering effects of strategic amnesia on the landscape and cultures of postcolonial Australia.[6]

I began this study by emphasizing the premise that "home" constitutes both a material and an ideological construct, signifying more than merely "[f]our walls and a ceiling" (Dickens, "A Cricket on the Hearth" 44). The notion that home—and consequently, identity—could be remade in the empire was of crucial importance to the Victorian emigrants who settled in Australia during the nineteenth century. This notion carried over into the twentieth century to the policies informing Aboriginal child removal through the assumption that, given an appropriate new "home," whether in an institution or family, an Aboriginal child could be remade in the image of the white Australians who were regarded as their "protectors." This transference of ideals from the realm of ideology to that of public policy again illustrates the portability of domesticity and the powerful and ultimately devastating role it played in the making of both transplanted British homes and the Australian nation. Ironically, it was the very reframing of home in Australia that enabled the pernicious dismantling of Aboriginal culture that occurred in the name of bringing Aboriginal children under the protection of an English-style domesticity.

It is only by understanding how British settlers and their descendants in Australia relied on ideologies of home to recreate their own colonial identities that we can begin to fathom the ultimately devastating role that portable domesticity played in contributing to the British civilizing mission, one of the most insidious aspects of imperialism. As Daiva Stasiulis and Nira Yuval-Davis assert, "the recent developments in indigenous politics across the globe whereby indigenous peoples have insisted upon the actualization of their unsurrendered rights is a reminder that settler societies cannot easily disengage from these formative histories of indigenous-European 'encounters'" (11). The tragic consequences of such encounters in Australia serve as a powerful indication of the crucial significance of what happens in the presumably private space of the domestic realm and the extent to which domestic concerns relentlessly cross over political and geographical lines. In grappling with a culture that fetishized domestic life as the Victorians did, we must interrogate the portability of domesticity, both in Britain and throughout the empire, precisely because as we have seen in the case of Antipodal England, domestic concerns invariably resist staying at home.

Notes

INTRODUCTION — "ANOTHER ENGLISH
HOUSE IN ANOTHER COUNTRY"

1. Throughout this study, I make a strategic distinction between England/English and Britain/British, since the former is often invoked in contemporary texts to refer to a self-contained entity/identity that is imagined as existing outside the confines of the empire.

2. For an analysis that similarly examines the importance of portable objects in helping Britons maintain a sense of national identity while traveling throughout the empire, see John Plotz's *Portable Property: Victorian Culture on the Move*. Published as *Antipodal England* was going to press, Plotz's book will no doubt offer many fruitful points of intersection with this study.

3. These studies include, among others, Deirdre David's *Rule Britannica: Women, Empire, and Victorian Writing*, Inderpal Grewal's *Home and Harem: Nation, Gender, Empire, and the Cultures of Travel*, Rita Kranidis's *The Victorian Spinster and Colonial Emigration: Contested Subjects*, Anne McClintock's *Imperial Leather: Race, Gender and Sexuality in the Colonial Contest*, Susan Meyer's *Imperialism at Home: Race and Victorian Women's Fiction*, Jenny Sharpe's *Allegories of Empire: The Figure of Woman in the Colonial Text*, and Carolyn Vellenga Berman's *Creole Crossings: Domestic Fiction and the Reform of Colonial Slavery*.

4. This definition comes from Daiva Stasiulis and Nira Yuval-Davis's edited collection, *Unsettling Settler Societies: Articulations of Gender, Race, Ethnicity and Class*, which examines relations between indigenous and settler/immigrant populations in ten different societies. Donald Denoon's work, *Settler Capitalism: The Dynamics of Dependent Development in the Southern Hemisphere*, focusing on a comparative analysis of common aspects of development in six settler nations from 1890–1914, is regarded as an important early work in the field. More recently, Caroline Elkins and Susan Pedersen's *Settler Colonialism in the Twentieth Century: Projects, Practices, Legacies*, and Annie E. Coombes' *Rethinking Settler Colonialism: History and Memory in Australia,*

Canada, Aotearoa New Zealand and South Africa have called for renewed examination of the implications of settler colonialism in the twentieth century for
both settler and indigenous populations.

5. A number of fascinating historical studies, by contrast, have focused
on nonfictional sources such as emigration statistics, society records, emigrant letters, and diaries. See Patricia Clarke's *The Governesses: Letters from the
Colonies, 1862–1882*, James Hammerton's *Emigrant Gentlewomen: Genteel Poverty and Female Emigration, 1830–1914*, Andrew Hassam's *Sailing to Australia:
Shipboard Diaries by Nineteenth-Century British Emigrants*, and Helen R. Woolcock's *Rights of Passage: Emigration to Australia in the Nineteenth Century*.

6. Rita S. Kranidis's 1999 study *The Victorian Spinster and Colonial Emigration: Contested Subjects* focuses on a metaphorical space she designates "Elsewhere" that served as an appropriate receptacle for unmarried women, while
her 1998 *Imperial Objects: Victorian Women's Emigration and the Unauthorized
Imperial Experience* features collected essays on various aspects of Victorian
women's emigration. Diana C. Archibald's 2002 study, *Domesticity, Imperialism, and Emigration in the Victorian Novel*, explores representations of women's
emigration to British settler colonies and the United States, examining how
well the ideal of the domestic woman translated across geographical lines.

7. To the best of my knowledge, since Coral Lansbury's 1970 study,
*Arcady in Australia: The Evocation of Australia in Nineteenth-Century English Lit-
erature*, there have been no new studies on the role of the Australian colonies
in the Victorian novel.

8. See Karen R. Lawrence's *Penelope Voyages: Women and Travel in the Brit-
ish Literary Tradition*, Sara Mills's *Discourses of Difference: An Analysis of Women's
Travel Writing and Colonialism*, and Mary Louise Pratt's *Imperial Eyes: Travel
Writing and Transculturation*.

9. For example, one contemporary reviewer of a novel written by Catherine Spence, a long-standing colonist who had emigrated from Scotland,
writes that "[t]his novel is no more Australian than results from the fact that
the author, having been resident in Australia, having a gift for novel writing, and writing about what she knew best, unavoidably wrote an Australian
novel" (qtd. in Thomson xv). The odd contortions through which Spence's
novel is deemed "Australian" are indicative of the ambivalence that makes settler writing contestatory in nature.

10. For other critics who have explored the interdependence between
home and colony, see McClintock, David, and Meyer's *Imperialism at Home*.

11. Although indigenous testimony regarding practices such as forcible
child removal came the forefront of public consciousness only in the 1990s,
when the Human Rights and Equal Opportunity Commission (HREOC)
began soliciting such testimony, historians emphasize that indigenous resistance to such policies has a long history (Whitlock 30).

12. For an examination of how the middle class was reflected and created
through political discourses, see Dror Wahrman's *Imagining the Middle Class:*

The Political Representation of Class in Britain, c. 1780–1840. For accounts that bring gender into the discussion of how the middle class came into being, see Leonore Davidoff and Catherine Hall's *Family Fortunes: Men and Women of the English Middle Class, 1780–1850,* and John Tosh's *A Man's Place: Masculinity and the Middle-Class Home in Victorian England.*

13. Statistics suggest that between 1788 and 1868, 162,000 convicts were transported from Britain to Australia (Arnstein, *Britain Yesterday and Today* 62).

14. Dror Wahrman argues, for instance, that in the early decades of the nineteenth century the "taming" of the middle class transformed it from a potentially revolutionary to a stabilizing force, one that represented the voice of public opinion.

15. Such portability is ironically represented in the following example from an emigrant guide, which advises male emigrants that women are valuable assets in the colonies: "A good wife will be found to be infinitely the most valuable part of his outfit, and will go far to insure success from the commencement" (Hursthouse 53).

16. Chisholm was responding to what was historically a disproportionate population of male emigrants in the Australian colonies. Hammerton notes, for instance, that "[b]y 1836 the New South Wales population included 2.6 males for every female, a clear consequence of the uneven effects of convict transportation" (*Emigrant Gentlewomen* 53).

CHAPTER 1 — HOUSEKEEPING AT SEA AND ON SHORE

1. Such an act is consistent with what Benedict Anderson identifies as a crucial feature of nationalism: the simultaneous operation of remembering certain aspects of the nation's history while forgetting others. For an extended discussion of the trope of "memory and forgetting" see chapter 11 in *Imagined Communities: Reflections on the Origin and Spread of Nationalism.*

2. Brown's creation of this double work of art was in keeping with a common practice among the members of the Pre-Raphaelite Brotherhood, who experimented with different methods of combining the "sister arts" of painting and poetry.

3. Lucy Rabin has speculated that Brown may have derived his idea for the framing of this painting from the porthole of a ship (228). This suggestion is interesting insofar as it introduces the role of the spectator into readings of the painting. The fact that the spectator's view of the ship is always cut off and fragmented suggests the violence of displacement as well as the inaccessibility of the emigrant experience for those who have not left their homes for another country.

4. Rabin suggests that the father is also framed by a halo in the ship fitting that looms above him, and that the haloes suggest Brown's Biblical allusion to Mary and Joseph's departure for Egypt (228).

5. This conception of women's power is obviously in keeping with John Ruskin's famous description of separate spheres elaborated in *Sesame and Lilies*.

6. As Rita Kranidis notes, "The extension of England's national boundaries intensified during the Victorian period, beginning with the New Colonial Policy of 1839, which facilitated the emigration from the British Isles of dramatically increasing numbers of people: Whereas 130,000 had emigrated in 1842, by 1847 250,000 had emigrated, a remarkable contrast to 1829, when there were only 30,000 emigrants" (*The Victorian Spinster* 21).

7. Charles Hursthouse argues that because emigration is on par in importance with birth, marriage, and death, "it appears to me that everyone who speaks or writes on such a subject is morally *bound* to use such language of moderation that the emigrant may actually realise in practice what he may hear in the lecture-room or read by his fireside. This 'language of moderation' I shall certainly use this evening, not only because it is right to do so, but because it is *expedient*" (28).

8. Another interesting example of this emphasis on hard work comes from George S. Baden-Powell: "There are endless ways of gaining really good livings in Australia; but there, as elsewhere, there are not any royal roads to fortunes. People must not imagine that the sacrifices they make in leaving home and undergoing a long voyage are to be necessarily repaid in a few years by a fortune. All they can do is to improve their condition of life; but they have to devote to it fully as much toil and industry as they would do in the old country" (453).

9. In another passage, the same guide inadvertently suggests that the overarching appeal of British national identity makes the blurring of class distinctions less important or less relevant in the context of emigration: "There is no better instrument for the amelioration of the condition of society in countries like our own so immediately, or so extremely available, so easily worked, or so certain and speedy in its results as emigration. Its demands are simple. It does not require high moral or intellectual attainments, or patronage, or favour. It simply demands men, women, and children of the ordinary stamp of character, possessed of British strength, British pluck, British determination, and British common sense to work out a prosperous future" (*Australian and New-Zealand Passengers' Guide* 4).

10. Writing in the eighteenth century, Samuel Johnson similarly evoked the multiple threats involved in sea travel by describing ships as "prison[s], with the chance of being drowned" (qtd. in Fraser 13).

11. For more detailed information on the layout and design of Victorian passenger ships, see Basil Greenhill and Ann Giffard's *Travelling by Sea in the Nineteenth Century: Interior Design in Victorian Passenger Ships*.

12. Caroline Chisholm also articulates the disciplinary function of the family aboard ships as one means of reinforcing traditional gender roles. By creating family collectives who travel together and look after one another, she imagines that "the pride of an Englishman would be roused: men would feel as men; mothers would look with pride upon their children" (14).

13. Like the Silver's guide, Hursthouse describes the voyage out as a period well-suited to domestic industry that is carefully coded according to acceptable gender roles: "A hundred days or so at sea afford an excellent opportunity for a course of useful reading, for improvement in any particular science or study . . . Schools and newspapers are frequently established, or an interesting journal may be kept, to send home to friends. Then you have a quiet rubber, chess, or backgammon, with an occasional dance on deck in the fine evenings. The sporting part of the company amuse themselves with gymnastics, albatross-shooting, rifle-practice, shark-catching, &c.; whilst the young ladies, in the mornings prosecuting crochet work, and fashioning divers coloured little bags and nets, as elegant as useless, would find the soft moonlight nights in the tropics most favourable to love-making, and to the construction of certain other nets, in which are captured the larger animals" (67–68).

14. Charles Dickens's description of the Micawbers and the Peggottys departing for Australia appeared in a chapter entitled "The Emigrants" in the eighteenth monthly number of *David Copperfield*, which was published in October 1850, seven months after the publication of "A Bundle of Emigrants' Letters." The sequencing of these publications supports the theory that Dickens was indeed influenced by Chisholm's emigration model.

15. Paradoxically, while Dickens respected Chisholm's work on emigration, he was critical of her domestic inefficiency, and she became the prototype for Mrs. Jellyby in *Bleak House*. After visiting her in March 1850, Dickens wrote to Angela Burdett-Coutts, explaining: "I dream of Mrs. Chisholm, and her housekeeping. The dirty faces of her children are my continual companions" ("A Bundle" 85).

16. An excellent example of such vulnerability can be found in Dickens's characterization of Mr. Jaggers in *Great Expectations*, a character whose involvement in the legal defense of London criminals leads him into the habit of obsessively washing his hands to counteract the perceived contamination from his lower-class clients.

17. According to the Victorian language of flowers, a primrose signifies the sentiment, "I can't live without you." Within this context, the image of the primrose is especially fitting in exemplifying the idea that the home nation remains indispensable and unforgettable within the emigrant culture of Australia. As in Brown's *The Last of England*, this drawing highlights the critical role of memory in helping to maintain the emigrant's connection to Britain and in preserving the kind of restraint and loyalty that Chisholm and Dickens describe.

18. Other interesting examples of this kind of nostalgia abound in descriptions of the voyage out. To cite only one additional example, Baden-Powell likewise explains that at the end of the voyage, "Emerging from the busy disorder of the cabins, to lend a hand at meals, surrounded by familiar faces, dishes, and attendant men and things, there steals over all a certain vague regret that the voyage's end is so close at hand, in utter disregard of the fact

that this same consummation has been so longed for during three or four months, spent happily on the whole, in spite of sundry little tiffs and quarrels" (12–13).

19. The reformation of the spinster and the fallen woman in the British colonies had a fictional precedent in Elizabeth Gaskell's 1848 novel, *Mary Barton,* and in Dickens's own philanthropic work. Mrs. Gummidge's transformation echoes that of Gaskell's Mrs. Wilson, whose temperamental nature towards Mary Barton is moderated to the point that "hardly a passing cloud dimmed the happy confidence of their intercourse" (449). Likewise, Jem Wilson and Mary Barton contemplate emigration as a possible means of redemption for Mary's Aunt Esther when Jem proposes that "she shall go to America with us; and we'll help her to get rid of her sins" (463). Although Esther dies in Britain before such a plan can be effected, this solution had a realistic counterpart in Dickens's own work with fallen women, which Gaskell admired. In 1846–7, Dickens worked with Angela Burdett-Coutts to establish Urania Cottage, a reformatory for fallen women. This philanthropic institution emphasized reformation by training women in domestic skills and then assisting them in emigrating to the colonies, where they could presumably begin new lives. In an article published in *Household Words* in April 1853 entitled "Home for Homeless Women," Dickens describes the effect the home has in literally transforming its inhabitants: "One of the most remarkable effects of the Home . . . is the extraordinary change it produces in the appearance of its inmates . . . It is considered doubtful whether, in the majority of the worst cases, the subject would easily be known again at a year's end, among a dozen, by an old companion" (136). When Mr. Peggotty returns to England, he similarly muses about how Emily has been "altered" since her emigration, explaining to David that he would be unlikely to recognize her in her present state.

20. Chisholm uses a commonly evoked familial lexicon to buttress this argument in *The A. B. C. of Colonization*: "we cannot really be great as a nation except every man be made to feel that his individual conduct is thrown into the national scale, unless he is made sensible that he forms one of the commonwealth, and is an acknowledged and known member of the community" (31).

21. Chisholm's emphasis on the importance of narrative to constructions of nationalism reinforces Anderson's argument that by representing people in calendrical, simultaneous time, the novel and the newspaper become an analogue for the nation, "which is also conceived as a solid community moving steadily down (or up) history" (26).

CHAPTER 2 — PERFORMING THE VOYAGE OUT

1. For the terms of this debate about "superfluous women," see William R. Greg's "Why Are Women Redundant?" and Francis Power Cobbe's "What Shall We Do with Our Old Maids?" Greg associates the problem of

"redundancy" explicitly with women of the upper-middle class who were "too spoiled to purchase love at the expense of luxury" (445–6). Women of the lower classes, he argued, were unlikely to remain single for long because they did not maintain the same elite standards with respect to marriage, while female servants resolved the problem of redundancy by fulfilling their natural roles within the domestic realm.

2. The men's impotency in fulfilling their roles as breadwinners is humorously associated with sexual impotency through several prominent phallic symbols, including two poles on the dock, one topped by a phallic protuberance and the other by a suggestively small, frayed mesh net. By contrast, the ship's thick red and white striped smokestack emits a billowing trail of steam that may symbolize the virility and power of the vessel that carries the women away.

3. From the Family Colonization Loan Society established in 1849 to the British Women's Emigration Association active between 1880 and 1914, the rhetoric of women's religious and moral authority enabled thousands of British women of all classes to emigrate to the settler colonies under the rubric of service to the empire. For an account of these organizations, see James Hammerton's *Emigrant Gentlewomen: Genteel Poverty and Female Emigration, 1830–1914*, chapters 4 and 6.

4. As early as 1829 Edward Gibbon Wakefield linked emigration with the problems associated with single middle-class women in *A Letter from Sydney: The Principal Town of Australasia*. For a discussion of Wakefield's thesis and for census figures reflecting the population imbalance between the sexes in the 1860s, see Hammerton's *Emigrant Gentlewomen*, chapter 1.

5. Rye and Lewin had slightly different ideas about how best to run their society. Rye envisioned a two-tier system of female emigration that would cater both to well-trained governesses and to lower middle-class women. For Rye, whether or not marriage or domestic service was an inevitable by-product of emigration was irrelevant. However, Lewin, who took over as Honorary Secretary when Rye left the FMCES in 1865 to focus her efforts on juvenile emigration from Britain to Canada, ultimately limited the scope of the society's work by accepting only those middle-class women who were seeking professional careers in the colonies. For a more detailed account of the formation and development of the FMCES, see Hammerton's *Emigrant Gentlewomen*, chapter 5.

6. The FMCES assisted women in emigrating to Australia, New Zealand, South Africa, India, Russia, Canada, and the United States. I will be focusing on letters written by women who emigrated to Australia and New Zealand, the most common destinations.

7. An article published in the *Times* on April 18, 1850 insisted that the majority of emigrants sent out "should not be mere heaps of pauperism, shovelled from our shores, but fairly selected portions of British society" (qtd. in Hammerton 98). By manipulating this existing discourse of colonialism, Rye created a new narrative for female emigration.

8. Through governmental emigration schemes in the early part of the century individuals were sometimes taken from the streets to fill quotas on emigrant ships, which consequently became sites of drunkenness and debauchery. By one account, "At one time, under the notorious pretext of remedying the disproportion of the sexes in these colonies, the streets of London, Liverpool, Dublin, and Cork were swept for female immigrants to be conveyed out to these colonies at our expense, till the streets of Hobart Town and Sydney became like the worst thoroughfares of the British metropolis" (Shaw 86). The work of the FMCES was thus instrumental in elevating the respectability of female emigration and in distancing it from its earliest associations with convict transportation and prostitution.

9. My analysis extends Judith Butler's argument about the cultural construction of gender to include the category of class. Drawing on Butler's conception of performance, I argue that middle-class identities are constructed through the repetition of a series of regulatory practices that sustain the illusion of a unified self.

10. According to Benedict Anderson, a nation "is imagined as a *community*, because, regardless of the actual inequality and exploitation that may prevail in each, the nation is always conceived as a deep, horizontal comradeship" (7). Although Anderson alludes here to the presence of inequality and exploitation, he dramatically minimizes their effects, for as Mary Louise Pratt has recently argued, gender inequality places women in a position of permanent instability in relation to the nation by creating "a deep cleavage in the horizontal fraternity, one that cannot easily be imagined away" ("Women, Literature and National Brotherhood" 31). In addition, as the writings of the FMCES emigrants show, class must also be inserted into an analysis of nationality, since class, like gender, is a locus of disruption in the horizontal comradeship that undergirds the imagined community.

11. Citations from the FMCES letters are taken both from Patricia Clarke's *The Governesses: Letters from the Colonies, 1862–1882* and from the original manuscript source held by The Women's Library at London Metropolitan University. The archival source includes two Letter Books with handwritten page numbers; when citing from the original manuscript I will provide both book and page numbers. I am indebted to Clarke's fascinating study for introducing me to these letters, but her intention is "not to interpret the letters, but to let the governesses speak for themselves" (xi). In fact, letters such as these have been previously overlooked as a valuable source for textual analysis. Rita Kranidis, for instance, asserts that despite being "potentially ideal primary texts for a study on female emigration," such letters "are not very helpful" and "can best be described as 'resisting' texts that do not lend themselves to extensive analysis" (*Victorian Spinster* 46). As my own examination of the FMCES letters suggests, however, this very resistance is often what makes the letters so interesting and revealing.

12. This number is exceptionally small when contrasted to the work of two female emigration schemes of the previous decade, whose combined efforts enabled 1,300 women to emigrate within the short span of only three years. In addition, it pales in comparison to the work of the British Women's Emigration Association, which assisted nearly 20,000 women to emigrate between 1880 and 1914. For more detailed accounts of these figures, see Hammerton's *Emigrant Gentlewomen*, chapters 4 and 6.

13. The FMCES emigrants challenged in a number of ways the neat binary oppositions commonly drawn between voluntary and assisted emigration. As part of "a surplus population" they belong to the category that *The Emigrant's Manual* labels "Unfit Emigrants"; however, they simultaneously match the description of those emigrants in the opposite category "who seek a new field of exertion as a better means of rising and going forward in the world than they can find at home" (22).

14. Consistent with an emphasis on self-help as opposed to philanthropy, the FMCES gave loans to their emigrants to pay for their passages, with the stipulation that they be repaid within two years and four months. The issue of debt is a recurrent theme in the FMCES letters partly because the emigrants often included payments or requests for extra time to repay their loans.

15. Clarke's analysis helps to account for the class dynamics associated with food and eating aboard ship: "First-class passengers dined at the captain's table; however, for others, the food and drink provided on board ship was very basic and many governesses advised intending emigrants to bring some supplies of their own, to add variety to the shipboard meals" (Clarke 44).

16. See Homi K. Bhabha's "DissemiNation" for a related discussion of how the imperative to forget the violence involved in the nation's past serves to consolidate the national will.

17. Charles Dickens describes a similar instance of amnesia in *David Copperfield* when Wilkins Micawber, prior to boarding a ship for Australia, reduces the import of emigration by figuratively erasing the distance between Britain and the colony: "It is merely crossing . . . merely crossing. The distance is quite imaginary" (659). Such a strategy is also fairly common in emigrant propaganda, as this example from *S. W. Silver & Co.'s Handbook for Australia and New Zealand* demonstrates: "The immigrant will discover that he has but come to another Britain over the Line, and that trades and professions similar to those at home are in full exercise there" (96).

18. As Robert Hughes explains, Australian nationalism was also born out of such forgetfulness: "After abolition, you could (silently) reproach your forebears for being convicts. You could not take pride in them, or reproach England for treating them as it did. The cure for this excruciating colonial double bind was amnesia—a national pact of silence" (xii).

19. As Patrick Brantlinger suggests, the energizing myths of Australian emigration—"Arcadian redemption versus social damnation"—left no possibility for return (*Rule of Darkness* 132).

20. The complexities of the governesses' role within the Victorian family have been ably delineated by Mary Poovey and others, but as Anne McClintock notes, such complexities are magnified within a colonial context: "The colonial governess was in every sense a threshold creature. Graced with an education, she did not have the opportunity to use it. Racially a member of the white elite, she was in reality a member of the serving class. She was protected by racial privilege but not by economic security" (277).

21. The trope of darkened or yellowed skin is frequently evoked to signify the taint of colonialism in the Victorian novel. See, for example, descriptions of two other returning emigrants, George Talboys in *Lady Audley's Secret* (36) and Angel Clare in *Tess of the d'Urbervilles* (313), both of whom bear complexions that are characteristically transformed in the colonies. I will explore this issue in more depth in chapter 3.

22. Inderpal Grewal similarly links the veil with inscrutability, arguing that the first step toward civilizing the colonies was to see into the harem and through the veil, thereby penetrating the opacity that marked Eastern cultures as "other" while simultaneously creating a transparent populace (50).

23. Trollope traveled extensively in Australia and New Zealand, publishing a travel book based on his experiences in 1873. His son Frederic, whom Trollope visited while in Australia, was the model for the central character in his short novel *Harry Heathcote of Gangoil*, which dramatizes the conflicts between squatters and free-selectors in Australia. Although such conflicts are reconciled in the happy ending of this novel, Frederic ultimately failed as a sheep farmer and had to sell his station at a great loss in 1875. Trollope's consequent disappointment may have inflected his more pessimistic vision in *John Caldigate* of the possibilities of colonization and empire.

CHAPTER 3 — THE FRAUDULENT FAMILY

1. Though the trade was abolished, slavery continued as "apprenticeship" for approximately six more years.

2. Also see Frantz Fanon, who suggests that reading the family as a microcosm for the nation is foundational to the process of European colonialism more generally: "In Europe the family represents in effect a certain fashion in which the world presents itself to the child. There are close connections between the structure of the family and the structure of the nation . . . In Europe and in every country characterized as civilized or civilizing, the family is a miniature of the nation" (141–42).

3. Deirdre David in *Rule Britannia: Women, Empire, and Victorian Writing*, for example, examines images of invasion and counterinvasion as colonized subjects infiltrate the mother country.

4. For criticism focused on Lady Audley's duplicity, see Anne Cvetkovich's *Mixed Feelings: Feminism, Mass Culture, and Victorian Sensationalism*, chapter 3, Helena Michie's *Sororophobia: Differences Among Women in Literature*

and Culture, pp. 63–71, and Susan David Bernstein's, *Confessional Subjects: Revelations of Gender and Power in Victorian Literature and Culture*, chapter 3. For criticism focused on Robert Audley, see Simon Petch's "Robert Audley's Profession" and Richard Nemesvari's "Robert Audley's Secret: Male Homosocial Desire in *Lady Audley's Secret*."

5. Thomas identifies 1868–74 as "the Claimant's moment" (93) with interest in his story tapering throughout the 1870s, but McWilliam has argued that the Claimant's story maintained a hold on the public imagination for a much longer period from 1867–1886.

6. For a comprehensive account of the Claimant's history and the trials, see Douglas Woodruff's early study, *The Tichborne Claimant: A Victorian Mystery* and Rohan McWilliam's recent work, *The Tichborne Claimant: A Victorian Sensation*, which is likely to become a seminal treatment of the topic.

7. Although transportation was officially abolished in 1857, the last convict ship did not sail to Australia until 1867.

8. Patrick Brantlinger similarly describes this prohibition against return: "Numerous characters in Victorian fiction experience secular rebirths in the Bush; even convicts can strike it rich and be redeemed, though they generally must stay in the land of their redemption. Those convicts who return to Britain . . . remain convicts whether they have completed their sentences or not, shadowed by crimes and guilt they cannot shake off" (*Rule of Darkness* 124).

9. In addition to this direct warning, *Clara Morison* includes a cautionary tale about Miss Ker, a woman who is the victim of a bigamous husband. Miss Ker functions in the novel as Clara's double, and her fate—she marries a man in Adelaide who already has a wife and four children living in Sydney—serves as a recurrent reminder for Clara to exercise caution with respect to her own suitor's affections (1: 204–5).

10. Recent criticism on *Jane Eyre* is also invested in measuring the extent of Rochester's accountability. See Gayatri Chakravorty Spivak's "Three Women's Texts and a Critique of Imperialism," Susan L. Meyer's "Colonialism and the Figurative Strategy of *Jane Eyre*," and Deirdre David's *Rule Britannia*, chapter 3.

11. See Elaine Showalter's "Family Secrets and Domestic Subversion: Rebellion in the Novels of the 1860s" for an extended discussion of "bigamy novels." Later in the century, I am thinking particularly of Thomas Hardy's novels, which often include marginal plots that connect emigration and bigamy.

12. Also see Anne McClintock, who argues that "[f]or the elite, a sun-darkened skin stained by outdoor manual work was the visible stigma not only of a class obliged to work under the elements for a living but also of far-off, benighted races marked by God's disfavor" (212).

13. Such a distinction between the superficial and psychic wounds of displacement is also evident in Thomas Hardy's *Tess of the D'Urbervilles* when Angel Clare returns from Brazil physically wasted by disease and bearing

a characteristically sickly complexion. Although Clare acknowledges prior to his departure that emigration is often a profitable commercial endeavor, he nonetheless laments that it "snaps the continuity of existence" (222). The violence of this image again invokes the sense of psychic trauma that George associates with displacement, as well as highlighting a distressing lack of continuity between the emigrant's life before and after his displacement.

14. It is interesting to note that sensationalism enters Dickens's otherwise realistic plot through the convict story and the realities of return.

15. While the lower-class homes in the novel offer evidence of domestic squalor, the aristocratic homes provide examples of what Paul Morrison calls the "domestic carceral," insofar as their pristine facades cover over the gothic secrets and repressive "domestic regulations" that imperil each family's prospects for domestic happiness (438).

16. See Cvetkovich, pp. 45–70, and Michie's *Sororophobia*, pp. 63–71.

17. Also see Eileen Cleere's more extended treatment of this topic in *Avuncularism: Capitalism, Patriarchy, and Nineteenth-Century English Culture.*

18. Pip is similarly positioned in relation to the marriage plot at the end of *Great Expectations.* Although he does not go to Australia himself, Pip's imbrication in Magwitch's colonial history renders him unable to reassimilate into normative domestic life in Britain. As a result, he goes to work as a clerk for the Eastern branch of Clarriker & Co. and is absorbed into the family as an adjunct to the marriage of his best friend, Herbert, and Herbert's wife, Clara.

19. David Wayne Thomas quotes a widely circulated statement from the press that was issued at the end of the civil trial which explains that the Claimant was backed "by 85 witnesses, comprising his own mother, the family solicitor, one baronet, six magistrates, one general, three colonels, one major, two captains, 32 no-commissioned officers and privates, four clergymen, seven tenants of the estate, 16 servants of the family, and 12 general witnesses, who all swore to his identity. The claim was denied by the oaths of only 17 witnesses" (qtd. in Thomas 90).

20. The passage from *Aurora Floyd* actually reads as follows: "I should think fellows with plenty of money and no brains must have been invented for the good of fellows with plenty of brains and no money, and that's how we continue to help our equilibrium in the universal see-saw" (190).

21. The jury in the criminal trial was ultimately persuaded by this theory, finding that the Claimant was not Roger Tichborne, but that he was Arthur Orton. In an effort to explain how Orton managed to perpetrate the fraud, Douglas Woodruff speculates that Roger Tichborne may have survived the wreck of the *Bella*, made his way to Australia, and subsequently encountered Arthur Orton. He goes on to suggest the possibility that Orton may have witnessed Tichborne's death in the bush, retained his papers and possessions, and subsequently plotted the imposture. Once he arrived back in Britain, the Claimant had nearly five years to accrue information about Roger Tichborne's life before he had to stand trial.

22. Such inequalities are responsible for prompting not only the emigration of the fictional George Talboys, who is disinherited after marrying below his station, but also that of Roger Tichborne, who exiled himself from Britain after his uncle refused to allow him to marry his first cousin, whom he loved, and thereby prevented the joining of the Tichborne and Doughty estates. The similarity of these two accounts is suggestive of fractures within the British family that are already present before emigration occurs, but that are subsequently heightened by virtue of displacement and return.

23. The prosecutor in the criminal trial at one point asserted that in the Claimant's testimony "[w]e have the most extraordinary medley of ignorance and knowledge" (Woodruff 347). The most bewildering gaps in the Claimant's knowledge had to do with his imperfect recollection of his education and with his failure to remember how to speak French. Criminologist Edgar Lustgarten addresses these same contradictions by explaining that the Claimant's story while "incredible if it was true, was yet more incredible if it was false" (qtd. in Rawling).

24. The supposition that Roger Tichborne possessed a "malformation" was based on numerous speculative connections: that Roger had been kept in frocks until the age of 12; that he had been nicknamed "small cock" at school and in the army; that a practical joke by fellow soldiers entailed tying a donkey to his bed; that he might not be able to have children and hence was not seen as a viable suitor for one of his cousins (McWilliam 199–200).

25. Such voyeurism was driven home for me as a critic while sitting in the British Library reading court testimony regarding "the malformation" in a document clearly designated "For the Perusal of Gentlemen Only."

26. Thomas Hardy's *Jude the Obscure* suggests that class considerations are quite important in determining whether bigamy is a criminal offense. After Arabella emigrates to Australia, remarries, and returns with her husband to Britain, her bigamy goes unremarked. As Jude puts it, "[t]here is this advantage to being poor and obscure people like us—that these things are done for us in a rough and ready fashion. It was the same with me and Arabella. I was afraid her criminal second marriage would have been discovered, and she punished; but nobody took any interest in her—nobody inquired, nobody suspected it" (322).

CHAPTER 4 — "VERILY THE ANTIPODES OF HOME"

1. Such propaganda is evident in the following passage from *S. W. Silver & Co.'s Handbook for Australia and New Zealand*, which represents marriage in the colonies as a process of inevitable transition: "The constant changing of single women into the ranks of the married makes room for new hands at service, in the house, or shop. It may appear paradoxical to say, though it is none the less true, that there is often a readier opening for young female immigrants in the old settled Colony, than in places where, from their scarcity, women may be thought to be more required" (97).

2. For a discussion of such anxieties, see Mary Poovey's *Uneven Developments: The Ideological Work of Gender in Mid-Victorian England*, chapter 5.

3. This possibility resurfaces later in the novel when Mr. Briggs, the lawyer, suggests that were John Eyre well, he would urge Jane to accompany Mr. Mason to Madeira.

4. The undesirability of this solution is evident in the very names associated with the position: the reader is obviously not meant to question why Jane resists going to Mrs. O'Gall of Bitternutt Lodge.

5. For a relatively optimistic reading of Brontë's resolution, see Deirdre David's *Rule Britannia: Women, Empire, and Victorian Writing*, chapter 3. David reads the ending as "a fantasy of rehabilitated wealth," arguing that although both Rochester and Jane's wealth is acquired through the practices of colonialism, "it may still serve to fashion a chastened colonial governance" (84).

6. For discussions of these intersections, see Gayatri Chakravorty Spivak's seminal essay, "Three Women's Texts and a Critique of Imperialism," along with Susan L. Meyer's "Colonialism and the Figurative Strategy of *Jane Eyre*," and David's *Rule Britannia*, chapter 3.

7. Charlotte Brontë's *Villette* seems to come closest to dramatizing such a fate, although the governess heroine is sent, not to the colonies, but to the Continent.

8. Through an analysis of Charlotte Brontë's *Jane Eyre* as well as feminist campaigns aimed at improving opportunities for female education and employment, Mary Poovey argues that the British governess highlighted the contradictions inherent in Britain's domestic ideals, specifically those associated with the ideology of separate spheres. Poovey writes that because the governess was positioned by virtue of the work she did between the middle-class mother and the working-class woman, she "belongs to both sides of the opposition: in her, the very possibility of an opposition collapses" (147). In her analysis of Victorian governess novels, Helena Michie explores images of the governess that show her wavering between the bodies of the leisure class lady and the female worker, thereby dramatizing the contradictions within her position. Michie argues that the role of the governess is actually figured in fiction as a disguise that must be penetrated by the hero and the reader. "Underneath the subdued costume of the governess," Michie writes, "is the delicate and sensitive body of the leisure-class heroine" (*The Flesh Made Word* 48).

9. Annie Hunt, a middle-class emigrant to Australia who was not a governess, exhibits a characteristic class bias when she alludes to the stigmas associated with needlework: "Fortunately I am not bound to this one means of getting a living [Law Copying] and have already found employment with my needle—this, however, will have its disadvantages because if I follow this for a living I could not stay in the Home on my present footing and I would not mix with the Dressmakers and Needlewomen here" (Clarke 122).

10. Citations from the FMCES letters in this chapter are taken from Patricia Clarke's *The Governesses: Letters from the Colonies, 1862–1882.*

11. By the time of her death in 1910, Spence was widely known as the "grand old woman of Australia" (Thomson ix).

12. Poovey discusses the governess primarily in terms of her perceived status as a social problem, while Anne McClintock focuses on the colonial governess' status as an abject figure. In her discussion of *Jane Eyre*, Michie alludes to a more positive reading of the governess, arguing that "Jane's ambiguous bodily position is both potentially transformative and dangerous" (*The Flesh Made Word* 50).

13. For a more detailed account of the formation and development of the FMCES, see chapter 5 of James Hammerton's *Emigrant Gentlewomen: Genteel Poverty and Female Emigration, 1830–1914*.

14. Such class consciousness is everywhere evident in Rye's letters, which often include similar allusions such as "the right set of girls" (*Times*, June 21, 1862) and "women . . . of a class very superior to those now sent" (*Times*, April 7, 1862).

15. For her pioneering critique of how the development of the female as individualist in the age of imperialism often occurs, as it does in this instance, at the expense of the native female, see Spivak's "Three Women's Texts and a Critique of Imperialism."

16. Clara's predicament is echoed by several FMCES emigrants who indicate that their letters of introduction are useless, as are their British teaching credentials. One governess laments that "Our Cook has £10 more than I do and I hold an English Certificate, [which] is as much value as waste paper here" (Clarke 120).

17. A similar thematic is evident in the representation of the governess in Mrs. Henry Wood's *East Lynne* (1861). After she is presumed dead, Lady Isabel Vane adopts a disguise and returns to her former home where she becomes a governess to her own children. Although her identity is at issue after she assumes the persona of the governess, Madame Vine, her gentility is always evident in spite of her disguise.

18. Pierre Bourdieu asserts: "To the socially recognized hierarchy of the arts, and within each of them, of genres, schools or periods, corresponds a social hierarchy of the consumers. This predisposes tastes to function as markers of 'class'" (1–2). For a detailed discussion of how such hierarchies function, see *Distinction: A Social Critique of the Judgement of Taste*.

19. Spence's implicit critique of Miss Waterstone and Miss Withering closely mirrors Jane Eyre's critique of Blanche Ingram: "She was not good; she was not original: she used to repeat sounding phrases from books: she never offered, nor had, an opinion of her own" (Brontë 210).

20. Clara's affinity for the Elliots clearly echoes Brontë's description of Jane's affinity for Mary and Diana Rivers: "I liked to read what they liked to read" (391).

21. As a young girl at Gateshead, Jane's reading material, including Bewick's *History of British Birds* and Swift's *Gulliver's Travels*, allows her to

travel imaginatively and to escape the painful confinement she experiences in the Reed household. Later at Moor House, her reading with the Rivers sisters temporarily grants Jane genteel status, but she subsequently returns to "a service of poverty and obscurity" when she becomes mistress at the village school (Brontë 396). Her status is elevated thereafter only when she receives news of her inheritance.

22. Clara's conventionally racist critique of Black Mary's history works to reinforce Clara's alliance to her British traditions, since she judges the narration according to the conventions of realism and domestic values: "It was uninteresting enough, but yet it did not seem true, so that it was unsatisfactory in all respects . . . and when she told Clara about the pickaninny she had had many moons ago, who had wasted away and died, she did not weep as an English mother would do, nor did her voice sink to sorrowful pathos; but she talked of it with indifference, till she had finished her recital" (1: 212).

23. Spence comments in her *Autobiography* on the strategic negotiations she engaged in as a colonial writer seeking also to appeal to an English audience: "If stories are excessively Australian they lost the sympathies of the bulk of the public. If they are mildly Australian, the work is thought to lack distinctiveness" (qtd. in Thomson x).

24. There are many conspicuous parallels between the two novels. Most obviously, Clara, like Jane, is an orphaned governess. When Spence's novel opens, Clara's father has just died and she and her sister have been left at the mercy of their uncle, who decides to assist Clara in emigrating to Australia while he retains her sister, Susan, as governess in his own family. Like Jane, Clara subsequently falls in love with a suitor who is unavailable for marriage, both because of differences in station and because of prior commitments. In *Clara Morison*, Reginald's engagement to an English woman named Julia serves as an impediment to their marriage, paralleling Rochester's secret marriage to Bertha Mason Rochester in *Jane Eyre*. The plots of both novels climax when opportune discoveries of lost cousins lead to the revelation of each heroine's genteel origins. After enduring a long series of "new servitude[s]" (Brontë 99), the protagonists are eventually restored to their appropriate stations through marriage to their previously unavailable suitors.

25. At the level of plot, Spence answers this self-reflexive question by allowing her hero to choose Clara over Julia, the quintessentially "lovely, accomplished English wife" (1: 60).

26. Like Brontë, Spence resists the romantic conventions that idealize women, whether for their beauty or their abilities, instead focusing on the grim realities of female work and vocation. Prior to Clara's entrance into domestic service, the narrator parodies the romance tradition and the surety with which idealized heroines overcome seeming obstacles: "They row boats without feeling fatigued, they scale walls, they rein in restive horses, they can lift the most ponderous articles, though they are of the most delicate and fragile constitutions, and have never had such things to do in their lives . . . It was

not so with Clara, however" (90). Whereas the narrator's examples above all relate to miraculous feats of physical strength performed by otherwise fragile women, the seemingly impossible tasks that Clara faces involve the work of domesticity—work which is presumed to be easy for women. By elaborating on Clara's difficulties in mastering the domestic skills necessary to become a good servant in Mrs. Bantam's household, Spence denaturalizes domestic work, thereby destabilizing the notion that domesticity is woman's sphere, domestic work a natural outcropping of female identity.

27. For readings that address the seemingly contradictory impulses of the novel's ending, see Sandra Gilbert and Susan Gubar's "A Dialogue of Self and Soul: Plain Jane's Progress" and Meyer's "Colonialism and the Figurative Strategy of *Jane Eyre*."

28. The trope of darkened skin signifying the taint of colonialism is prevalent in innumerable instances in Victorian novels. For a nuanced reading of how this trope is employed in *Jane Eyre*, see Meyer, 259–261.

29. Compare Reginald's speech to Rochester's banter after he has proposed to Jane for the first time: "But listen—whisper—it is your time now, little tyrant, but it will be mine presently: and when once I have fairly seized you, to have and to hold, I'll just—figuratively speaking—attach you to a chain like this . . . Yes, bonny wee thing, I'll wear you in my bosom, lest my jewel I should tyne" (Brontë 303).

CONCLUSION — PORTABLE DOMESTICITY
AND STRATEGIC AMNESIA

1. This term was first coined in Peter Read's 1981 work, *The Stolen Generations: The Removal of Aboriginal Children in New South Wales, 1883–1969*.

2. Although it is difficult to pinpoint the exact number of children who experienced removal given a variety of complex factors, Read's succinct calculation of the human costs of such policies hints at their wide-reaching scope: "To put it another way, there is not an Aboriginal person in New South Wales who does not know, or is not related, to one or more of his/her countrymen who were institutionalized by the whites" (*A Rape of the Soul* 67–68).

3. The Commission was charged with examining four main issues, which ranged from an analysis of past laws, practices, and policies that allowed for forcible child removal; to the question of state-sponsored compensation for those affected; to the current laws, practices, and policies regarding the placement and care of indigenous children, particularly through welfare and juvenile justice systems ("Bringing Them Home," Background to the Inquiry). In conducting their Inquiry, the Commission relied on public evidence from individuals and organizations representing various contingencies within the community, including indigenous people, state and territory governments, non-government agencies, and churches. They also relied on confidential

evidence from indigenous people affected by removal as well as adoptive and foster parents.

4. Reynolds notes that "[g]iven the widespread conviction that Aboriginal children would automatically benefit from living with Europeans in almost any circumstances and be 'uplifted' in the process, it is not surprising that individual colonists and their families 'adopted' Aboriginal children, acquired in a variety of ways but all illustrating the increasing powerlessness of indigenous communities" (160).

5. In addition to these harmful psychological consequences, recent studies show no significant educational or economic advantage for indigenous children who were taken from their families versus those who were not; indeed, statistics suggest that members of the former group are no more likely to be employed or to have higher incomes than their peers who were not removed from their families ("Bringing Them Home," Scope of the Inquiry).

6. Although the discriminatory legislation that codified the practice of child removal in the twentieth century was overturned in all Australian states and territories by the 1960s, the Commission's investigation into current practices suggests that indigenous children are still disproportionately represented in the juvenile welfare and justice systems, suggesting some degree of ongoing marginalization and social, legal, and economic vulnerability in the larger culture. The Inquiry found, for instance, that indigenous children are six times more likely to be removed for welfare reasons and 21 times more likely to be in juvenile detention than non-indigenous children, a discrepancy that may reflect a combination of factors including but not limited to discrimination and cultural bias ("Bringing Them Home," Frequently Asked Questions).

Works Cited

"Alarming Prospect—The Single Ladies off to the Diggings." Cartoon. Bodleian Library, Oxford.

Alloula, Malek. *The Colonial Harem*. Minneapolis: U of Minnesota P, 1986.

Anderson, Benedict. *Imagined Communities: Reflections on the Origin and Spread of Nationalism*. New York: Verso, 1991.

Archibald, Diana C. "Angel in the Bush: Exporting Domesticity through Female Emigration." *Imperial Objects: Essays on Victorian Women's Emigration and the Unauthorized Imperial Experience*. Ed. Rita S. Kranidis. New York: Twayne, 1998. 228–247.

———. *Domesticity, Imperialism, and Emigration in the Victorian Novel*. Columbia: University of Missouri Press, 2002.

Armstrong, Nancy. *Desire and Domestic Fiction: A Political History of the Novel*. New York: Oxford UP, 1987.

Arnstein, Walter L. *Britain Yesterday and Today: 1830 to the Present*. Lexington, MA: D. C. Heath, 1996.

———. "Victoria, Queen of England (1819–1901)." *Victorian Britain: An Encyclopedia*. Ed. Sally Mitchell. New York and London: Garland, 1988. 835–837.

Australian and New-Zealand Passengers' Guide. Rpt. in "Hetherington's Universal Register." London: F. W. Hetherington, 1885.

Baden-Powell, George S. *New Homes for the Old Country. A Personal Experience of the Political and Domestic Life, the Industries, and the Natural History of Australia and New Zealand*. London: Richard Bentley and Son, 1872.

Berman, Carolyn Vellenga. *Creole Crossings: Domestic Fiction and the Reform of Colonial Slavery*. Ithaca: Cornell UP, 2006.

Bernstein, Susan David. *Confessional Subjects: Revelations of Gender and Power in Victorian Literature and Culture*. Chapel Hill: U of North Carolina P, 1997.

Bhabha, Homi K. "DissemiNation: Time, Narrative, and the Margins of the Modern Nation." *Nation and Narration*. Ed. Homi K. Bhabha. New York: Routledge, 1990. 291–322.

————. *The Location of Culture*. New York: Routledge, 1994.

Bourdieu, Pierre. *Distinction: A Social Critique of the Judgment of Taste*. Trans. Richard Nice. Cambridge: Harvard UP, 1984.

Braddon, Mary Elizabeth. *Aurora Floyd*. New York: Oxford UP, 1996.

————. *Lady Audley's Secret*. New York: Oxford UP, 1987.

Brantlinger, Patrick. "Cultural Studies versus the New Historicism." *English Studies/Culture Studies: Institutionalizing Dissent*. Eds. Isaiah Smithson and Nancy Ruff. Urbana: U of Illinois P, 1994. 43–58.

————. *Rule of Darkness: British Literature and Imperialism, 1830–1914*. Ithaca: Cornell UP, 1988.

"Bringing Them Home: Report of the National Inquiry into the Separation of Aboriginal and Torres Strait Islander Children from Their Families April 1997." *Australian Human Rights Commission*. December 11, 2008. December 27, 2008. <http://www.hreoc.gov.au/social_Justice/bth_report/report/index.html>

Brontë, Charlotte. *Jane Eyre*. New York: Penguin, 1996.

————. *Villette*. New York: Bantam, 1986.

Brown, Ford Madox. *The Exhibition of WORK, and other Paintings by Ford Madox Brown. 1865. The Art of Ford Madox Brown*. By Kenneth Bendiner. University Park, PA: Pennsylvania State UP, 1998. 131-156.

Brown, Ford Madox. *The Last of England*. 1852–55. Birmingham Museums & Art Gallery, Birmingham.

Butler, Judith P. *Gender Trouble: Feminism and the Subversion of Identity*. New York: Routledge, 1990.

Chadfield, P. B. *Out at Sea; or, The Emigrant Afloat, Being a Hand Book of Practical Information for the Use of Passengers on a Long Sea Voyage*. Derby: Chadfield and Son, 1862.

Chisholm, Caroline. *The A. B. C. of Colonization*. London: John Ollivier, 1850.

Clacy, Mrs. Charles. *A Lady's Visit to the Gold Diggings of Australia 1852–53*. London: Angus and Robertson, 1963.

————. "A Bush Fire." *Lights and Shadows of Australian Life*. 2 vols. London: Hurst and Blackett, 1854.

Clarke, Patricia. *The Governesses: Letters from the Colonies, 1862–1882*. London: Hutchinson, 1985.

Cleere, Eileen. *Avuncularism: Capitalism, Patriarchy, and Nineteenth-Century English Culture*. Stanford: Stanford UP, 2004.

————. "The Shape of Uncles": Capitalism, Affection, and the Cultural Construction of the Victorian Family. Diss., Rice University, 1996.

Cobbe, Francis Power. "What Shall We Do with Our Old Maids?" *Fraser's Magazine* Nov. 1862: 594–610.

Coombes, Annie E. "Introduction: Memory and History in Settler Colonialism." *Rethinking Settler Colonialism: History and Memory in Australia, Canada, Aotearoa New Zealand, and South Africa*. Ed. Annie E. Coombes. New York: Manchester UP, 2006. 1–12.

Cvetkovich, Anne. *Mixed Feelings: Feminism, Mass Culture, and Victorian Sensationalism.* New Brunswick, NJ: Rutgers UP, 1992.

David, Deirdre. *Rule Britannia: Women, Empire, and Victorian Writing.* Ithaca and London: Cornell UP, 1995.

Davidoff, Leonore and Catherine Hall. *Family Fortunes: Men and Women of the English Middle Class, 1780–1850.* Chicago: U of Chicago, 1987.

Denoon, Donald. *Settler Capitalism: The Dynamics of Dependent Development in the Southern Hemisphere.* New York: Oxford UP, 1983.

Dickens, Charles. "A Bundle of Emigrants' Letters." *Uncollected Writings From Household Words, 1850–1859.* Ed. Harry Stone. Vol. 2. Bloomington: Indiana UP, 1968. 85–96.

———. "A Cricket on the Hearth." *The Christmas Books.* Ed. Michael Slater. Vol 2. New York: Penguin, 1985. 21–120.

———. *David Copperfield.* New York: Oxford UP, 1983.

———. *Great Expectations.* New York: Bantam, 1981.

———. "Homes for Homeless Women." *'Gone Astray' and Other Papers from Household Words, 1851–59.* Ed. Michael Slater. Vol. 3. London: Dent, 1998. 127–141.

Doyle, Martin. *Hints on Emigration to Upper Canada: Especially Addressed to the Middle and Lower Classes in Great Britain and Ireland.* Dublin: Curry, 1834.

"The Ears of Sir Roger and the Claimant." Illustration. *True Briton* 30 May 1874.

Elkins, Caroline and Susan Pedersen, eds. *Settler Colonialism in the Twentieth Century: Projects, Practices, Legacies.* New York: Routledge, 2005.

The Emigrant's Manual. Emigration in its Practical Application to Individuals and Communities. Edinburgh: William and Robert Chambers, 1851.

Evans, H. Smith. *A Guide to the Emigration Colonies: Including Australia, Tasmania, New Zealand, Cape of Good Hope, Natal, Canada, and the other British Possessions of North America. Also the United States and California. Compiled from Official Documents: Being the Substance of a Lecture Delivered at the Mechanics' Institution Southampton Buildings.* London: Letts, Son, and Steer, 1851.

Fanon, Frantz. *Black Skin, White Mask.* Trans. Charles Lam Markmann. New York: Grove Weidenfeld, 1991.

FMCES records. Ms. Letter Book 1, 1862–1877, Letter Book 2 (numbered 3), 1877–1882. The Women's Library, London Metropolitan University.

Foucault, Michel. *Discipline and Punish: The Birth of the Prison.* Trans. Alan Sheridan. New York: Vintage, 1979.

Fraser, James, Surgeon. *The Emigrant's Medical Guide.* London: Simpkin, Marshall, and Co., 1853.

Gaskell, Elizabeth. *Mary Barton.* New York, Penguin, 1985.

Gilbert, Sandra M. and Gubar, Susan. "A Dialogue of Self and Soul: Plain Jane's Progress." *The Madwoman in the Attic: The Woman Writer and the*

Nineteenth-Century Literary Imagination. New Haven: Yale UP, 1979. 336–71.

Greenhill, Basil and Ann Giffard. *Travelling by Sea in the Nineteenth Century: Interior Design in Victorian Passenger Ships.* New York: Hastings House, 1974.

Greg, William R. "Why Are Women Redundant?" *National Review* 28 Jan. and April 1862: 434–460.

Grewal, Inderpal. *Home and Harem: Nation, Gender, Empire, and the Cultures of Travel.* Durham and London: Duke UP, 1996.

Hammerton, A. James. *Emigrant Gentlewomen: Genteel Poverty and Female Emigration, 1830–1914.* Totowa, NJ: Rowman and Littlefield, 1979.

———. "'Out of Their Natural Station': Empire and Empowerment in the Emigration of Lower-Middle-Class Women." *Imperial Objects: Essays on Victorian Women's Emigration and the Unauthorized Imperial Experience.* Ed. Rita S. Kranidis. New York: Twayne, 1998. 143–169.

Hardy, Thomas. *Jude the Obscure.* New York: Bantam, 1981.

———. *Tess of the D'Urbervilles.* New York: Norton, 1979.

Hassam, Andrew. *Sailing to Australia: Shipboard Diaries by Nineteenth-Century British Emigrants.* Manchester, Eng.: Manchester UP, 1994.

Hetherington, Frederick Wallace. *Hetherington's Useful Handbook for Intending Emigrants. Life at Sea and the Immigrant's Prospects in Australia and New Zealand.* London: Hetherington, 1884.

Hughes, Robert. *The Fatal Shore.* London: Collins Harvill, 1987.

Hursthouse, Charles Flinders. *Emigration. Where to Go and Who Should Go. New Zealand & Australia (as Emigration Fields) in contrast with Canada and the United States.* London: Trelawny Saunders, 1852.

Kranidis, Rita S. *The Victorian Spinster and Colonial Emigration: Contested Subjects.* New York: St. Martin's, 1999.

———, ed. *Imperial Objects: Victorian Women's Emigration and the Unauthorized Imperial Experience.* New York: Twayne, 1998.

Lansbury, Coral. *Arcady in Australia: The Evocation of Australia in Nineteenth-Century English Literature.* Melbourne: Melbourne UP, 1970.

Lawrence, Karen R. *Penelope Voyages: Women and Travel in the British Literary Tradition.* Ithaca: Cornell UP, 1994.

A Literary & Pictorial Record of the Great Tichborne Case Containing a Complete History of this Cause Célèbre, with Numerous Engravings from Sketches and Photographs, Reprinted from The Graphic, and Facsimile Autographs of Letters, Now Published for the First Time. London: Graphic, 1874.

Mackenzie, Eneas. *The Emigrant's Guide to Australia: With a Memoir of Mrs. Chisholm.* London: Clarke Beeton, 1853.

Maconochie, Captain. *Emigration, with Advice to Emigrants; Especially Those with Small Capital. Addressed to the Society for Promoting Colonization.* London: John Ollivier, 1848.

Magarey, Susan. Introduction. *Clara Morison: A Tale of South Australia during the Gold Fever.* By Catherine Helen Spence. Adelaide: Wakefield, 1986. v–x.

McClintock, Anne. *Imperial Leather: Race, Gender and Sexuality in the Colonial Contest.* New York: Routledge, 1995.

McWilliam, Rohan. *The Tichborne Claimant: A Victorian Sensation.* London: Hambledon Continuum, 2007.

Mereweather, Rev. John Davies. *Life on Board an Emigrant Ship Being a Diary of a Voyage to Australia.* London: T. Hatchard, 1852.

Meyer, Susan L. "Colonialism and the Figurative Strategy of Jane Eyre." *Victorian Studies* 33.2 (1990): 247–68.

———. *Imperialism at Home: Race and Victorian Women's Fiction.* Ithaca: Cornell UP, 1996.

Michie, Helena. *The Flesh Made Word: Female Figures and Women's Bodies.* New York: Oxford UP, 1987.

———. *Sororophobia: Differences Among Women in Literature and Culture.* New York: Oxford UP, 1992.

Miller, D. A. *The Novel and the Police.* Berkeley: U of California P, 1988.

Mills, Sara. *Discourses of Difference: An Analysis of Women's Travel Writing and Colonialism.* New York: Routledge, 1991.

Morrison, Paul. "Enclosed in Openness: Northanger Abbey and the Domestic Carceral." *Texas Studies in Literature and Language* 33.1 (Spring 1991): 1–23.

Nemesvari, Richard. "Robert Audley's Secret: Male Homosocial Desire in *Lady Audley's Secret.*" *Studies in the Novel* 27 (1995): 515–28.

Petch, Simon. "Robert Audley's Profession." *Studies in the Novel* 32.1 (2000): 1–13.

Pettman, Jan Jindy. "Race, Ethnicity and Gender in Australia." *Unsettling Settler Societies: Articulations of Gender, Race, Ethnicity and Class.* Eds. Daiva Stasiulis and Nira Yuval-Davis. London: Sage, 1995. 65–94.

Plotz, John. *Portable Property: Victorian Culture on the Move.* Princeton: Princeton UP, 2008.

Poovey, Mary. *Uneven Developments: The Ideological Work of Gender in Mid-Victorian England.* Chicago: U of Chicago, 1988.

Pratt, Mary Louise. *Imperial Eyes: Travel Writing and Transculturation.* New York: Routledge, 1992.

———. "Women, Literature and National Brotherhood." *Nineteenth-Century Contexts* (1994): 27–47.

"Probable Effects of Over [sic] Female Emigration, or Importing the Fair Sex from the Savage Islands in Consequence of Exporting all our own to Australia!!!!!" Cartoon. Bodleian Library, Oxford.

Rabin, Lucy. *Ford Madox Brown and the Pre-Raphaelite History-Picture.* New York: Garland, 1978.

Rae, W. F. [anon.]. "Sensation Novelists: Miss Braddon." *North British Review* ns 4 (1865): 92–105.

Rawling, Gerald. "The Man Who Might Have Been: Was He the Tichborne Heir?" *British Heritage* 1.2 (1980): 48–57.

Read, Peter. *A Rape of the Soul So Profound: The Return of the Stolen Generation.* Melbourne: Allen and Unwin, 2000.

———. *The Stolen Generations: The Removal of Aboriginal Children in New South Wales, 1883–1969.* Sydney: New South Wales Ministry of Aboriginal Affairs, 1981.

Reynolds, Henry. *An Indelible Stain? The Question of Genocide in Australia's History.* New York: Viking, 2001.

Roe, Michael. *Kenealy and the Tichborne Cause: A Study in Mid-Victorian Populism.* Carlton, Victoria: Melbourne UP, 1974.

Ruskin, John. *Sesame and Lilies.* New York: Chelsea House, 1983.

Rye, Maria S. "Female Middle Class Emigration." *Times* 29 April 1862: 14.

———. "Female Middle Class Emigration." *Times* 21 June 1862: 12.

———. "Miss Rye's Emigrants." *Times* 29 May 1863: 5.

———. "The Employment of Women." *Times* 7 April 1862: 9.

Said, Edward. *Culture and Imperialism.* New York: Knopf, 1993.

Sharpe, Jenny. *Allegories of Empire: The Figure of Woman in the Colonial Text.* Minneapolis: U of Minnesota P, 1993.

Shaw, John, M. D. *A Tramp to the Diggings: Being Notes of a Ramble in Australia and New Zealand in 1852.* London: Richard Bentley, 1852.

Showalter, Elaine. "Family Secrets and Domestic Subversion: Rebellion in the Novels of the 1860s." *The Victorian Family: Structure and Stresses.* Ed. Anthony S. Wohl. New York: St. Martin's, 1978. 101–118.

Silver, Stephen William. *S. W. Silver & Co.'s Colonial and Indian Pocket Book Series and Voyager's Companion. No. 1 The Cape, Free State, and Diamond Fields.* London: S. W. Silver & Co., 1879.

———. *S. W. Silver & Co.'s Handbook for Australia and New Zealand.* 5th ed. London: S. W. Silver & Co., 1886.

"Sir Roger Doughty Tichborne, Bart.? Baronet or Butcher." Men of the Day, No. 25. Chromolithograph. *Vanity Fair* 10 June 1871: 226.

Slemon, Stephen. "Unsettling the Empire: Resistance Theory for the Second World." *World Literature Written in English* 30.2 (Autumn 1990): 30–41.

Spence, Catherine Helen. *Clara Morison: A Tale of South Australia during the Gold Fever.* 2 vols. London: John W. Parker and Son, 1854.

Spivak, Gayatri Chakravorty. "Three Women's Texts and a Critique of Imperialism." *"Race," Writing, and Difference.* Ed. Henry Louis Gates, Jr. Chicago: U of Chicago, 1986. 262–80.

Stasiulis, Daiva and Nira Yuval-Davis. "Introduction: Beyond Dichotomies—Gender, Race, Ethnicity and Class in Settler Societies. *Unsettling Settler Societies: Articulations of Gender, Race, Ethnicity and Class.* Eds. Daiva Stasiulis and Nira Yuval-Davis. London: Sage, 1995. 1–38.

Tait, J. S. *Emigration by Colony for the Middle Classes.* Edinburgh: Crawford & M'Cabe, 1885.

Thomas, David Wayne. *Cultivating Victorians: Liberal Culture and the Aesthetic.* Philadelphia: U of Pennsylvania P, 2003.

Thomson, Helen, ed. Introduction. *The Portable Catherine Helen Spence.* New York: U of Queensland, 1987. ix–xxv.

"To Emigrants!" Advertisement. *The British Journal* 2.9 September 1852.

"Topics of the Week." *Graphic* 14 Feb. 1874: 154.

"Topics of the Week." *Graphic* 21 Feb. 1874: 166.

"Topics of the Week." *Graphic* 14 Mar. 1874: 239.

Tosh, John. *A Man's Place: Masculinity and the Middle-Class Home in Victorian England.* New Haven, CT: Yale UP, 1999.

Tracts: Canada: The Land of Hope for the Settler and Artisan, the Small Capitalist, the Honest, and the Persevering. With a Description of the Climate, Free Grants of Land, Wages, and its General Advantages as a Field for Emigration. By the Editor of the "Canadian News." 3rd edition. London: F. Algar, 1862.

Trollope, Anthony. *Australia and New Zealand.* 2 vols. London: Dawsons, 1968.

———. *Harry Heathcote of Gangoil: A Tale of Australian Bushlife.* New York: Oxford UP, 1992.

———. *John Caldigate.* New York: Oxford UP, 1993.

Wahrman, Dror. *Imagining the Middle Class: The Political Representation of Class in Britain, c. 1780–1840.* Cambridge: Cambridge UP, 1995.

Wakefield, Edward Gibbon. *A Letter from Sydney: The Principal Town of Australasia.* London: J. Cross, 1829.

Weitzer, Ronald. *Transforming Settler States: Communal Conflict and Internal Security in Northern Ireland and Zimbabwe.* Berkeley: U of California P, 1990.

"Welcome Given in Melbourne Australia to a Primrose from England." Illustration. *Illustrated London News* 16 October 1858: 355.

Whitlock, Gillian. "Active Remembrance: Testimony, Memoir and the Work of Reconciliation." *Rethinking Settler Colonialism: History and Memory in Australia, Canada, Aotearoa New Zealand, and South Africa.* Ed. Annie E. Coombes. New York: Manchester UP, 2006. 24–44.

Wills, W. H. "Safety for Female Emigrants." *Household Words* 3 (1851): 228.

Wood, Mrs. Henry. *East Lynne.* New Brunswick, NJ: Rutgers UP, 1984.

Woodruff, Douglas. *The Tichborne Claimant: A Victorian Mystery.* New York: Farrar, 1957.

Woods, R. I. *British Population History: From the Black Death to the Present Day.* Ed. Michael Anderson. Cambridge: Cambridge UP, 1996.

Woolcock, Helen R. *Rights of Passage: Emigration to Australia in the Nineteenth Century.* New York: Tavistock, 1986.

Woolf, Virginia. *A Room of One's Own.* New York: Harcourt, 1981.

"Would You Be Surprised to Hear? I Am Sir Roger Tichborne." London: Disley, n.d.

"The Yarn of the Claimant." London: H. G. Clarke and Co., n.d.

Index

Printed in Great Britain
by Amazon